THE DOCTRINE OF HUMAN DEPRAVITY
Introduction

This book is likely to meet with a decidedly mixed reception. Some of our readers will probably be very disappointed when they see the title, deeming the subject quite unattractive and unedifying. If so, they are to be pitied, and we would fain cherish the hope that God may bless these contents unto them. Medicine is proverbially unpleasant, but there are times when all of us find it necessary and beneficial. Others will be thankful that, by Divine grace, we seek to glorify God rather than please the flesh. And surely that which most glorifies God is to declare "*all* His counsel," to insist on that which puts man in his proper place before Him, and to emphasize those portions and aspects of the Truth which our generation is most in need of. As we shall endeavour to show, our theme is one of immense doctrinal importance and of great practical value. Since it is a subject which occupies so prominent a place in God's Word, no apology is needed for our engaging in such a task.

It is our deep conviction that the vital question most requiring to be raised today is this: Is man a totally and thoroughly depraved creature by nature? Does he now enter the world completely ruined and helpless, spiritually blind and dead in trespasses and sins? According as is our answer to *that* question, so will be our views on many others. It is upon the basis of this dark background that the whole Bible proceeds. Any attempt to modify or abate, repudiate or tone down the teaching of Scripture thereon is fatal. Put the question in another form: Is man now in such a condition that he cannot be saved without the special and direct intervention of the Triune God on his behalf? In other words, is there any hope for him apart from his personal election by the Father, his particular redemption by the Son, and the supernatural operations of the Spirit within him? Or, putting it in still another way: If man be a totally depraved being, can he possibly take the first step in the matter of his return unto God?

The Scriptural answer to that question makes evident the utter futility of the schemes of social reformers for "the moral elevation of the masses," the plans of politicians for the peace of the nations, and the ideologies of dreamers to usher in a "golden age" for this world. It is both pathetic and tragic to see many of our greatest men putting their faith in such chimeras. Divisions and discords, hatred and bloodshed, cannot be banished while human nature is what it is. But during the past century the steady trend of a deteriorating Christendom has been to underrate the evil of sin and overrate the moral capabilities of men. Instead of proclaiming the heinousness of sin, there has been a dwelling more upon its inconveniences, and the abasing portrayal of the lost condition of man as set forth in Holy Writ has been obscured, if not obliterated, by flattering disquisitions upon human advancement. If the popular religion of "the churches"—including nine-tenths of what is termed "Evangelical Christianity"—be tested at this point, it will be found that it clashes directly with man's fallen, ruined, and spiritually dead condition.

There is therefore a crying need today for sin to be viewed in the light of God's Law and Gospel, so that its exceeding sinfulness may be demonstrated, and the dark depths of human depravity exposed by the teaching of Holy Writ—that we may learn what is connoted by those fearful words, "dead in trespasses and sins." The grand object of the Bible is to make God known unto us, to portray man as he appears in the eyes of his Maker, and to show the relation of one to the other. It is therefore the business of His servants not only to declare the Divine character and perfections, but also to delineate the original condition and apostasy of man, as well as the Divine remedy for his ruin. Until we really behold the hole of the pit in which by nature we lie, we can never properly appreciate Christ's so-great salvation. In man's fallen condition we have the awful disease for which Divine redemption is the only cure, and our estimation and valuation of the provisions of Divine grace will necessarily be modified in proportion as we modify the need it was meant to meet.

It was truly pointed out by one of the Puritans that "The end of the ministry of the Gospel is to bring sinners unto Christ. Their way to this end lies through the sense of their misery without Christ. The ingredients of this misery are our sinfulness, original and actual; the wrath of God, whereto sin has exposed us; and our impotency to free ourselves either from sin or wrath. That we may therefore promote this great end, we shall endeavour, as the Lord will assist, to lead you in this way, by the sense of misery to Him who alone can deliver from it. Now the original of our misery being the corruption of our nature, or original sin, we thought fit to begin here, and therefore have pitched upon these words as very proper for our purpose: 'Behold, I was shapen in iniquity, and in sin did my mother conceive me' " (from introduction of David Clarkson's sermon on Psalm 51:5—around 1660).

This subject is indeed a most *solemn* one, and none can fitly write or preach thereon unless his own heart be deeply awed thereby. It is not something from which any man can detach himself and expatiate thereon as though *he* were not directly involved in it, still less as from a higher level looking down upon those whom he denounces. Nothing is more incongruous and ill-becoming than for a young preacher glibly to rattle off passages of Scripture which portray his own vile-

THE DOCTRINE OF HUMAN DEPRAVITY

by

A.W. Pink

OLD PATHS GOSPEL PRESS

P.O. Box 318 • Choteau, MT 59422
Phone or Fax: (406) 466-2311

**OLD PATHS
gOSPEL PRESS**

P.O. Box 318 • Choteau, MT 59422
Phone or Fax: (406) 466-2311

THE DOCTRINE OF HUMAN DEPRAVITY
TABLE OF CONTENTS

Introduction 3
Its Origin 9
Its Imputation 37
Its Consequences.. 59
Its Transmission... 80
Its Nature... 87
Its Enormity 116
Its Extent 131
Its Ramifications... 152
Its Evidences... 173
Its Corollaries.. 188
Its Remedy.. 211
Conclusion 234

ness by nature. Rather should they be read or quoted with the utmost gravity. "As no heart can sufficiently conceive, so no tongue can adequately express the state of wretchedness and ruin into which sin has cast guilty, miserable man. In separating him from God, it severed him from the only source of all happiness and holiness. It has ruined him body and soul: the one it has filled with sickness and disease; in the other it has defaced and destroyed the image of God in which it was created. It has made him love sin and hate God" (J. C. Philpot).

The doctrine of total depravity is a very *humbling* one. It is not that man leans to one side and needs propping up, nor that he is merely ignorant and requires instructing, nor that he is run down and calls for a tonic: but rather that he is undone, lost, spiritually dead. Consequently, he is "without strength," thoroughly incapable of bettering himself; exposed to the wrath of God, and unable to perform a single work which can find acceptance with Him. Almost every page of the Bible bears witness to this truth. The whole scheme of redemption takes it for granted. The plan of salvation taught in the Scriptures could have no place on any other supposition. The impossibility of any man's gaining the approbation of God by works of his own appears plainly in the case of the rich young ruler who came to Christ. Judged by human standards, he was a model of virtue and religious attainments, yet, like all others who trust in self-efforts, he was ignorant of the spirituality and strictness of God's Law, and when Christ put him to the test his fair expectations were blown to the winds, and "he went away sorrowful" (Matt. 19:22).

It is therefore a most *unpalatable* doctrine. It cannot be otherwise, for the unregenerate love to hear of "the greatness, the dignity, the nobility of man." The natural man thinks highly of himself and appreciates only that which is flattering. Nothing pleases him more than to listen to that which extols human nature and lauds the state of mankind, even though it be in terms which not only repudiate the teaching of God's Word, but which are flatly contradicted by common observation and universal experience. And many there are who pander to him by their lavish praises of the excellency of civilization and the steady progress of the race. Hence, to have the lie given to the popular error of "Evolution" is highly displeasing to its deluded votaries. Nevertheless, the first office of God's servants is to stain the pride of all that man glories in, to strip him of his stolen plumes, to lay him low in the dust before God. However repugnant such teaching be, he must faithfully discharge his duty, "whether they will hear, or whether they will forbear" (Ezek. 3:11).

This is no dismal dogma invented by the Church in "the dark ages," but *a truth of Holy Writ.* Said the much-used George Whitefield, "I look upon it not merely as a doctrine of Scripture—the great Fountain of Truth—but a very fundamental one, from which I hope God will suffer none of you to be enticed." It is a subject to which great prominence is given in the Bible. Every part of the Scriptures has much to say upon the awful state of degradation and slavery into which the Fall has brought man. The corruption, the blindness, the hostility of all Adam's descendants unto everything of a spiritual nature are constantly insisted upon. Not only is man's utter ruin fully described, but his powerlessness to save himself from the same. In the declarations and denunciations of the Prophets, of Christ, and His Apostles, the bondage of all men unto Satan and their complete impotence to turn unto God for deliverance are repeatedly set forth—not indirectly and vaguely, but emphatically and in great detail. This is one of a hundred proofs that the Bible is no human invention, but a communication from the Thrice Holy One.

It is a *sadly neglected* subject. Notwithstanding the clear and uniform teaching of Scripture thereon, man's ruined condition and alienation from God are but feebly apprehended and seldom heard in the modern pulpit, and are given little place even in what are regarded as the centres of orthodoxy. Rather is the whole trend of present-day thought and teaching in the opposite direction, and even where the Darwinian hypothesis has not been accepted, its pernicious influences are often seen. In consequence of the guilty silence of the modern pulpit, a generation of churchgoers has arisen which is deplorably ignorant of the basic truths of the Bible, so that perhaps not more than one in a thousand has even a mental knowledge of the chains of hardness and unbelief which bind the natural heart, or of the dungeon of darkness in which they lie. Instead of faithfully telling their hearers of their woeful state by nature, thousands of preachers are wasting their time by relating the latest news of the Kremlin or development of the atom bomb.

It is, therefore, a *testing* doctrine, especially of the preacher's soundness in the Faith. A man's orthodoxy on this subject determines his viewpoint of many other doctrines of great importance. If his belief *here* be a Scriptural one, then he will clearly perceive how impossible it is for men to improve themselves—that Christ is their only hope. He will know that unless the sinner be born again there can be no entrance for him into the Kingdom of God. Nor will he entertain the idea of the fallen creature's free will unto good. He will be preserved from many errors. "I never knew a person verge toward the Arminian, the Arian, the Socinian, the Antinomian schemes, without first entering diminutive notions of human depravity or blameworthiness" (Andrew Fuller). Said the well-equipped theological instructor,

J. M. Stifler, "It cannot be said too often that a false theology finds its source in inadequate views of depravity."

It is a doctrine of great *practical* value as well as doctrinal importance. The foundation of all true piety lies in a correct view of ourselves and our vileness, and a Scriptural belief of God and His grace. There can be no genuine self-abhorrence or repentance, no real appreciation of the saving mercy of God, no faith in Christ, without it. There is nothing like a knowledge of this doctrine so well calculated to undeceive vain man and convict him of the worthlessness and rottenness of his own righteousness. Yet the preacher who is sensible of the plague of his own heart knows full well that *he* cannot present this Truth in such a way as to make his hearers actually realize and feel the same, so as to make them out of love with themselves and cause them to renounce forever all hope in themselves. Therefore, instead of relying upon his faithfulness in presenting the Truth, he will be cast upon God to apply it graciously in power to those who hear him and bless his feeble efforts.

It is an exceedingly *illuminating* doctrine. It may be a melancholy and humiliating one, nevertheless, it throws a flood of light upon mysteries which are otherwise insoluble. It supplies the key to the course of human history and shows why so much of it has been written in blood and tears. It supplies an explanation of many problems which sorely perplex and puzzle the thoughtful. It reveals why the child is prone to evil and has to be taught and disciplined unto anything that is good. It explains why every improvement in man's environment, every attempt to educate him, all the efforts of social reformers, are unavailing to effect any radical betterment in his nature and character. It accounts for the horrible treatment which Christ met with when He wrought so graciously in this world, and why He is still despised and rejected of men. It enables the Christian himself better to understand the painful conflict which is ever at work within him, and which causes him so often to cry, "Oh, wretched man that I am!"

It is therefore a most *necessary* doctrine, for the vast majority of our fellows are ignorant of the same. God's servants are sometimes thought to speak too strongly and dolefully of the dreadful state of man through his apostasy from God, but the fact is that it is impossible to exaggerate in human language the darkness and pollution of man's heart or to describe the misery and utter helplessness of a condition such as the Word of Truth describes in these solemn passages: "But if our Gospel be hid, it is hid to them that are lost: in whom the god of this world hath blinded the minds of them which believe not, lest the light of the glorious Gospel of Christ, who is the image of God, should shine unto them" (2 Cor. 4:3, 4). "Therefore they *could not believe,* because . . . He hath (judicially) blinded their eyes, and hardened their heart; that they should not see with their eyes, nor understand with their heart, and be converted, and I should heal them" (John 12:39, 40). This is yet more evident when we contrast the state of souls of those in whom a miracle of grace is wrought—see Luke 1:78, 79.

It is a salutary doctrine—one which God often uses to bring men to their senses. While we imagine that our wills have power to do what is pleasing to God, we never abandon dependence on self. Not that a mere intellectual knowledge of man's fall and ruin is sufficient to deliver from pride. Only the Spirit's powerful operations can effect that: yet He is pleased to use the faithful preaching of the Word unto that end. Nothing but a felt sense of our lost condition lays us in the dust before God.

THE DOCTRINE OF HUMAN DEPRAVITY
Its Origin

That something is radically wrong with the world of mankind requires no laboured argument to demonstrate. That such has been the case in all generations is plain from the annals of history. This is only another way of saying that something is radically wrong with man himself, for the world is but the aggregate of all the individual members of our race. Since the whole of anything cannot be superior to the parts comprising it, it necessarily follows that the course of the world will be determined by the characters of those who comprise it. But when we come to inquire exactly what it is that is wrong with man, and how he came to be in such a case, unless we turn to God's inspired Word no convincing answers are forthcoming. Apart from that Divine revelation no sure and satisfactory reply can be made to such questions as: From where have been derived the unmistakable imperfections of human nature? What will furnish an adequate explanation of all the manifold evils which attend man's present state? Why is it that none is able to keep God's Law perfectly, do anything which is acceptable to Him while in a state of nature?

To ascertain how sin, which involves all men in it, came into the world is a matter of no little importance. To discover why it is that all men universally and continually are unrighteous and ailing creatures supplies the key to many a problem. Look at human nature as it now is: depraved, wretched, subject to death. Ask philosophy to account for this, and it cannot do so. None can deny the fact that men are what they ought not to be, but how they became so, human wisdom is unable to tell us. To attribute our troubles to heredity and environment is but an evasion, for it leaves unanswered the question, How came it that our original ancestors and environment were such as to produce what now exists? Look not only at our prisons, hospitals, and cemeteries, but also upon the antipathy which is ever to be seen between the righteous and the wicked, between those who fear God and those who fear Him not. The antagonism between Cain and Abel, Ishmael and Isaac, Esau and Jacob, is repeatedly duplicated in every age and clime—and the Bible alone traces that antagonism to its fountain head.

The more judicious of the ancients recognized and bemoaned the universal tendency of men to be law-breakers, but were entirely unaware of its real source. They were agreed that the practice of virtue was the chief thing necessary for the promotion of man's good, but they had to lament an irregular bent in the wills and corruption in the affections of their disciples, which rendered their precepts of little mankind, who have the noblest faculties of any beings on earth, should yet generally pursue their destruction with as much eagerness as the beasts avoid it. Plato, in the second book of his Republic, complained that men by their natures are evil and cannot be brought to good. Trully acknowledged that "man is brought forth into the world, in body and soul, exposed to all miseries and prone to evil, in whom that Divine spark of goodness, and wisdom, and morality, is opposed and extinguished." They realized that all men were poisoned, but how the poison came to be in the human constitution they knew not. Some ascribed it to fate; others to the hostile influences of the planets; still others to an evil angel which attends each man.

Most certainly we cannot attribute man's natural inordinancy and defectiveness unto his Creator. To do so would be the rankest blasphemy, as well as giving the lie to His Word, which declares that "God hath made man upright" (Eccl. 7:29). Even on a much lower ground, such a conclusion is self-evidently false: it is impossible that darkness should issue from the Father of light, or that sin should come from the ineffably Holy One. It is infinitely better to confess our ignorance than to be guilty of grossest impiety—to say nothing of manifest absurdity—by placing the onus upon God. But there is no excuse for anyone to be ignorant thereon: the Holy Scriptures supply a definite solution to this mystery, and show that the entire blame for his present wretchedness lies at man's own door. And therefore, to say that man is a sinful creature, or even to allow that he is totally depraved, is but to acknowledge half of the truth, and the least humbling half at that. Man is a *fallen* creature. He has departed from his original state and primitive purity. So far from man's having ascended from something inferior to an ape, he has descended from the elevated and honourable position in which God first placed him; and it is all-important to contend for this, since it alone satisfactorily explains *why* man is now depraved.

Man is not now as God made him. He has lost the crown and glory of his creation, and has plunged himself into an awful gulf of sin and misery. By his own perversity he has wrecked himself and placed an entail of woe upon his posterity. He is a ruined creature as the result of *his apostasy from God*. This requires that we should consider, first, man in his original estate, that we may perceive his folly in so lightly valuing the same and that we may form a better conception of the vastness, and vileness of his downward plunge, for that can only be gauged as we learn what he fell *from* as well as *into*. By his wicked defection man brought himself into a state as black and doleful as his original one was glorious and blessed. Second, we need to consider most attentively what it has pleased the Holy Spirit to record about the Fall itself, pondering each detail described in Genesis 3, and the amplifications of them supplied by the later Scriptures: looking unto God graciously to grant us an understanding of the same. And then, third, we shall be in a better position to view the fearful consequences of the Fall and perceive how the punishment was made to fit the crime.

Instead of canvassing the varied opinions and conflicting conjectures of our fallible and fallen fellows concerning the original condition and estate of our first parents, we shall confine ourselves entirely to the Divinely inspired Scriptures, which are the only unerring rule of faith. From them, and them alone, can we ascertain what man was when he first came from the hands of his Creator. First, His Word makes known God's intention *to* bring him into existence: "And God said, Let Us make man in Our image, after Our likeness" (Gen. 1:26). There are two things exceedingly noteworthy in that brief statement, namely the repeated use of the pronoun in the plural number, and the fact that its language suggests the idea of a conference between the Divine Persons at *this point* of the "six days" work. We say at this point, for there is nothing resembling it in the record of what occurred during the previous days. Thus, the Divine conference here conveys the impression that the most important stage of creation had now been reached, that man was to be the masterpiece of the Divine workmanship, the crowning glory of the mundane sphere—which is clearly borne out in his being made in the Divine image.

It is the usage of the plural number in Genesis 1:26, which, in our judgment, intimates the first signification of the term "image." God is a trinity in unity, and so also is the man that He made: consisting, in his entirety, of "spirit and soul and body" (1 Thess. 5:23)—while in some passages, "spirit" and "soul" are used as synonyms—in Hebrews 4:12, they are distinguished. The fact that the plural number occurs *three* times in the brief declaration of Genesis 1:26, supplies confirmation that the *one* made in Their likeness was also a threefold entity. Some scholars consider that we have an allusion to this feature of man's constitution in the Apostle's statement, "In Him we live, and move, and have our being" (Acts 17:28), pointing out that each of those three verbs has a philological significance: the first to our animal life, the second (from which is derived the Greek word used by ethical writers for the passions—such as fear, love, hatred, and the like) not, as our English verb suggests, to man's bodily motions in space, but to his *emotional* nature—the soul; the third to that which constitutes our essential being (the "spirit")—the intelligence and will of man.

"So God created man in His own image, in the image of God created He him; male and female created He them" (Gen. 1:27). This announces the actual accomplishment of the Divine purpose and counsels referred to in the preceding verse. The repetition of statement, with the change of the pronoun from the plural to the singular number, imports a second signification to the term "image." Viewing it more generally, it tells of the *excellency* of man's original nature, though it must needs be explained consistently with that infinite distance there is between God and the highest creature. Whatever was this glory which God placed upon Adam, it is not to be understood that he was made to participate in the Divine perfections. Nor is the nothingness of the best of finite beings any disparagement when they be compared with God: for whatever likeness there is to Him, either as created, regenerated, or glorified, there is at the same time an infinite disproportion. Further, this excellency of man's original nature must be distinguished from that glory which is peculiar to Christ, who, so far from being said to be "made in the image of God," "*is* the Image of the invisible God" (Col. 1:15), "the express Image of His Person" (Heb. 1:3). There is a oneness and equality between the Father and the Son which in nowise pertains to any "likeness" between God and the creature.

Examining the term more closely, "the image of God" in which man was made refers to his *moral nature*. Calvin defined it as being "spiritual," that it "includes all the excellence in which the nature of man surpasses all the other species of animals," and "denotes the integrity Adam possessed"; that it may be more clearly specified "in *the restoration* which we obtain through Christ." Without an exception, all the Puritans we have consulted say substantially the same thing, regarding this "image of God" as moral rectitude, a nature in perfect accord with the Divine Law. It could not be otherwise: for the Holy One to make a creature after *His* likeness would be to endow him with holiness. When it is said of the regenerate that he has been "*renewed* in knowledge after the image of Him that created him" (Col. 3:10), that clearly implies the *same* image in which man was originally made, and which sin has defaced. Not only did that "image" consist of knowledge (i.e. of God) but, as Ephesians 4:24 informs us, of "righteousness and true holiness" also. Thus, man's original state was far more than one of innocence (sinlessness, harmlessness), which is mainly a negative thing.

That man was created in positive holiness is also taught in Ecclesiastes 7:29, "God hath made (not is now "making") man *upright*": not only without any improper bias, but according to rule—straight with the Law of God conformed to his will. As Boston expressed it, "original righteousness was con-created with him." The same Hebrew word occurs in "good and upright is the LORD" (Psa. 25:8). We have dwelt the longer on this point because not only do Romanists and Socinians *deny* that man was created a spiritual (and not merely natural) and holy (not simply innocent) being, but some hyper-Calvinists—who prefer logic and "consistency" with *their own* principles to the Word of God—do so too. One error inevitably leads to another: to insist that the unregenerate are under no obligation to perform *spiritual* acts obliges them to infer the same thing of Adam. To conclude that "if Adam fell from a holy and spiritual condition, then we must abandon the doctrine of final perseverance" is to leave out Christ and lose sight of the superiority of the covenant of grace to the original one of works.

"And the LORD God formed man of the dust of the ground, and breathed into his nostrils the breath of life, and man became a living soul" (Gen. 2:7). This supplies us with additional information upon the making of Adam. First, the matter of which his body was formed: to demonstrate the wisdom and power of God in making out of such material so wondrous a thing as the human body, and to teach man his humble origin and dependence upon God. Second, the quickening principle bestowed which was immediately from God, namely an intelligent spirit, of which the Fall did not deprive him (Eccl. 12:7)—that "the breath of life" included reason or the faculty of understanding is clear from "the *life* was the *light* of men" (John 1:4). Third, the effect thereof: his body was now animated and made capable of vital acts. Man's body out of the dust was the workmanship of God, but his soul was an immediate communication from "the Father of spirits" (Heb. 12:9), and thereby earth and Heaven were united in him.

"And the LORD God said, It is not good that the man should be alone: I will make him an help meet for him.... And the LORD God caused a deep sleep to fall upon Adam, and he slept: and He took one of his ribs, and closed up the flesh instead thereof. And the rib, which the LORD God had taken from man, made He a woman, and brought her unto the man" (Gen. 2:18, 21-22). It seems that God chose this mode of making the woman, instead of forming her also out of the dust, to express the intimate union which was to take place between the sexes—to denote their mutual relation and dependence, and to show the superiority of man to the woman. Those two were so made that the whole human race, physically considered, were contained in them and to be produced from them, making them all literally "of one blood" (Acts 17:26).

"And God blessed them, and God said unto them, Be fruitful, and multiply, and replenish the earth, and subdue it: and have dominion over the fish of the sea, and over the fowl of the air, and over every living thing that moveth upon the earth" (Gen. 1:28). Those words intimate that there was yet another meaning to "the image of God," for the position of headship and authority which He conferred upon Adam shadowed forth the Divine *sovereignty*. Psalm 8:5, 6, tells us, "Thou hast made him a little lower than the angels, and hast crowned him with glory and honour. Thou madest him to have dominion over the works of Thy hands. Thou hast put all things under his feet." Adam was constituted God's viceroy on earth, the government of all inferior creatures being conferred upon him. That was further demonstrated when the Lord brought all before Adam for him to give names to them (Gen. 2:19, 20), which not only evinces that he was a rational creature, endowed with the power of choice, but manifested his superiority over all mundane creatures, a propriety in them, and liberty to use them unto God's glory and his own good.

But more. God not only endowed Adam with righteousness and holiness, thereby fitting him to fulfill the end of his creation by glorifying the Author of his being; bestowed upon him the gift of reason, which distinguished him from and elevated him above all the other inhabitants of the earth; conferred upon him the charter of dominion over them; but brought him into a pure and *beautiful environment*. "And the LORD God planted a garden eastward in Eden, and there He put the man whom He had formed...and the LORD God took the man, and put him in the garden of Eden (which the Septuagint renders "the paradise of joy") to dress it and keep it" (Gen. 2:8, 15)—Genesis 3:24 confirms the fact that "the garden of Eden" was distinct from the earth. The whole world was given him for a possession, but Eden was the special seat of his residence, a place of pre-eminent delight. It presented to his view the whole earth in miniature, so that he might, without travelling long distances, behold the lovely landscape which it afforded. It epitomized all the beauties of nature, and was, as it were, a conservatory of its fairest vegetation and a storehouse of its choicest fruits.

That the garden of Eden was a place of surpassing beauty, excelling all other parts of the earth for fertility, is evident from other Scriptures. When prophesying, in a day of wretchedness and barrenness, the bountiful spiritual blessings which would attend the Gospel era, Ezekiel used this figurative but graphic language: "This land that was desolate is become like the garden of Eden" (36:35). Still plainer was the promise of Isaiah 51:3: "For the LORD shall comfort Zion: He will comfort all her waste places: and He will make her wilderness like Eden, and her desert like the garden of the LORD: joy and gladness shall be found therein, thanksgiving and the voice of melody." From those words it is clear that nothing was wanting in Eden, in its pristine glory, to give the most complete happiness to man. That it was a place of perfect bliss is further evident from the fact that Heaven itself—the habitation of the blessed—is called "paradise" in Luke 23:43; 2 Corinthians 12:4; Revelation 2:7—may we not see in that *threefold* allusion (there are no others!) a pledge for the complete satisfaction of the glorified man's spirit and soul and body?

In the statement that the Lord God put the man into the garden of Eden "to dress it and keep it," several things are imported and implied. First, and most obviously, that God takes no pleasure in idleness, but in an active industry. That such an appointment was for Adam's good cannot be doubted and sure it is that regular employment preserves *us* from those temptations which so often attend indolence. Second, that secular employment is by no means inconsistent with perfect holiness, or a person's enjoying intimate communion with God and the blessings arising therefrom; though Adam's work would, of course, be performed without any of the fatigue and disappointment which accompany such today. The holy angels are not inert, but "ministering spirits" (Heb. 1:14); yea, of the Divine Persons Themselves, our Lord declared, "My Father worketh hitherto, and I work" (John 5:17); thus this employment assigned Adam was also a part of his conformity to God. Third, it implied the duty of keeping his own heart—the garden of his soul—with all diligence (Prov. 4:23), tending its faculties and graces so that he might ever be in a condition to pray, "Let my Beloved come into His garden and eat His pleasant fruits" (Song. 4:16).

Further, in the "dress it"—Hebrew "serve," "till"—we are taught that God's gracious bestowments are to be highly treasured and carefully cultivated by us: "neglect not the gift that is in thee" (1 Tim. 4:14), "stir up the gift of God, which is in thee" (2 Tim. 1:6). In the additional "and to *keep it*," we believe there was a tacit warning given by God unto Adam. Not only does the English term convey that thought, but the Hebrew word *(shainar)* here used requires it. Nineteen times it is rendered "preserve," twelve times "take heed," four times "watch," and once it is actually translated "beware." Thus it signified a caution against danger, putting Adam on his guard, bidding him be on the look out against the encroaching of an enemy. The Dutch Puritan, Herman Witisus, pointed out that the "keeping of Paradise virtually engaged him of all things to be anxiously concerned not to do anything against God, lest as a bad gardener be should be thrust out of the garden, and in that discover a melancholy symbol of his own exclusion from Heaven." Finally, in that "paradise" is one of the names of Heaven, we may conclude that the earthly one in which Adam was placed was a pledge of that celestial blessedness which, had he survived his probation and preserved his integrity, he had become possessed of.

In addition to the institution of marriage (Gen. 2:23-25; 1:28), God appointed the weekly Sabbath. "On the seventh day God ended His work He had made, and He rested on the seventh day from all His works which He had made. And God blessed the seventh day and sanctified it, because that in it He had rested from all His work which God created and made" (2:2, 3)—should any raise the cavil that the term "Sabbath" is not found in those verses, we would remind them that in Exodus 20:11, Jehovah Himself expressly terms that first "seventh day" of rest "the Sabbath day." The word "blessed" signifies *to declare blessedness:* thus, on the frontispiece of His Word, God would have every reader know that special Divine blessing attends the observance of the Sabbath. The word "sanctified" means that it was a day set apart for sacred use. For Adam it would be a means for his more intimate communion with God, wherein he would enjoy a recess from his secular employment and have opportunity of expressing his gratitude for all those blessings of which he was the partaker.

Though Adam had been made in the image of God, taken into communion with Him, fitted to rejoice in all the manifestations of His wisdom and goodness which surrounded him in Eden, nevertheless he was capable of falling. Since it is a point which has sorely puzzled many of the Lord's people, how it was possible for a holy person, devoid of any corruption, *to sin,* we will endeavour to explain. First, Adam's liability to fall lay in the fact that he was but a *creature.* As such he was entirely dependent upon Him "which holdeth our soul in life" (Psa. 66:9). As our natural life continues only so long as God sustains it, so it was with Adam's spiritual life: he stood only so long as he was Divinely upheld. Moreover, as a creature, he was but finite, and therefore possessed of no invincible power with which to repel opposition. Nor was he endowed with omniscience, so that he had been incapable of being deceived or mistaking an evil for an apparent good. Thus, though man's original condition was one of high moral excellence, with no evil tendency in any part of his nature, yea, with nothing in him which in the least deviated from the moral law, yet, being but a creature, he was capable of falling.

Second, Adam's liability to fall lay in his *mutability.* Changeableness is the very law or radical characteristic of the creature, to distinguish it from the Creator. God alone is "with Whom is no variableness, neither shadow of turning" (James 1:18). Therefore, it is that "He cannot be tempted with evil" (James 1:13) i.e., induced to sin: a statement which clearly implies that the creature as such *has* a capacity to be so tempted—not only a depraved creature, but even an unfallen one. Immutability and impeccability (non-liability to sin) are qualities which essentially distinguish the Creator from the creature—the angels possess neither, as the fall of at least one-third of their number (Rev. 12) demonstrated. Further, as the excellent Goodwin pointed out, God alone acts from His own power, whereas the creature acts by a power given to him which is distinct from himself. "God's own goodness and happiness is His ultimate end, therefore He can never act but holily, for He acts by Himself, and for Himself, and so cannot fail in acting, but is holy in all His ways and works, and cannot be otherwise." But man neither acts immediately by his own power nor is himself the legitimate end of his acting, but rather God. Thus, with all his faculties, man may falter when using them.

Third, Adam's liability to fall lay in the *freedom of his will*. He was not only a creature and a rational creature, but also a moral one. Freedom of will is a property which belongs to man as a rational and responsible being. As we cannot separate understanding from the mind, neither can we liberty from the will, especially in connection with things within its own sphere, and most especially still when considering that all the faculties of man's soul were in the state of perfection before the Fall. With Adam and Eve the freedom of the will consisted in a power of choosing or embracing what appeared agreeable to the dictates of their understandings, to be good, or in refusing and avoiding what was evil; and that without any constraint or force laid upon them to act contrary to the dictates thereof. Such freedom also supposed a power to act pursuant to what the will chooses, otherwise it could not obtain the good desired or avoid the evil detested, and in such cases its "liberty" would be little more than a name. Freedom of action is opposed to that which is involuntary or compelled, and the will is both self-inclining and self-determining in the acting, both internally and externally; for then only can it, strictly speaking, be said to be free.

Our first parents had that freedom of will, or power to retain their integrity. This is evident from the clearly revealed fact that they were under an indispensable obligation to yield perfect obedience unto God, and liable to deserved punishment for the least defect thereof: therefore, they must have been given a power to stand, a liberty of will to choose that which was conducive to their happiness. The same thing is also evident from the difference there is between man's primitive and present state. As fallen, man is now by a necessity of nature inclined to sin, and accordingly he is denominated "the servant of sin" (John 8:34)—a slave to it, entirely under its dominion—but it was far otherwise with Adam, whose nature was holy and furnished with everything necessary to his yielding that obedience demanded of him. Nevertheless, his will being free, it was capable of complying with an external temptation to evil, though so long as he made a right use of his faculties he would defend himself and reject the temptation with abhorrence. It pleased God to leave our first parents without any immediate help *ab extra,* to the freedom and mutability of their own will. But that neither made Him the author of their sin nor brought them under any natural necessity of falling.

Before considering the probation under which Adam was placed, and the test to which his loyalty and subjection to God was submitted, it should be pointed out that Scripture requires us to regard him as far more than a private person—the consequences of whose action would be confined to himself. As we purpose showing, that is made very plain from the event itself. Adam was more than the father of the human race. By Divine constitution he was made the *covenant head* of all his natural seed, so that what be did was Divinely regarded and reckoned as being done by them—just as Christ came into the world as the covenant Head of all His spiritual seed, acting and transacting in their name and on their behalf. God willing, this will be considered more fully under the next division of our subject, when we shall treat of the imputation of his offence to all his posterity. Suffice it now to point out that in Romans 5:14, Adam is expressly called "the figure of Him that was to come." In what was he a type of the Redeemer? The principal respect in which he was distinguished from all other creatures lay in his being the federal head and legal representative of all his offspring. This is confirmed by 1 Corinthians 15:45-49, where the first Adam and the last Adam are designated "the first man" and "the second man," for they were the only two who sustained that covenant and federal relation unto others before God.

"And the LORD God planted a garden eastward in Eden; and there He put the man whom He had formed. And out of the ground made the LORD God to grow every tree that is pleasant to the sight, and good for food; the tree of life also in the midst of the garden, and the tree of knowledge of good and evil" (Gen. 2:8, 9). That is the first mention of those two notable trees, and it is to be duly observed that, like all the others surrounding them, they were both pleasing to the eye and suitable for eating. Thus God not only provided for Adam's profit, but his pleasure also, that he might serve Him with delight. "And the LORD God commanded the man, saying, Of every tree of the garden thou mayest freely eat: but of the tree of the knowledge of good and evil thou shalt not eat of it: for in the day that thou eatest thereof thou shall surely die" (Gen. 2:16, 17). This, as the following verses indicate, took place *before* Eve was created, and thus the Covenant of Works was made with Adam alone as the head of our race. Far more was implied in those words than is actually expressed, as we hope to show when considering them more closely under our next division. Meanwhile, a few general remarks thereon may be of interest.

"The tendency of such a Divine precept is to be considered. Man was thereby taught: (1) That God is Lord of all things—that it is unlawful for man even to desire an apple but with His leave. In all things, therefore, from the greatest to the least, the mouth of the Lord is to be consulted as to what He would or would not have done by us. (2) That man's trite happiness is placed in God alone, and nothing to be desired but with submission to God, and in order to employ it for Him. So that it is *He* only on whose account all other things appear good and desirable to man. (3) Readily to be satisfied without even the most delightful and desirable things, if God so commands; and to think that there is much more good in obedience to the Divine precept than in the enjoyment of the most delightful thing in the world. (4) That man was not yet arrived to the utmost pitch of happiness, but to expect a still greater good after his course of obedience was over. This was hinted by the prohibition of the most delightful tree, whose fruit was, of any other, greatly to be desired and this argued some degree of imperfection in that state in which man was forbidden the enjoyment of some good" (H. Witsius).

In forbidding Adam to eat of the tree of knowledge of good and evil his Maker asserted His dominion and enforced His authority. That it was proper for Him to do so cannot be lawfully questioned, and as the sole Proprietor of the garden it was fitting that He should emphasize His rights by this restriction. Moreover, man having been created a rational creature and endowed with freedom of will, he was a fit subject for command, and accordingly was placed under law. Thereby Adam's loyalty and subjection to his Creator and Lord was put to the test. Trial of his obedience was made to discover whether the will of God was sacred to him. It was both meet and just that he remain in the state of holiness in which God had made him, if he would continue to enjoy His favour. Thus he was placed on probation, made the subject of Divine government. Adam was not an independent creature, for he did not create himself: being made by God, he owed a debt to Him, he was a mortal being, and therefore responsible to serve and please God. The commandment given to him was no arbitrary infliction, but a necessary injunction for making evident and enforcing the relationship in which man stood to God.

The particular injunction laid upon our first parents (Gen. 2:17) has been a favourite subject of ridicule by the opponents of Divine revelation. They who are wise in their own conceits have deemed it unworthy of the Almighty to interpose His authority in a matter so trifling, and have insisted it is incredible to believe that He exposed Adam and Eve to the hazard of ruining themselves and all their progeny by eating the food of a particular tree. But a little reflection ought to show us that there was nothing in that prohibition unbecoming over all creatures here below, it was surely fitting that He should require some peculiar instance of homage and fealty to Him as a token of his dependence and an acknowledgment of his subjection to his Maker—to whom he owed the most absolute submission and obedience. And what mark of subjection could be more proper than being interdicted to partake of one of the fruits of Paradise? Full liberty was granted him to eat of all the rest, and that single abstention was well suited to teach our first parents the salutary lesson of self-denial and of implicit resignation to the good pleasure of the Most High.

In addition to what was noted by Witsius, it may be pointed out that the character of this prohibition taught Adam and Eve to keep their sensitive appetites in subjection to the reasoning faculty. It showed them they must subordinate their bodily inclinations unto finding their highest delight in God alone. It intimated that their desire after knowledge must be kept within just bounds, that they must be content with what God deemed to be really proper and useful to them, and not presume to pry with an unwarrantable curiosity into things which did not belong to them, and which God had not thought well to reveal unto them. It was not sinful *per se* (in itself abstractedly considered) for Adam and Eve to eat of the tree of knowledge of good and evil, but only because the Lord God had expressly forbidden them to do so. Accordingly, solemn warning of the dire consequences that would certainly follow their disobedience was given, for even in Eden man was placed under the holy awe of Divine threatening, which was a hedge placed around him for his protection. Man's supreme felicity lies in God Himself and the enjoyment of His favour and in Eden he was forbidden to seek satisfaction in any other object. In that single restriction upon his liberty was his integrity put to the proof.

So far from that arrangement being unworthy of the Divine majesty, such an enforcing of His will and authority upon the creature of His hand was most becoming. It was not only necessary in the nature of the case if the responsibility of a free agent was to be enforced, and his subjection to the Divine government insisted upon, but the very triviality of the object withheld from our first parents only served to give greater reality unto the trial to which they were subjected. As Professor Dick pointed out, "It is manifest that the prohibition did not proceed from malevolence or an intention to impair the happiness of man: because, with this single reservation, he was at liberty to appropriate the rich variety of fruits with which Paradise was stored. It is certain that, situated as he was, no command could be easier, as it properly implied no sacrifice, no painful privation, but simple abstinence from one out of many things; for who would deem it a hardship, while he was sitting at a table covered with all kinds of delicate and substantial foods, to be told that there was one, and only one, that he was forbidden to taste? It is further evident that no reason could be assigned why Adam should not eat the fruit of the tree of knowledge of good and evil but the Divine prohibition.

"The fruit was as good for food as that of any tree, and as pleasant to the eye; and there was nothing sacred in it which would have been profaned by human touch. Hence you will perceive that if God had an intention to make trial of the newly formed subject, He could not have chosen a more proper method, as it indicated nothing like a harsh or tyrannical exercise of authority, and was admirably fitted to ascertain whether His simple command would be to him instead of all other reasons for obedience. It is not a proper trial of reverence for a superior when the action which he prescribes is recommended by other considerations. It is when it stands upon the sole foundation of his authority; when, having no intrinsic goodness, it becomes good only by his prohibition; when the sole inducement to perform it is his command. It is in these circumstances it is known whether we duly feel and recognize our moral dependence upon him. The morality of an action does not depend upon its abstract nature, but upon its relation to the Law of God. Men seem often to judge of actions as they judge of material substances—by their bulk. What is great in itself, or in its consequences, they will admit to be a sin; but what appears little they pronounce to be a slight fault, or no fault at all.

"Had Adam, it has been remarked, been possessed of preternatural power, and wantonly and wickedly exerted it in blasting the beauty of Paradise, and turning it into a scene of desolation, men would have granted that he was guilty of a great and daring offence, for which a curse was justly pronounced upon him. But they can see no harm in so trifling a matter as the eating of a little fruit. Nothing, however, is more fallacious than such reasoning: the essence of sin is the transgression of a law, and whether that law forbids you to commit murder or to move your finger, it is equally transgressed when you violate the precept. Whatever the act of disobedience is, it is rebellion against the Lawgiver: it is a renunciation of His authority, it dissolves that moral dependence upon Him which is founded on the nature of things, and is necessary to maintain the order and happiness of the universe. The injunction therefore to abstain from the tree of knowledge of good and evil was a proper trial of our first parents, and the violation of it deserved the dreadful punishment which was denounced and executed. He was put to the test whether the will of God was sacred in his eyes, and he was punished because he gave preference to his own will." Our apology for making a longer quotation than we are accustomed to do from the writings of others. The one just given is of particular weight and importance and greatly needed in this day. We hope the reader will give it a second and more careful perusal.

It only remains for us to add now that the foundation of Adam's obligation to render such obedience unto God lay, first, in his relations to Him. As his Maker, his Governor, his Benefactor, it behooved him to render full subjection to His revealed will. Second, in the privileges and favours bestowed upon him: these required that he should express his gratitude and thanksgiving by doing those things which were pleasing in His sight. Third, in his endowments, which qualified him so to do: created in God's image, with a nature that inclined his will unto obedience—ability and obligation then being co-extensive. Fourth, in the relation he sustained to the race: as the head and father of all his progeny, their welfare or ruin was bound up in how he conducted himself, thus greatly augmenting his responsibility to abstain from wrong-doing. Fifth in that the command forbidding Adam to eat of the tree of knowledge was accompanied by a solemn threat of dire punishment to be inflicted in case of disobedience. Not only should that have acted as an effectual deterrent, but the penalty necessarily implied a promise: since death would be the sure result of disobedience, life would be the reward of obedience— not only a continuation of the blessedness and happiness which he then enjoyed in fellowship with his Maker, but such an augmentation of the same as He might be pleased further to make in the exercise of His bounty. That also ought to have served as a powerful incentive unto continued fidelity. Thus there was every reason why Adam should have preserved his integrity.

Though created in the image and likeness of God, man was not endowed with infallibility. In body perfectly sound, in soul completely holy, in circumstances blissfully happy, still man was but a mutable creature. Pronounced by God "very good" (Gen. 1:31) on the day of his creation, man's character was not yet *confirmed* in righteousness, and therefore he was (like the angels) placed on probation and subjected to trial—to show whether or not he would render allegiance to his Lord. Though "made upright," he was not incapable of falling; nor did it devolve upon God to keep him from so doing. This is clear from the event, for had there been any obligation upon God, His faithfulness and goodness had preserved Adam. Nor would He have upbraided our first parents had their defection been due to any breach of *His* fidelity. As moral agents, Adam and Eve were required to maintain their pristine purity unsullied, to walk before God in unswerving loyalty and loving submission. But a single restriction was put upon their liberty, which was necessary in order to the testing of their fealty and the discharge of their responsibility.

Alas, man in honour did not abide. He valued at a low rate the approbation of his Maker and the inestimable privilege of communion with Him. He chafed against the love-lined yoke that had been laid upon him. Quickly did he supply tragic evidence of his mutability and disrupt the tranquillity of Paradise. The beauty of holiness in which the parents of our race were arrayed was soon succeeded by the most revolting depravity. Instead of preserving their integrity, they fell into a state of sin and misery. They were speedily induced to violate that commandment of God's—obedience to which was the sole condition of their continued felicity. Not for long did they enjoy their fair heritage. Notwithstanding the ideal conditions in which they were placed, they became dissatisfied with their lot, succumbed to their very first testing, and evoked the holy displeasure of their Benefactor. How early did the fine gold become dim! How soon did man forfeit the favour of his Maker, and plunge himself into an ocean of wretchedness and woe! How swiftly was the sun of human happiness eclipsed by man's own folly!

It has been generally held among devout students of God's Word that our first Parents remained unfallen for but a very brief season. Such a view is in full accord with the general Analogy of Faith, for it is a solemn and humbling fact that whenever God has been pleased to place anything in the hands of human responsibility, man has proved unfaithful to His trust; that when He has bestowed some special favour upon the creature, it has not been long before he has sadly abused the same. Even a considerable part of the angels in Heaven "kept not their first estate," though how soon they apostatized, the Scriptures do not disclose. Noah, when he came forth on to a judgment-swept earth to be the new father of the human race, defiled his escutcheon at a very early date and brought a curse upon his son. Within the space of but a few days after Israel had solemnly entered into a covenant with Jehovah at Sinai, they were guilty of the horrible sin of idolatry, so that the Lord complained to Moses, "They have turned aside *quickly* out of the way which I commanded them: they have made themselves a molten calf, and have worshipped it" (Exo.

32:8)—how tragically did that portend the whole of their future national history!

No sooner were the "times of the Gentiles" inaugurated by Nebuchadnezzar's being made "a king of kings" (Dan. 2:37), so that his dominion was "to the end of the earth" (4:22), than pride led to his downfall. While he was boasting "Is not this great Babylon that I have built for the house of the kingdom by the might of my power, and for the honour of my majesty?" a voice from Heaven announced, "They shall drive thee from men, and thy dwelling shall be with the beasts of the field; they shall make thee to eat grass as oxen, and seven times shall pass over thee until thou know that the most High ruleth in the kingdom of men, and giveth it to whomsoever He will" (Dan. 4:30, 32). Alas, what is man? Even the honour of the primitive Christian Church was speedily tarnished by the sin of Ananias and Sapphira. Thus it has been all through the piece, and there is no evidence to show that at the commencement of human history Adam and Eve were any exception. Rather are there clear indications to the contrary, so that God had reason to say of them also "they have turned aside quickly out of the way."

Personally, we doubt if our first parents preserved their integrity for forty-eight hours, or even for twenty-four. In the first place, they were bidden to "be fruitful and multiply" (Gen. 1:28), and had they complied with that injunction and the blessing of God had attended the same, then *a sinless child* had been begotten and conceived, which, following the fall of Adam and Eve, would be born into a depraved family—a terrible anomaly, involving the utmost confusion. Second, if those words concerning Christ are to be taken without qualification, "that in *all* things" He might have the preeminence (Col. 1:16), then He is the only One who kept the Sabbath perfectly on this earth, and consequently Adam fell before the seventh day ended! Third, in Psalm 49:12, the Hebrew word for "man" is *Adam*—the same as in Genesis 2 and 3 and Job 31:33, while that for "abode" signifies "to stay or lodge for a night." Manton rendered it "Adam being in honour abideth not for a night," and Thomas Watson (in his *Body of Divinity)* said, "Adam, then, it seems, did not take up one night's lodging in Paradise—quoted by Spurgeon in his *Treasury of David.* Fourth, the Devil "was a manslayer from the beginning," (John 8:44)—not from the beginning of time, for there was no man *to* slay during the first five days, but "from the beginning" *of human history.* In the morning holy; by night a sinner!

It is the melancholy and disastrous episode of the Fall itself we are now to consider. The event is described in Genesis 3, upon which George Whitefield rightly said, "Moses unfolds more in that chapter than all mankind would have been capable of finding out of themselves though they had studied it to all eternity." It is indeed one of the most important chapters in all the Bible, and it should be pondered by us frequently with prayerful hearts. Here commences the great drama which is now being enacted on the stage of human history, and which well-nigh six thousand years have not yet completed. Here is given us the Divine explanation of the present debased and ruined condition of the world. Here we are shown how sin entered it, together with its present effects and dire consequences. Here we have discovered to us the subtle devices of our great enemy the Devil, and are shown how we permit him to gain an advantage over us. On the other hand, it is a most blessed chapter, for it reveals the grace and mercy of God, and assures us that the head of the serpent will yet be crushed by the victorious Seed of the woman—Romans 16:20, telling us that His redeemed will also participate in Christ's glorious triumph. Thus we see, from the commencement, that in wrath our God "remembered mercy"!

A careful reading of Genesis 3 indicates that much is there compacted into an exceedingly small space. The historical account of this momentous incident is given with the utmost conciseness—so very different from how an uninspired pen had dealt with it! Its extreme brevity calls for the careful weighing of every word and the implications of each clause. That there is not a little contained "between the lines" is plainly intimated in the Lord's words to Adam, "Because thou hast hearkened to the *voice* of thy wife" (v. 17), yet the preceding verses nowhere tell us that she even spoke to him! Again, from the judgment pronounced upon the serpent, "upon thy belly shalt thou go" (v. 14), we may warrantably infer that previously it had stood erect. Again, from that part of the Divine sentence passed upon the woman, "thy desire shalt be subject to thy husband, and he shall rule over thee" (v. 16), it is to be concluded that Eve had acted unbecomingly and exerted all undue influence and authority in inducing Adam to eat of the forbidden fruit. Thus if we fail to ponder thoroughly every detail and meditate thereon, we are certain to miss not a little of interest and importance.

"Now the serpent was more subtle (wiser) than any beast of the field which the LORD God had made" (Gen. 3:1). Great care needs to be taken in the interpreting of this sentence. On the one hand, we must not give free rein to our imagination; on the other, it is not to be hurriedly and thoughtlessly skimmed over. Other passages require to be compared in order for their light to be thrown thereon, if a fuller understanding is to be obtained of it. Personally we believe that the statement refers to a *literal* "serpent," yet as being the instrument of a superior being. We consider that the terms of verse 14 make it clear that an actual serpent is here in view, for the Lord's words there are only applicable to that beast itself: "Because thou hast done this, thou art cursed above all cattle . . . upon thy belly shalt thou go, and dust shalt thou eat all the days of thy life." Nevertheless, what immediately follows in verse 15 makes it equally plain that more than a beast of the field was involved, namely Satan. Putting the two statements together, we gather that Satan made use of a literal serpent as his mouthpiece in the beguiling of Eve—as the Lord spoke through the mouth of Balaam's ass (Num. 22:30).

Confirmation of what has just been said is found in John 8:44, where our Lord declared that "*the Devil is* a murderer (or more literally "man-slayer") from the beginning"—designating him such because by his wiles he brought death upon our first parents. Moreover, in Revelation 12:9, and 20: 2, Satan is called "that old serpent" in manifest allusion to the transaction of Genesis 3. "And he said unto the woman, Yea, hath God said, Ye shall not eat of every tree of the garden?" The thoughtful reader is at once struck by the abruptness of this remark, and is almost forced to conclude that the serpent was replying to what Eve had said previously, for his opening "Yea" plainly implies something going before and with which it was connected. This leads us to raise the question, *Where was Eve* when she was thus addressed and assailed? With many others, we believe the answer is, Standing before the very tree whose fruit had been forbidden them to eat! It is apparent from the immediate sequel that she was at least within sight of the tree, and it was from her beholding of it that the serpent took occasion to speak about and commend it unto her.

We also agree with those who have concluded that Adam was *not with Eve* when the serpent first engaged her in conversation, though we know that soon after he had rejoined her. Ridgley, George Whitefield, Gill, and many others held that Eve was alone when she confronted the serpent. For ourselves, we base that belief upon what we are told in 1 Timothy 2:13, 14, where the Holy Spirit has emphasized the fact that the woman was *first* in the transgression, and then became the seducer of the man. That could hardly be said had Adam been present from the beginning, for in such a case he had been *a partaker* of her evil doing—by suffering her to yield to the temptation instead of making every effort in causing her to reject it. Furthermore, it is to be carefully noted that when the guilty couple were arraigned before their Maker, Eve passed no blame upon her husband for making no attempt to dissuade her, but instead sought to throw the onus on the serpent. Nor did the Lord Himself charge Adam with any complicity in his wife's crime, as He surely would have done had Adam been a passive spectator. The serpent, then, tempted Eve in the absence of her husband.

We consider that Eve's being alone, and more especially her near approach unto the fatal tree, casts considerable light on what then occurred. "Had she kept close to the side out of which she was lately taken, she had not been so exposed" (Matthew Henry); and had she kept away from that which threatened certain death, she had been upon safer ground. Satan cannot injure any of us while we are walking with God and are treading the paths of righteousness. We are expressly told that there is no lion "in the way of holiness," that no ravenous beast "shall be found *there*" (Isa. 35:8, 9). No, we have to step out of that way and trespass on the Devil's territory before he can "get an advantage of us" (2 Cor. 2:11). That is why we are so emphatically enjoined, "Enter not into the path of the wicked, and go not in the way of evil men. *Avoid it,* pass not by it, turn from it" (Prov. 4:14, 15). We certainly do not regard Eve as being guilty of any sin at this initial stage, but the sequel shows plainly that she incurred great danger and exposed herself to temptation by approaching so near unto that tree whose fruit had been Divinely prohibited, and we need not be surprised to discover, as she also did, that that ground was already occupied by the serpent! Such has been recorded for our learning and warning.

"And he said unto the woman, Yea, hath God said, Ye shall not eat of every tree in the garden?" The serpent must have looked a very different object then from the repulsive reptile it now is, not only standing erect, but—in keeping with his pre-eminence above all other beasts, and as the Hebrew word intimates—of a striking and beautiful appearance. Apparently he then stood before the tree of the knowledge of good and evil, and it seems more than likely that he personally took and ate of its fruit in Eve's presence. His so doing evoked from her some ejaculation of surprise or look of horror, which explains why he then said what he did. As Samuel Hopkins long ago pointed out, "It is probable that the serpent told the woman that by eating of the fruit of that tree he had obtained the use of reason and the faculty of speech which she now saw in exercise—and therefore said that, from his own experience, he could assure her that if she would eat of this fruit she would be so far from dying that she would reach to a higher degree of perfection and knowledge." While such an inference must not be pressed dogmatically, we have long felt it possesses much probability, and that it is an illuminating one.

Quite recently we discovered that in his "Family Bible" that devout and renowned scholar, John Brown, of Haddington, wrote concerning the serpent's words to Eve, "Perhaps he pretended that himself had acquired what knowledge he had above other beasts by eating of this forbidden fruit. It is certain that he attempted to confirm his contradiction of the threatening by a solemn appeal to God." This requires us to examine closely the tempter's words. It is to be noted that the margin of our Bibles gives an alternative rendering: "Yea, *because* God hath said," which regards his language as a declaration rather than a query—Genesis 13:9; Psalm 35:10; Matthew 26:53; Luke 22:35, are other examples where a strong affirmation and appeal is put (for the sake of emphasis) in the form of an interrogation. Considering it thus here, we may regard the serpent's opening words to Eve as answering her previous expression of surprise. Is it "because God hath said" that you are so startled at seeing me eating the fruit? Thomas Scott also pointed out, "Indeed we cannot satisfactorily account for the woman's entering into conversation with the serpent, and showing no marks of surprise or suspicion, unless we admit a supposition of this kind." It is one of the first duties of an expositor to show the *connection*, explicit or implicit, of each statement of Holy Writ.

"And he said unto the woman, Yea, hath God said, Ye shall not eat of every tree of the garden?" Therein we perceive the guile and enmity of the enemy. His allusion to the Divine restriction made it appear much greater and more severe than it actually was. The Lord had in fact made a free grant for them to eat *freely* of "every tree of the garden" with but a single exception (Gen. 2:16, 17). Thus, Satan sought to bring reproach upon the Divine Law by misrepresenting it! It was as though he said, "Can it be that your Maker has given you appetites and also placed before you the means of gratifying them, only to mock you? You surely must have misunderstood His meaning!" We therefore regard this opening utterance of the serpent's as an attempt not only to make Eve doubt God's veracity, but also to cause her to suspect the Divine beneficence. *That* is the poison Satan is ever seeking to inject into our hearts: to distrust God's goodness—especially in connection with His prohibitions and precepts. That is really what lies behind all evil lusting and disobedience: a discontent with our position and portion, a craving for something which God has wisely withheld from us. The more clearly we perceive the precise *nature* of the serpent's poison the better enabled are we to *judge* its workings within ourselves. Hearken not to any suggestion that God is unduly severe with you! Put from you with the utmost abhorrence anything which causes you to doubt God's lovingkindness. Allow nothing to make you call into question His love.

Its Origin

In review, we have called attention to the exceeding brevity of the narrative of Genesis 3 and the need for us to weigh carefully every word in its opening verses and ponder the implication of each clause. We pointed out that not a little is contained "between the lines" and therefore, while we must refrain from reading into it what is *not* there, we must be careful not to overlook anything of importance which *is* there, either explicit or implicit—by definite statement or necessary inference. We also gave our reasons for believing that Eve was away from the side of her husband, and that it was because she had entered dangerous ground by approaching so closely unto the fatal tree that she was there confronted by the serpent and subjected to temptation. Further, we intimated that the sentence passed upon the serpent by the Lord in verse 14 warrants us to conclude that before he seduced the woman he stood erect, and that his form and appearance at that time were very different from the present repulsiveness of that reptile. We also made reference to the opinion of many reputable writers that there seems reason to think that Eve beheld the serpent himself eating of the forbidden fruit, that such a spectacle evoked from her an ejaculation of surprise, and that this alone accounts for the abruptness of his opening statement.

"And he said unto the woman, Yea, hath God said, Ye shall not eat of every tree of the garden?" (Gen. 3:1). As Matthew Henry pertinently pointed out, "Satan tempted Eve that, by her, he might tempt Adam; so he tempted Job by his wife, and Christ by Peter. It is his policy to send temptations by unsuspected hands, and theirs that have most interest in us and influence over us." Eve's suspicions ought at once to have been aroused when the serpent introduced such a subject for conversation, and she should have turned away immediately from him. "Those that would keep from harm, must keep out of harm's way" (Henry). Or, as one infinitely greater than any human commentator bids us, "Go *from* the presence of a foolish man when thou perceivest not in him the lips of knowledge" (Prov. 14:7). And again, "Cease, my son, to hear the instruction that causeth to err from the words of knowledge" (Prov. 19:27). The serpent's opening word was designed to produce in Eve a spirit of discontent. It was really a sly insinuation which amounted to this: If you cannot eat of all the trees, you might as well eat of none—as Ahab, with all his royal possessions, was dissatisfied while denied Naboth's vineyard; and Haman, though he had found favour with the king, petulantly exclaimed "all of this availeth me nothing" so long as Mordecai refused to pay him deference.

If Eve were not already secretly desiring the forbidden fruit, would she have paid any attention to the cunning query made to her?

We very much doubt it. Still less can we conceive of her entering into a discussion with the serpent on the subject. Dalliance with temptation always implies a lusting after the object presented. Had she been content with God's grant in Genesis 2:16, and were she satisfied with the knowledge He had given her by creation, she would have *abhorred* the false knowledge proposed by the tempter, and that would have precluded all parleying with him! That is more than a supposition of ours, for it is obviously confirmed by what follows. Compare her conduct with Christ's, and observe how very differently He acted! He steadfastly refused to enter into any debate with the Devil. He did not dally with temptation, for He had no desire for anything but the will of God. Each time He firmly repulsed the enemy's advances by taking His stand upon God's Word—as Eve ought to have done—and concluded by thrusting away Satan's solicitation with the utmost detestation. A greater contrast cannot be imagined: the woman's Seed met Satan's temptation with holy loathing; the woman was in a condition to respond to the serpent's wiles with unholy delight.

"And the woman said unto the serpent, We may eat of the fruit of the trees of the garden; but of the fruit of the tree which is in the midst of the garden, God hath said, Ye shall not eat of it, neither shall ye touch it, lest ye die" (Gen. 3:2, 3). Instead of fleeing in dread from the serpent, Eve conferred with him, which, as the outcome showed, was both foolish and fatal. Satan is much wiser than we are, and if we attempt to meet his own ground and argue with him the result will be disastrous. His evil influence had already begun to affect Eve injuriously, as appears from a close examination of the first part of her reply. The Lord had said, "Of every tree of the garden thou mayest *freely* eat," and Eve's omission of that word "freely" was both significant and ominous—indicating that the generosity of the Divine grant was not influencing her heart as it should. But on the other hand we do not agree with those who charge her with *adding* to God's word in verse 3, for while the "neither shall ye touch it" was not distinctly expressed in Genesis 2:17, nevertheless it was clearly and necessarily implied—how could she eat of the fruit without "touching" it?—the one act requires the other.

There is a very important principle involved in what has just been pointed out: one which it behooves us to understand clearly and make conscience of. That principle may be stated thus: when God forbids any act He at the same time forbids everything tending thereto and leading up to it. Our Lord made that very plain in His sermon on the mount, as He enforced the spirituality and strictness of the Law when repudiating the errors of the Jewish religious leaders, who were guilty of modifying its holy requirements. He insisted that "thou shalt not kill" is by no means to be restricted unto the bare act of murder: that it also prohibits every evil exercise of the mind and heart preceding it—such as hatred, ill-will, malice. In like manner He declared that "thou shalt not commit adultery" included very much more than interdicting unlawful intercourse between the sexes, but, even impure imaginations and desires. That commandment is broken as soon as there is an unchaste lusting or even looking. God demands very much more than merely keeping clean the outside of the cup and platter (Matt. 23:25, 26). So too "thou shalt not steal" includes not even *thinking* of so doing, nor handling what is not yours—still less borrowing anything when you have no intention of returning it.

Eve, then, was quite right in concluding that the Divine commandment forbidding them to *eat* of the tree of the knowledge of good and evil comprehended "neither shall ye touch it," for the act of eating involves not only the desire and intention so to do, but the touching, handling, plucking, and placing of the fruit in the mouth. But we are not so sure about the exact force of her words "lest ye die." Many have supposed she was there toning down the Lord's "thou shalt surely die" of 2:17. They may be right, but we are not at all sure. "Kiss the Son, *lest* He be angry" (Psalm 2:12) is obviously not the language of uncertainty. The Hebrew for "lest" here is *pen* and in Genesis 24:6, is rendered "that . . . . not." If the reader will compare John 3:20; 12:42; 1 Corinthians 1:17; he will see that the force of "lest" in these passages is "otherwise." Gill also states that Eve's employment of the "lest" is "not at all conclusive that she expressed any doubt, since the word may also be used of the event of anything as in Psalm 2:12, and hence may be rendered "that ye die not." We therefore prefer to leave it as "an open question."

"And the serpent said unto the woman, Ye shall not surely die" (v. 4). Perceiving his advantage, that he had now gained Eve's ear, the tempter grew bolder and flatly contradicted the Divine threatening. He began by seeking to instill a doubt—Is it so or not?—by casting a reflection upon the Divine goodness and making Eve dissatisfied with God's most liberal grant; and then he denied that there was any danger in eating of the fruit. First he had, by implication, slandered God's character; and now he told a downright lie. If, as we believe was the case, he had himself eaten of the forbidden tree in the woman's presence, then his action would lend colour to his falsehood. It was as though he said, You need not hesitate, God is only seeking to frighten you. You can see for yourself the fruit is quite harmless, for I have partaken of it without suffering any ill effects. Thus does the great enemy of souls seek to persuade man that he may defy God with impunity, inducing him when "he heareth the words of this curse" to "bless himself in his heart, saying, I shall have peace, though I walk in the imagination of mine heart, to add drunkenness to thirst" (Deut. 29:19).

No excuse can be made for Eve now. If she had acted foolishly in approaching so near to the fatal tree, if her suspicions were not at once aroused by the serpent's opening remark, she certainly ought to have been deeply horrified, and turned away immediately, when she heard him giving the lie to the Lord her God. If Joseph "fled" from his temptress (Gen. 39:12), much more reason had Eve now to run from the serpent with loathing. Instead, she remained to hear him add, "For God doth know that in the day ye eat thereof, then your eyes shall be opened, and ye shall be as gods, knowing good and evil" (v. 5). Therein he declared that not only would no harm be suffered, but they would be the gainers by heeding his suggestion and doing as he had done. A threefold promise or inducement was set before the woman. First, that by eating of this fruit their capacity of discernment and perception would be considerably increased, for that is the force of "your eyes shall be opened"—those of their bodies were so already, therefore his reference must be to the eyes of their understanding. Second, their position would be improved and their power enlarged: they should be as "gods" or angels. Third, their wisdom would be much augmented: "knowing good and evil"—as though that were most desirable. And all of this *at once*—"then," without any delay.

It will be observed from the above that the serpent addressed himself not to Eve's bodily appetites but to the noblest part of her being, by the inducement of such an increase of wisdom as would elevate our first parents above their then condition and fit them to be meet companions for the celestial creatures. Therein lay the force of his temptation: seeking to fan a desire for forbidden knowledge and self-sufficiency—to act independently of God. From then until now, Satan's object has been to divert men from the only Source of wisdom and cause them to seek it from him. Nevertheless, the bait dangled before Eve in nowise hid the barb he was using to catch her. Taking together the whole of his statement in verses 4 and 5, the serpent not only charged God with making a threat which He had no intention of fulfilling, but also accused Him of being tyrannical in withholding from them what He knew would be for their good. Said he, You need have no fear that God will be as severe and rigorous as His language sounded. He is only seeking to intimidate you. He is well aware that if you eat this fruit, your knowledge will be greatly enlarged, but this He is unwilling should be your portion, and therefore He is seeking to prevent it by this unreasonable prohibition.

"And when the woman saw that the tree was good for food, and that it was pleasant to the eyes, and a tree to be desired to make one wise, she took of the fruit thereof, and did eat" (v. 6). Ere examining the details of this tragic verse, let us carefully consider two questions, and endeavour to supply answers thereto. First, why did not the Divine threat in Genesis 2:17 deter Eve from disobeying God? David declared, "Thy Word have I hid in mine heart (to be awed thereby, to put it into practice), that I might not sin against Thee" (Psa. 119:11). It is clear from Genesis 3:3, that God's word was at least in Eve's thoughts when the serpent accosted her: then how was it that it did not preserve her from sin? Surely the answer is that she did not make use of it, but instead dallied with temptation, parleyed with God's enemy, and believed his lie; and therein is to be found a most solemn warning for us. If we would have God deliver us from the destroyer, then we must determine to shun every occasion of evil and, as Joseph, flee from temptation when it is presented to us. If we really take to heart the solemn failure and fall of Eve, then we shall pray with ever-increasing earnestness, "Lead me not into temptation," and if Thou art pleased for me to be tested, "deliver me from evil."

Second, in 2 Corinthians 11:3, we are informed that "the serpent beguiled (or "cheated") Eve through his subtlety," and in 1 Timothy 2:14, that she was "deceived." How then are we to explain what is recorded of her in Genesis 3, where the historical account seems to make it very plain that she committed the act after due deliberation, with her eyes wide open? Wherein was she "deceived" if she knowingly disobeyed God? The answer is that, as soon as she ceased to be regulated by the light of God's word, her imagination became filled with the false impressions presented to her by Satan, and her foolish mind became darkened. Unholy lustings were begotten within her. Her affections and appetites overrode her judgment, and she was persuaded to disbelieve what was true and believe what was false. Oh, the "deceitfulness of sin" (Heb. 3:13), which calls good evil and bitter sweet. She was beguiled by consenting to listen to another voice than God's, and because she disregarded her allegiance to her husband. Oh, my reader, the prelude to every fall from grace is the alienation of the heart from Christ (the Christian's spiritual Husband), with the consequent beclouding of the judgment. When the truth be rejected, error is welcome. Satan, in his efforts to induce souls to seek their happiness in departing from God, ever adapts his temptations to the cases and circumstances of the tempted.

"And when the woman saw that the tree was good for food, and that it was pleasant to the eyes" (Gen. 3:6). Let it be duly considered at what point this statement comes in the narrative: not at the commencement, but after all that is recorded in the preceding verses had transpired! Let us also observe the *order* of those two clauses. We would naturally expect to find it said that Eve saw the tree was "pleasant to the eyes" *before* mention being made that it was "good for food." Why, then, are the two things reversed? Does not the raising of these queries the better enable us to understand exactly what is meant by "*when* the woman *saw* that the tree was good for food"? The time-mark must not be ignored, for it cannot be without significance. We suggest that it looks back to the foregoing action of the serpent, which we believe to be clearly implied in the context, namely her seeing him personally eat of the forbidden fruit. How else could she perceive the tree was "good for food" before she had herself partaken of it? Does not the third clause of the verse confirm and clinch this interpretation, for how else could Eve possibly know the fruit was "to be desired to *make one wise*" unless she had previously witnessed what appeared to her to be an ocular demonstration of the same?

Is it not evident, then, that the words "And when the woman saw that the tree *was good* for food" signify that since she had beheld the serpent eating thereof without dying or even suffering any injury she need have no fear to emulate him; yea, could infer that it was from his so doing that he had acquired the faculty of reason and the power of speech, and she too would be much advantaged by partaking of the same? Instead of acting faith on the word of God, she walked by sight, only to discover—as her sons and daughters often do—that *appearances* are very deceptive. Moreover, she saw "that it was pleasant to the eyes": there was nothing in the outward appearance of the fruit to denote that it was unfit for eating; on the contrary, it looked attractive. In Genesis 2:9, we read that "out of the ground made the LORD God to grow every tree that is pleasant to the sight, and good for food," and, as the remainder of that verse shows, the tree of the knowledge of good and evil was no exception. All creation was beautiful and agreeable to the senses, but by her yielding to the serpent's temptation, *that* tree was now particularly appealing unto Eve: she had a secret hankering after it and unlawfully coveted the same.

Had there been any uncertainty in her mind, her course was plain—to consult her husband, which is ever the wife's duty and privilege. Instead, we are told that she saw the tree was "to be desired to make one wise." That is to say, she judged it entirely by what the serpent had told her—and not by what God had said—as a reference to the preceding verse shows. She was flattered with the false hope which the enemy had held out to her. She first gave credence to his "ye shall not surely die." Next she was attracted by the prospect of becoming like the "gods" or angels. And then, on her believing the promise of augmented knowledge, lustful longing consumed her. The Hebrew word for "desired" in Genesis 3:6, is the one that is rendered "thou shalt not covet" in Exodus 20:17. It is the same thing as is termed "concupiscence" in Romans 7:8, and "lust" in James 1:15. Indeed, we may see how that latter passage traces for us in detail the course of Eve's downfall, and how in turn her conduct solemnly illustrates James 1:14, 15. "But every man is tempted, when he is drawn away (from the path of rectitude) of his own lust (as Eve evidently was in approaching the forbidden tree), and enticed (as she was by the serpent). Then when lust hath conceived (in her by the seductive promises of the serpent), it bringeth forth sin (externally); and sin, when it is finished (i.e. the outward act is completed), bringeth forth death"!

"God's commandment, in its full form, was, Thou shalt not lust after but abhor the knowledge of good and evil, thou shalt not choose but refuse it. The prohibition in the instance of the Eden statute, as in that of the Ten Commandments, involved both the inward desire and the outward act, both inclination and volition" (W. Shedd). Note well that the holiness of Christ is described as a *refusing* of the evil and choosing the good (Isa. 7:15). He who *desires* the prohibited evil does in effect *choose* it; as he who hates another violates the Sixth Commandment though he does not actually slay him. The fruit was *not* to be "desired" by Eve, for God had forbidden her to eat it. Instead of desiring, she should have *dreaded* it, but she turned from God as her everlasting portion and chief end. In lusting after what God had prohibited, she preferred the creature to the Creator. Unspeakably solemn warning for us. If we estimate things by our senses or by what others say of them, instead of accepting God's valuation, we are certain to err in our judgment. If we resort to carnal reasoning, we shall quickly persuade ourselves that wrong is right. Nothing is *good for you, my* reader, save that which you can receive from *God's* hand and thank Him for it!

"She took of the fruit thereof, and did eat" (Gen. 3:6) without consulting Adam. So strong was the unlawful lusting of her heart that she could no longer abstain, and thus she committed the overt act, thereby completing "the transgression." Yes, "*she* took of the fruit thereof, and did eat"—it was not the serpent who put it into her mouth! Satan may tempt, but *force* anyone, he cannot. It was by her own free act she took of the fruit, and therefore she could rightly blame none but herself. By this time Adam had rejoined her, for we are told that she "gave also unto her husband *with her*"—the first time he is mentioned in the sacred narrative as being by her side! Such is the vile nature of sin: ourselves yielding to temptation, and then becoming the tempters of others—seeking to drag them down to our level. "And he did eat," instead of refusing what his God-defying wife proffered him. He "was not deceived" (1 Tim. 2:14), which, if possible, made his guilt the greater. He "hearkened unto the voice of his wife" (Gen. 3:17): probably she repeated to him what the serpent had said unto her, commending the fruit, and possibly pointing out that they must have misunderstood the Lord's words, since she had eaten and was still alive.

Thus did man apostatize from God. It was a revolt from his Maker, an insurrection from His supremacy, a rebelling against His authority. He deliberately resisted the Divine will, rejected God's word, deserted His way. Thereby he was despoiled of his primitive excellence and forfeited all his happiness. Adam cast himself and all his posterity into the deepest gulf of woe and wretchedness. Such, my reader, was the *origin* of human depravity. Genesis 3 gives us the Divinely inspired account of how sin entered this world, and supplies the only adequate and satisfactory explanation both of its six thousand years' history and of its present-day condition.

THE DOCTRINE OF HUMAN DEPRAVITY
Its Imputation

We are now to consider the bearing which Adam's sin had upon his posterity, and the different effects which it entailed and produced—though the latter will come before us in another chapter (D.V.), wherein we shall treat more specifically with the consequences of the Fall. What we are here to examine particularly requires us to turn unto and look more closely at what was briefly alluded to in *Part 2 of Its Origin*, namely that in Eden Adam acted not simply as a private person, the results of whose conduct affected none but himself, but rather that he transacted as a public person, so that what he did directly concerned and judicially involved others. Adam was very much more than the father of the human race: he was also their legal agent, standing in their stead. His descendants were not only in him seminally as their natural head, but were in him also morally and legally as their moral and forensic head. In other words, by Divine constitution and covenant arrangement, Adam acted as the federal representative of all his children. By an act of His sovereign will, it pleased God to ordain that Adam's relation to his natural seed should be like unto that which Christ sustained to His spiritual seed—the one acting on the behalf of many.

The whole human race was placed on probation in the person of its legal representative and covenant head. This is a truth of great importance, for it casts light not only upon much in Scripture, but upon human history, too. While Adam retained the approbation of God and remained in fellowship with Him, the whole of his constituency did likewise. Had he survived the appointed trial, had he faithfully and fitly discharged his responsibility, had he continued in obedience unto the Lord God, then *his* obedience had been reckoned to *their* account, and they had entered into and been fellow partakers of the reward bestowed on him. Contrariwise, if the head failed and fell, then all his members fell in and with him. If he disobeyed, then his disobedience was charged unto those whom he represented, and the frightful punishment pronounced upon him fell likewise on those on whose behalf he transacted. Justice required that the whole human race should be legally regarded and dealt with as sharing the guilt of its representative, and subjected to the same penalty as was inflicted upon him. In consequence of this arrangement, when Adam sinned, we sinned, and therefore, "by the offence of one judgment came upon all men to condemnation" (Rom. 5:18).

Instead of placing each member of the human race on probation separately and successively, it pleased God to put the whole of them on formal trial once and for all in the person of their head. Probably it will make it easier for the reader to grasp the nature of Adam's legal relation unto his descendants if we make use of a simple contrast and analogy, which have been employed by other writers on this subject. God did not treat with mankind as with a field of corn, where each stalk stands on its own individual root; but rather has He dealt with our race as with a tree—all the branches of which have one common root. While the root of a tree remains healthy and unharmed, the whole of it flourishes. But if an axe strikes at and severs the root, then the whole of the tree suffers and falls—not only the trunk, but all the branches, and even its smallest twigs wither and die. Thus it was in connection with the Eden tragedy. When Adam's communion with his Maker was broken, all his posterity were alienated from His favour. This is no theory of human speculation, but a fact of Divine revelation: "Wherefore, as by one man sin entered into the world, and death by sin; and so death passed upon all men, for that all have sinned" (Rom. 5:12).

Adam, then, occupied a unique position. At his creation all his unborn children were germinally created in him. Not only so, but God entered into a solemn covenant with him in their name. The entire human family was represented by him and stood in him before the Lord. The future well-being of his progeny was suspended on his conduct. He was therefore placed on trial, to show whether he would promote the interests of his Creator, or refuse to be subject to His government. Some test must needs be given him in order for the exercise of his moral agency and the discharge of his responsibility. He was made to love and serve God, being richly endowed and fully capacitated thereunto. His supreme blessedness and continued happiness consisted in his so doing. In what follows we shall submit scriptural proof that Adam *did* transact on the behalf of his descendants, and so stood in their stead before the Divine Law that what *he* did was, in effect, what *they* did. Or, as Manton expressed it, "We saw the forbidden fruit with his eyes, gathered it with his hands, ate it with his mouth; that is, we were ruined by those things as though we had been there and consented to his acts."

We propose to show, first, that Adam was the federal head of the race. Second, that he entered into a covenant with God on their behalf. Third, that the guilt of his original sin was Divinely imputed to his descendants. Concerning the first we shall confine ourselves unto two proof texts. "Death reigned from Adam to Moses, even over them that had not sinned after the similitude of Adam's transgression, who is *the figure of Him* that was to come" (Rom. 5:14). That is truly an astonishing statement. Occurring in such a setting it is really startling and should at once arrest our attention. With what accuracy and propriety could it be said that the father of our fallen race foreshadowed the Lord Jesus? Adam, when tempted yielded and was overcome; Christ, when tempted resisted and overcame. The former was cursed by God, the latter was owned by Him as the One in whom He was well pleased. The one is the source of sin and corruption to all his posterity, but the other is a fount of holiness unto all His people. By Adam came condemnation, by Christ comes salvation. Thus they are as far apart as the poles. Wherein, then, was Adam a "figure" of the coming Redeemer?

The Greek word for "figure" in Romans 5:14, signifies "type," and in the scriptural sense of that term, a type consists of something very much more than a casual resemblance between two things or an incidental parallel between them. There is a *designed* likeness, the one being Divinely intended to shadow forth the other. From all eternity it was foreordained that the first man should prefigure the incarnate Son of God. Again we ask, In what particular respect? Certainly not in his conduct. Nor in his natural constitution, as consisting of sprit and soul and body, for in that matter all who lived before Christ was born might as properly be called figures of Him. The whole context makes it clear that it was in the *official position* which he occupied that Adam was a type of the Lord Jesus—as the federal head and legal representative of others. If Romans 5:12-19 be read attentively, it will be seen that all through it the fact which is there given the greatest prominence is that of the one acting on behalf of the many, the one affecting the destiny of the many. What the one did is made the legal ground of what befalls the many. As the disobedience and guilt of Adam entailed condemnation for all who were legally one with him, so the obedience and righteousness of Christ has secured the justification of all in whose place He served as Surety.

The other passage by which it may be proved that Adam sustained the relation of federal head to his posterity is 1 Corinthians 15:45-49. "And so it is written, The first man Adam was made a living soul: the last Adam was made a quickening spirit . . . . The first man is of the earth, earthy; the second man is the Lord from Heaven . . . . And as we have borne the image of the earthy, we shall also bear the image of the heavenly." Here again, despite marked contrasts between the type and the Antitype, there is that which is common to both of them. A mundane origin had the one: the other's was celestial. The former was but a man; the latter was "the Lord." The first Adam was made "a living soul," the last Adam is a Quickener of others. In the one "all die," in the other, "shall all be made alive" (v. 22). But that which marked each alike was his *representative character*—he was the head of an appointed seed, communicating his distinctive "image" to them. Adam is designated "the first man" not simply because he was the first in order—like the first day of the week—but because he was the first to act as the legal representative of a race. Christ is called "the second man," though He lived so long afterward, because He was the second to sustain a federal relation to an appointed seed, and "the last Adam" because there is to be no further covenant head.

We turn next to show that a *covenant* was entered into between the Lord God and Adam. Our first appeal is unto Genesis 2:16, 17, but before considering that passage let us remind the reader of the extreme brevity of the early chapters of Genesis, and that more is definitely implied by their contents than is distinctly expressed. Let us also point out what are the principal elements in a covenant. A covenant is a formal compact and mutual arrangement between two or more parties whereby they stand solemnly bound unto each other to perform the conditions contracted for. On the one side there is a stipulating of something to be done; on the other side a restipulation of some thing to be done or given in consideration thereof. There is also a penalty included in the terms of the agreement—some evil consequence which shall result unto the party who violates or fails to carry out his engagement. That penalty is added as a security. Where it is not expressly stated, it is implied by the promissory clause, just as the promise is to be necessarily inferred from a mention of the punishment therein (cf. Gen. 31:43-53; Matt. 26:14-16).

"And the LORD God commanded the man, saying, Of every tree of the garden thou mayest freely eat. But of the tree of the knowledge of good and evil, thou shalt not eat of it; for in the day that thou eatest thereof thou shalt surely die" (Gen. 2:16, 17). Here are all the constituent elements of a covenant. First, here are the contracting parties: the Lord God and man. Second, here is the condition defined and accepted. As the Creator and Governor of His creatures, it behooved God to exercise His authority; owing his being to Him, Adam was in duty bound to comply, and as a sinless and holy person he would heartily consent to the stipulation. Third, there was a penalty prescribed, which would be incurred if Adam failed to carry out his part of the compact. Fourth, there was by clear implication a promise made and reward assured—"do this, and thou shalt live"—to which Adam was entitled upon his rendering the obedience required. Where there is a stipulation and a restipulation between two parties, and a binding law pertaining to the same, there is a covenant (cf. Gen. 21:22-32).

Adam was placed not only under Divine Law, but under a Covenant of Works. The distinction is real and radical. A law requires obedience, and a punishment is threatened, in proportion to the nature of the offence, in case of disobedience. A subject is bound to obey the law, but he cannot be justly deprived of that which he has a natural right to, except in case of disobedience. On the other hand, while obedience to the law gives him a right to impunity, yet nothing more; whereas a covenant gives a person the right, upon his fulfilling the conditions thereof, to the reward or privilege stipulated therein. A king is not obliged to advance a loyal subject unto great honour; but if, as an act of favour, he has promised to elevate him upon his yielding obedience in some particular instance, then he would have a right to it—not as yielding obedience to a law, but as fulfilling the terms of a covenant. Thus Mephibosheth had a natural and legal right to his life and to the estate which had descended to him from his father, because he had lived peaceably and had not rebelled against David. But *this* did not entitle him to the special favour which the king conferred upon him, of sitting at his table continually (2 Samuel 9:13). *That* was the result of a covenant between David and Jonathan, in which David had promised to show kindness unto his house after him (1 Sam. 20:11-17, 42).

We consider that it should be obvious to the thoughtful reader that Adam had the promise of life upon his performing the condition agreed, for "in the day thou eatest thereof thou shalt surely die" necessarily implied the converse—If thou eatest not thereof thou shalt surely live. Just as "thou shalt not steal" inevitably requires "thou shalt act honestly and honourably," and as "rejoice in the Lord" includes "murmur not against any of His dealings with thee." So according to the simplest laws of construction, the threatening of death as the consequence of eating affirmed the promise of life unto obedience. This is an essential feature of a covenant—a reward guaranteed upon the fulfillment of its terms. Let it also be duly noted that the threat denounced in Genesis 2:17, not only signified God's intention to punish sin, but was also designed as a motive unto obedience, and therefore it included in it a promise of life upon man's maintaining his integrity. Again, had Adam been given no such promise, then he had been *without* a well-grounded hope for the future, for the hope which makes us not ashamed is always grounded upon the Divine promise (Rom. 4:18-20). Finally, Romans 8:10 expressly states that the commandment was *"to life"*—adapted to and setting before its complier such a prospect.

A few words need to be said here upon *the nature of* that "life" which was promised unto Adam. In his original state he was already possessed of spiritual life: what then did the reward consist of? Two different answers have been returned by the best of the theologians. First, that it was the *ratifying* of the life which he then had. Adam was placed on probation, and it was his response to the test that had been given him which would determine whether or not he remained in the favour of God, in communion with Him, and continued to enjoy his earthly heritage; whether they should be *confirmed,* and would then become the inalienable portion both of himself and his posterity. Such was the view long entertained by this writer. But of late we incline much more to the second alternative, namely that by the "life" promised Adam we are to understand a yet higher degree of happiness than he then possessed, even heavenly blessedness. Those benefits which Christ came into the world to procure for His people, and which are assured to them by the Covenant of Grace, are, for substance, the same as those which man would have enjoyed had he not fallen. This we consider is clear from those prophetic words of Christ: "I *restored* that which I took not away" (Psa. 69:4); and again, "The Son of man is come to seek and to save that which was lost" (Luke 19:10). He came to secure "eternal life" (with all that that means), and therefore *that* had been man's portion had he maintained his integrity.

The same may also be concluded from the nature of that "death" denounced in Genesis 2:17. When God said, "In the day that thou eatest thereof thou shalt surely *die,*" something far more dreadful than the loss of physical, or even spiritual life was involved, even the "second death," namely eternal punishment and suffering in the lake of fire. Contrariwise, the "life" promised included more than physical immortality or even the confirmation of spiritual life, even everlasting life, or unclouded fellowship with God in Heaven forever. We also concur with many able expositors that Romans 8:3. 4, treats of the same thing "The law" there looks back to that which was written on man's heart at the beginning—of which the Sinaitic was but a transcript. The statement that the Law was "weak through the flesh" alludes to the delectability of Adam. What the Law "could not do " with *such* material was to produce an indefeasible righteousness. Therefore God, in His sovereign grace, sent His own incarnate Son, impeccable and immutable, to make full atonement for the guilt of His people and bring in an "everlasting righteousness" (Dan. 9:24) for them. In a word, Christ performed that perfect obedience which the first man failed to render, and thereby obtained for all His seed the award of the fulfilled Law.

What has last been pointed out should remove any misconception that the view we have just propounded derogates in the slightest degree from the glory of the Saviour. Romans 8:3, 4, is treating of something far more essential and weighty than whether or not Christ, by His infinite merits, obtained for us something more than we lost in Adam: undoubtedly He did—our *establishment* in righteousness, our glorification, etc. Rather does that passage intimate what was the highest motive and ultimate end which God had before Him when He foresaw, foreordained and permitted our fall in Adam. *Christ* is the grand Centre of all the Divine counsels, and the magnifying of Him their principal design. Had God withheld Adam from sinning, all his race had been eternally happy. But in that case Adam had been their saviour and benefactor and all his seed had gloried *in him,* ascribing their everlasting felicity to his obedience. But such an honour was far too much for any finite creature to bear. Only the Lord from Heaven was worthy of it. Accordingly God designedly made the flesh of the first man "weak" or mutable and suffered his defection, in order to make way for His laying our help "upon One that is *mighty*" (Psa. 89:19), that we might owe our endless bliss unto Him! Moreover, that obedience which Christ rendered to the Law magnified it and made it infinitely more honourable than could the conformity to it of any mere creature.

Returning now to the scriptural evidence that God entered into a covenant with Adam. In Hosea 6:7, we read that God complained of Israel, "But they *like men* have transgressed *the covenant,* they have dealt treacherously against Me" (margin)—the Hebrew word for "men" there is Adam, as in Job 31:33. Adam, then, *was* placed under a covenant, the requirement or condition of which was his continued subjection unto God—whether or not the Divine will was sacred in his eyes. But he failed to love God with all his heart, held His high authority in contempt, disbelieved His holy veracity, deliberately and presumptuously defied Him. Thereby he "transgressed the covenant" and "dealt treacherously" with his Maker. In like manner did Israel, centuries later transgress the covenant which they entered into with the Lord at Sinai, preferring their own will and way, lusting after those false gods which He had forbidden under pain of death. Finally, let it be pointed out that the fact of Adam's having stood as the covenant head of his race is conclusively demonstrated by the penal evils which come upon his children in consequence of his fall. From the dreadful curse entailed upon all his descendants, we are
compelled to infer the covenant relationship which existed between him and them—for the Judge of all the earth, being righteous, will never punish where there is no crime. "In Adam all *die*," because in him all *sinned.*

Having proved from Scripture that God constituted Adam the covenant head and federal representative of his race, we are now to show that the guilt of his original sin was imputed unto all his posterity. Were there no explicit statements to that effect in the Bible we should be obliged to infer the same, for with *those* principles such a conclusion is inevitable. If the one was acting in the name and on the behalf of many, then the latter are legally responsible for what he did and must suffer the consequences of his conduct, be it good or evil. Had Adam survived the test to which he was subjected, had he remained obedient to his Maker and Lord, then his obedience had been reckoned to the account of all his seed, and they had been joint partakers of his reward. But if he revolted from the Divine government and preferred his own will and way, then the punishment he incurred must be visited also upon the whole of his constituency. Such a procedure is neither merciful nor unmerciful, but a matter of *righteousness*. Justice requires that the penalty of a broken law shall be visited upon its transgressors. A precept without penalty is simply advice, or at most a request, and compliance therewith merely a species of self-pleasing, and not submission unto authority. To divest the Divine Law of its sanction would be to reduce God to a mere supplicant—begging His creatures to behave themselves.

Not only had God the sovereign right to constitute Adam the covenant head of his race; not only was it strictly and legally just that its members should be held accountable for what he did, whether it issued in their weal or woe; but consider the *meetness* of such an arrangement. Since the loyalty and subjection of man to his Maker must be put to the proof, only two alternatives were possible: either the human race must be placed on probation in the person of a suitable representative and responsible head, or each individual member must enter upon probation for himself. "The race must either have stood in a full-grown man, with a full-orbed intellect, or stood as babies, each entering his probation in the twilight of self-consciousness, each deciding his destiny before his eyes were half-opened to what it all meant. How much better would that have been? How much more just? But could it not have been some other way? There was no other way. It was either the baby, or it was the perfect, well-equipped, all-calculating man—the man who saw and comprehended everything. That man was Adam" (G. S. Bishop).

Fresh from the hands of his Creator, with no sinful heredity behind and no depraved nature within him, but instead endowed with holiness and indwelt by the Spirit of God, Adam was well equipped for the honourable position assigned him. His fitness to serve as our head, and the ideal circumstances under which the decisive test was made, must forever close every honest mouth from objecting against the Divine arrangement and the fearful consequences which Adam's failure has brought down upon us. It has been well said that, "Had we been present, had we and all the human race been brought into existence at once, and had God proposed to us that we should choose one who was to be our representative, that He might enter into covenant with him on our behalf—should not we, with one voice, have chosen our first parent for this responsible office? Should we not have said, 'He is a perfect man and bears the image and likeness of God—if anyone is to standfor us, let it be this man Adam'? Since the angels which stood for themselves fell, why should we wish to stand for ourselves? And if it be reasonable that one stand for us, why should we complain when God has chosen the same person for this office that we should have chosen had we been in existence and capable of choosing ourselves?" (G. S. Bishop).

Ere proceeding farther, let it be insisted upon that God is nowise to be blamed for Adam's fall. After a thorough and extensive investigation Solomon declared, "This only have I found, that God hath made man upright; but they have sought out many inventions" (Eccl. 7:29). There the streams of human folly and iniquity are all traced back to their fountain-head of corruption. Man was created without irregularity or blemish; but he departed from his original rectitude. And why? Because he vainly supposed he could *better himself.* "They," that is, Adam and Eve, at first, followed by their crazed descendants, "sought out many inventions." Significant and suggestive words! What are "inventions" but devices to improve things? And what gives rise to such attempts but dissatisfaction with present conditions? Our first parents thought to find a superior way of happiness by kicking off their traces. Instead of being content with what their Maker had given and appointed them, they preferred their own will to God's, their inventions rather than His institutions. They forsook their rest in the Lord and sought to improve their case. They promised themselves liberty, only to become the slaves of Satan.

The course taken by our first parents is that which has been followed ever since by all their children, as is intimated in the change from the singular number to the plural in Ecclesiastes 7:29. As indicated above, we do not (as most expositors) regard the prime reference in that passage as being to the "aprons of fig leaves" which Adam and Eve sewed together, but rather to their original sin in being *dissatisfied* with the state in which God had placed them—vainly imagining to improve their lot by leaning unto their own understanding, following the desires of their hearts and responding to the evil solicitation of the serpent. Thus it has been, and still is, with their descendants. They have turned from the Creator to the creature for their comfort: having forsaken the Living Fountain, they engage themselves in hewing out "cisterns that can hold no water" (Jer. 2:13)—preferring the "far country" to the Father's house. Their search after wisdom, their mad quest for pleasure, their pursuit of wealth and worldly honours, are but so many "inventions" or attempts to better their lot, and proofs of a restless and dissatisfied heart! Had our first parents been content with the goodly heritage which their Maker assigned them, they would not have coveted that which He had prohibited. And today the remedy for covetousness is contentment—see Hebrews 13:5.

We therefore subscribe unhesitatingly to the dictum of Calvin, "It is clear that the misery of man must be ascribed wholly to himself, since he was favoured with rectitude by the Divine goodness, but has lapsed into vanity through his own folly." God expressly forbade Adam to eat of the tree of knowledge of good and evil. He plainly warned him what would be the consequence of disobedience. Though He made man a mutable creature, yet not evil—Adam had ability to stand as well as to fall. He was fully capable of loving God as his chief good and of moving toward Him as his last end. There was light in his understanding to know the rule he was to conform unto. There was perfect harmony between his reason and his affections. It was therefore easier for him to continue in obedience to the precept than to swerve from it. Though man was created with defect, yet he was not determined by God influencing his will, by any positive act, to apostasy. God did not force him, but suffered him to act freely. He did not withdraw any grace from him, but left him to that power with which He invested him at his creation. Nor was God under any obligation to sustain him supernaturally or withhold him from sinning. God created Adam in a righteous state, but Adam deliberately cast himself and his posterity into a forlorn state.

Adam took things into his own hands, revolted from God, trampled His Law beneath his feet. It behooves us to consider well the relation between that foul deed and the universal miseries consequent thereon, for it supplies the clue to all the dark confusion which perplexes us within and without. It tells us why infants die, why they are estranged from God from the womb (Psa. 57:3), and why each of us is born into this world with a heart that is deceitful above all things and desperately wicked. It is because Adam forfeited his Maker's approbation and incurred His awful displeasure, with all the terrible effects thereof. In Adam *we* broke the Covenant of Works: we offended in his offence and transgressed in his transgression; and thereby departed from God's favour and fell under His righteous curse. "Thus man apostatized, God was provoked, the Holy Spirit forsook His polluted temple, the unclean spirit took possession, the Divine image was defaced and Satan's image imposed in its place" (Thomas Scott). Through the sin of its head the race was ruined and fell into a state of most horrible moral leprosy. Ours is a fallen world: averse to God and holiness, iniquity abounding in it, death reigning over it, lust and crime characterizing it, suffering and misery filling it.

Accordingly it is written, "Wherefore, as by one man sin entered into the world, and death by sin; and so death passed upon all men, for that all have sinned" (Rom. 5:12). In the light of Genesis 3 that is surely a strange and startling statement, for that chapter makes it clear that Eve fell before Adam did! Why then is it not said, "by one woman," or at least "by one man and woman sin entered the world"? Because, as Thomas Goodwin long ago pointed out, "Moses tells us the *history* of Adam's fall, and Paul explains the *mystery* and the consequences thereof": in other words Romans 5 opens to us the significance and scope of the Eden tragedy. The opening word of verse 12 indicates that a logical proposition is there advanced, which is confirmed by the "as" and "so." The reason why no notice is taken of Eve is that throughout what follows the Apostle is treating of the *condemnation* of all mankind, and not of the vitiation of human nature. That condemnation is due solely to our having revolted from God in the person of our legal representative, and since Adam alone sinned in *that* capacity no mention is made of Eve—headship always pertains to the man and not to the woman.

Before proceeding farther, let us say a few words upon the *relation* of this most important passage. In the preceding chapters Paul had dealt at length with the depravity and sinfulness of mankind (especially in 1:18-32; 3:10-20) and had declared that even Christians in their unregenerate days were ungodly, without strength—enemies to God (5:6, 10)—here he shows *why* they were so, Adam's offence being the cause and source thereof. Second, he had refuted the proud but erroneous view of the Jews, who regarded themselves as holy because the seed of a holy father (2:17-3:9), and consequently they utterly lacked a true estimate of their desperate condition by nature and practice or a sense of their dire need of Divine grace—here the Apostle takes them back to a higher ancestor than Abraham, even Adam, who was equally the father of Jew and Gentile, both alike sharing his guilt and inheriting his curse. Third, Paul had presented the grand doctrine of justification by faith (3:21-31) and had illustrated the same by the cases of Abraham and David—here he shows Adam was a "figure" of Christ (5:14), that the one sustained an analogous relation to his race as the other did to His seed, that each transacted as the one for the many, and that therefore the Gospel principle of *imputation* (Christ's righteousness reckoned to the account of the believer) is no novelty, but identical with the one on which God acted from the beginning.

To proceed. Observe that it is not "through" but "by one man." But exactly what is meant by "*sin* entered the world"? Three explanations are possible. First, sin as an *act* of disobedience: by one man's rebellion against God began. But Genesis 3 shows otherwise: transgression of God's law was initiated by Eve! Second, sin as a principle of *depravity*: by one man originated our sinful nature. This is the view generally taken. But it is equally untenable, for the corruption of our nature is as much by the mother as by the father. Moreover, if such were the force of "sin" in the first clause, then the closing one would perforce read, "for that all are *sinful*." Furthermore verses 13 and 14 explain and furnish proof of what is asserted in verse 12, and it would be meaningless to say "a sinful *nature* is not *imputed*." Finally, all through this passage "sin" and "righteousness" are contrasted, and righteousness here is judicial and not experiential, something reckoned to our account and not infused into us. "Righteousness" in this passage signifies not a holy nature but conformity to the Law's demands; and therefore "sin" cannot be corruption of nature but rather the cause of our condemnation. Thus, third, by one man *guilt* entered into the world, exposing the race unto God's wrath.

"By one man sin *entered.*" Sin is here personified as an intruding enemy, coming as a solemn accuser as well as a hostile oppressor. It entered "the world," not the universe, for Satan had previously apostatized. "And *death* by sin," which is not to be limited to mere physical dissolution, but must be understood of the penal consequences of Adam's offence. All through this passage death is opposed unto "life," and life includes very much more than physical existence or even immortality of soul. When God told Adam, "In the day that thou eatest thereof thou shalt surely die," He signified, first, die *spiritually,* that is be alienated from the source of Divine life. Second, in due course, die *physically*: "thy body shall go to corruption and return to the dust. Third, die *eternally,* suffer "the second death" (Rev. 20:14), be cast into the lake of fire, there to suffer forever, unless a miracle of grace redeems and delivers thee—of which there is no record anywhere in Holy Writ.

"And so death *passed* upon all men" because of their complicity in the one man's sin. It is not that "death" as a principle of evil gained admittance and polluted the nature of his offspring, but that the penal sentence of death was pronounced upon them. Having been charged with his transgression they must suffer the consequence of the same.

The Apostle's design was to show the *connection* between the one man's sin and the resultant misery of the many. By his disobedience all men were constituted sinners—guilty criminals before God—and therefore sharers of the sentence passed upon Adam. "In Adam all die" (1 Cor. 15:22). Those words explain the "by man came death" of the preceding verse, and show that all die by virtue of their relation to the covenant head of our race—die because of their legal union with him. Even physical death is far more than "nature's debt," or the inevitable outcome of our frail constitution: it is a *penal affliction,* a part of sin's "wages." We are subject to mortality because we were "in Adam" by federal representation—we partake of his fallen nature because we are partners of his guilt and punishment. We are born into this world neither as innocent creatures nor to enter upon our probation: rather do we come into it as *culprits* condemned to death by the Divine Law.

Every man, woman and child is adjudged guilty before God. The ground of our condemnation is something *outside* of ourselves. Inward corruption and alienation from God are the consequences and not the cause of our condemnation. Antecedent to any personal act of ours (as such), we stand accursed by the Divine Law. Since "death" came as the result of "sin," since it is the penal sentence upon it, that sentence cannot be passed upon any save those who are *guilty.* If, then, death was "passed upon *all* men," it must be because all are guilty, all participated legally in Adam's offence. Clear and inevitable as is that inference, we are not left to draw it ourselves. The Apostle expressly states it in the next words: "for that all have sinned"—"for that" or "because," in consequence of. Here then is the Divinely given reason *why* the death penalty is passed upon "all men"—because "all have sinned," or, as the margin and the R.V. more accurately render it, "in whom all sinned." The Apostle is not here saying that all men sinned personally, but *representatively.* The Greek verb "sinned" is in the aorist tense, which always looks back to a past action which has terminated. The curse of the Law falls upon us, first, not because we are sinful, but because we were federally guilty when our covenant head sinned.

In Romans 5:12, the Apostle was not referring to the corrupting of man-kind. It is true that as a result of our first parents' sin the springs of human nature were polluted; but this is not what Paul was writing of. Instead he went behind *that,* and dealt with the cause of which moral depravity is but one of the effects. A corrupt tree can indeed produce nothing but corrupt fruit, but why are we *born* with corrupt hearts? Such is more than a terrible calamity: it is *a penal infliction* visited upon us because of our prior criminality. Punishment presupposes guilt, and the punishment is given to all because all are guilty, and since God accounts all guilty, then they must be participants in Adams offence. Well did George Whitefield say, "I beg leave to express my surprise that any person of judgment should maintain human depravity, and not immediately discover its necessary connection with the imputation, and how impossible it is to secure the justice of God without having recourse to it; for certainly the corruption of human nature, so universal and inseparable, is one of the greatest punishments that could be inflicted upon the species . . . . Now if God has inflicted an evident punishment upon a race of men perfectly innocent, which had neither sinned personally nor yet by imputation; and thus while we imagine we honour the justice of God by renouncing imputation, we in fact pour the highest dishonour upon that sacred attribute."

Death, penal death, has been passed upon all men because all sinned in Adam. That the "all have sinned" cannot signify their own personal transgressions is clear: because the manifest design of Romans 5:12, is to show that *Adam's sin is* the cause of death; because physical death (a part of sin's wages) is far more extensive than personal transgression—as appears from so many dying in infancy; and because such an interpretation would destroy the analogy between Adam and the One of whom he was "the figure," and would lead unto this comparison: as men die because they sin personally, so all earn eternal life because they are personally righteous! Equally evident is it that "all have sinned" cannot mean death comes upon men because they are depraved, for this too would clash with the scope of the whole passage: if our *subjective* sinfulness be the ground of our condemnation, then our subjective holiness (and not Christ's merits) is the ground of our justification. It would also contradict the emphatic assertion of verse 18: "by the offence of one judgment came upon all men to condemnation." Thus we are *obliged* to understand the "all have sinned" of verse 12 as meaning all sinned *in Adam*.

If the federal headship of Adam and the imputation of his sin unto all his posterity be repudiated, then what *alternative* is left us? Only that of the separate testing of each individual. If the race were not placed on probation in the first man, then each of his offspring must stand trial for himself. But the conditions of such a trial make success impossible, for each probationer would enter upon it in a state of spiritual death! The human family is either suffering for the sin of its head or it is suffering for nothing at all. "Man is born unto trouble," and from it there is no escape. What then is the explanation of the grim tragedy now being enacted on this earth? Every effect must have a previous cause. If we be not born under the condemnation of Adam's offence, then why are we "by nature the children of wrath" (Eph. 2:3)? "Now either man was tried and fell in Adam, or he has been condemned without trial. He is either under the curse (as it rests upon him from the beginning of his existence), for Adam's guilt, or for no guilt at all. Judge which is more honouring to God: a doctrine which, although profoundly mysterious, represents Him as giving man an equitable and most favourable probation in his federal head, or that which makes God condemn him untried, even before he exists" (R. L. Dabney).

We have carefully considered the solemn teaching of Romans 5:12, and we now propose to examine the verses which immediately follow, for they are not only of deep importance in connection with the present aspect of our subject, but their meaning is very little apprehended today, for they receive scarcely any notice either in the pulpit or the religious press. In Romans 5:13, 14, the Apostle takes no notice of our personal transgressions, but shows the effects of *Adam's* sin. His design in these verses is to intimate that the *universality* of physical death can only be satisfactorily accounted for on the ground that it is a penal infliction because of the first man's offence. The argument of verse 13 is as follows: the infliction of a penal evil presupposes the violation of a law, for death is the wages *of* sin. The violation of the Mosaic law does not account for the universality of death, because multitudes died before *that* law was given. As therefore death implies transgression, and the law of Moses explains not all of death's victims, then it clearly and necessarily follows that the whole human race is subject to the penal consequence of the primitive law being transgressed by their first father.

"For until the law sin was in the world." The opening "For" imports that the Apostle is now about to furnish proof of the assertion made in verse 12. "The law" here has reference to the Mosaic. "Sin," as all through this passage, signifies guilt or the judicial ground of condemnation, and not the corruption of human nature. "The world" includes the entire race: all were accursed, and are so regarded and treated by the Judge of all the earth. Having stated in Romans 5:12 that all mankind participated in Adam's original sin, and that in consequence all share in its punishment, Paul pauses to vindicate and amplify his assertion that "all sinned in" Adam. The method he follows is by reasoning backward from effect to cause. The argument is somewhat involved and calls for close attention, yet there is no difficulty in following its course if we perceive that it moves back from death to sin, and from sin to law—the one, in each case, being necessarily implied by the other. Sin was in the world before the law of Moses was given, as was evident from the fact that death held universal sway from Eden to Sinai—witness the oft-repeated "and he died" in Genesis 5. Thus far the argument *is* simple, but the next point is more difficult.

"But sin is not imputed when there is no law" (Romans 5:13). The meaning of this clause has been missed by many, through failing to follow the course of the Apostle's reasoning. They have imagined it signifies that, though sin was in the world prior to Moses, yet it was not reckoned to the account of those who were guilty. Such an idea is not only erroneous but manifestly absurd. Where sin exists the Holy One must deal with it as sin. And He did so from earliest times, as the flood demonstrated. "Sin is not imputed when there is no law." Why? Because "sin" or guilt is the correlative of "law." Sin or condemnation implies the law: one cannot be without the other—"sin is the transgression of the law" (1 John 3:4). None is guilty where no law exists, for criminality presupposes the violation of a statute. Thus, for any to be adjudged guilty is the same thing as saying he has broken the law. This prepares us for verse 14, where proof is adduced that a law, given previous to Moses, *had been violated,* and consequently God dealt with sinners as sinners long before the time of Moses.

"Nevertheless death reigned from Adam to Moses." Though it be truth that there is no sin where there is no law, and that where there is no law transgressed there can be no death, yet it is a Divinely certified fact that death reigned during the first twenty-five centuries of human life. Therefore the conclusion is so self-evident that Paul leaves his readers to draw it—the human race must have transgressed an earlier law than the Mosaic. Thus verse 14 clinches the interpretation we have given of verses 12 and 13. Since men died prior to the Sinaitic transaction, there must be some other reason and ground for their exposure to death. Note well "death *reigned*": it held undisputed and rightful sway. If then men were justly subject to its power, they must have been criminals. Death is far more than a calamity: it is a punishment, and that argues the breaking of a law. If men were punished with death from the beginning, then it inevitably follows that they were law transgressors from the beginning. Moreover, death furnished proof that sin *was* "imputed"—because men were guilty of Adam's offence.

"Even over them that had not sinned after the similitude of Adam's transgression" has reference unto those who in their own persons and conduct had never violated any law by which their exposure to death could be accounted for. The word "even" here suggests a contrast. Generally speaking, death had reigned from Adam to

Moses over all alike; but, to particularize, it did so even over a class who had not (in their own persons) sinned as Adam had. If we bear in mind that in verses 13 and 14 Paul is proving his assertion (at the end of verse 12) that death comes on all because of the first man's sin, then his line of reasoning is easier to follow. The word "even" here implies that there was a particular class who it *appears* ought to have been exempted from the dominion of sin, namely *infants*. Thus the death of infants supplied a conclusive proof of the doctrine here inculcated. Physical death is a penal infliction, and falling as it does on infants it must be because of Adam's sin. On no other ground can their demise be accounted for. *They* furnish the climacteric demonstration that all sinned in Adam and suffer the penal consequences of his offence.

At the close of Romans 5:14 the Apostle stated that Adam was "the figure of Him that was to come"—he foreshadowed Christ as the federal Head and legal Representative of His people. In verses 15-17 it is pointed out that there were contrasts as well as resemblances between the first man and Christ. "But not as the offence, so also is the free gift" (v. 15). The Fall differed radically from the restoration: though they are alike in their far-reaching effects they are quite unlike in the nature of those effects. "For if through the offence of one many be dead"—literally "many died," legally. The "many" includes infants, and since they die because of the one man's offence, that proves they are adjudged guilty of it, and therefore that God imputed it unto them, for He never punishes where there is no sin.

"Much more the grace of God, and the gift by grace, which is by one man, Jesus Christ, hath abounded unto many" (v. 15). Here the first contrast is drawn—between justice and grace. The "much more" does not mean numerically, for Christ cannot restore more than Adam ruined, and he encompassed the downfall of all his posterity. Nor does this "much more" signify that grace is more abundant and efficacious than the offence in its effects—*that* is brought out in verse 20. No, it is employed *argumentatively,* as a logical inference and as a note of certainty. If God willed it that one man should ruin many, much more can we suppose it to be agreeable that His Son should rescue many. If many be suffering from the offence of Adam, much more should we expect that many will benefit from the merits of Christ. Thus it is not a "much more" either of quantity or quality, but of assurance and certainty. If it were a meet arrangement in the Divine government that the principle of representation should operate though it entailed the curse, much more may we look for that principle to operate in producing blessing. If Scripture teaches the imputation of sin, we should not stumble when we find it affirming the imputation of righteousness. If God dealt in inflexible justice with the original sin, then, from all we know of Him, much more may we look for a display of the riches of His grace through Christ.

"And not as it was by one that sinned, so is the gift: for the judgment was by one to condemnation, but the free gift is of many offences unto justification" (Rom. 5:16). Here the second contrast is drawn. Though there be a close resemblance between ruin and redemption, in that each was accomplished by the one man, yet there is a great difference between the scope of their respective effects. The destroying power of the former went not beyond the one sin of Adam, whereas the restoring power of the latter covers our countless iniquities. How vastly more extensive, then, is the reach of the "free gift"! Thus this verse explains itself—the second clause interpreting the first. The Divine sentence of condemnation fell upon the entire human family because of the single offence of their head, but believers are justified by Christ from many offences—"having forgiven you *all* trespasses" (Col. 2:13). Christ does very much more than remove the guilt which came upon His people for the first man's sin: He has also made full satisfaction or atonement for all their personal sins—who gave Himself for us, that He might redeem us from all iniquity" (Titus 2:14).

"For the judgment was by one to condemnation." Each term requires to be carefully weighed. The word "judgment" obviously signifies a judicial sentence—pronounced by God—and that judgment was "to condemnation" and *not*, be it noted, to "corruption" or vitiation of nature. The judgment "was by one"—not (here) by one man, but rather by one sin, for it is set over against the "many offences" which we have personally committed. Thus it is expressly asserted that judgment came by Adam's initial transgression, and if all be condemned for that sin then all must be accounted guilty of it, for the righteous Judge will not condemn the innocent. "But the free gift is of many offences unto justification"—where sin abounded grace did much more abound. The finished work of Christ not only provides for the cancellation of original sin, but acquits from the accumulated guilt of all our sins. Moreover, believers in Christ are not merely pardoned, "but justified"—exonerated, pronounced righteous by the Law. They are not only restored to their unfallen state, but given a title to enjoy the full reward of Christ's obedience. As Adam's posterity participate in his guilt, depravity, and death, so Christ's seed receive through Him righteousness, holiness, and eternal life.

"For if by one man's offence death reigned by one (better, "by the offence of the one man death reigned"); much more they which receive abundance of grace and of the gift of righteousness shall reign in life by one, Jesus Christ" (Rom. 5:17). Here is the third contrast—death and life, issuing from the two heads. Here again the central truth of the whole passage is reiterated: death comes on men not because their natures have been corrupted, nor because of their own personal transgression, but as a judicial sentence passed on account of Adam's crime. It is here expressly said that death reigned "by (because of) the one man's offence," and therefore everyone over whom death has dominion must be regarded as guilty. The word "reigned" here is very impressive and emphatic: those who die are looked upon as death's *lawful subjects*, for it is regarded as their king. In other words, death has a legal claim upon all men. The forceful language of Hebrews 2:14, 15 contains the same concept: "that through death He (Christ) might destroy him that had the power (authority) of death, that is, the devil; and deliver them," i.e., free death's lawful prisoners. Note how this verse indirectly confirms Romans 5:14—death could have no dominion over infants unless they were charged with Adam's sin.

"Much more they which receive abundance of grace," etc. The "much more" of this verse emphasizes a different thought from that of verse 15. There it refers to God dealing with Adam and his posterity consistently with His own perfections: if God could righteously condemn all mankind because of the disobedience of their first parent, then much more could He justify the seed of Christ (Isa. 53:10) on the ground of the obedience of their Representative. But here the "much more" has reference to the *modus operandi* of condemnation and justification. If death has come upon us as a judicial infliction for an offence in which we did not actively participate, then much more shall we share the reward of Christ's righteousness which we voluntarily "receive" by faith. There is a double thought conveyed by "the gift of righteousness," which it is important to observe, for most of the commentators have missed the second. First, it signifies that righteousness is entirely *gratuitous*, neither earned nor merited. Second, it implies that it is *imputed*, for a "gift" is something which is transferred from one person to another. Not only pointless but senseless is the objection that if righteousness were transferred from Christ to us it would leave Him without any. Does God's gift of life unto sinners leave Him without any life?

"Shall reign in life by one, Jesus Christ." They who by faith receive the gift of His righteousness are not only saved from the consequences of the Fall, but are partakers of eternal life and made joint-heirs with Christ and sharers of His celestial glory. They who have been wholly under the power of death are not only completely freed from it and spiritually quickened, but as one with the King of kings they are made "kings unto God" (Rev. 1:6). They are not reinstated in the earthly paradise, but shall be brought to honour and glory and immortality in Heaven—given title to a state of eternal and supernal blessedness. The careful student should have observed both a threefold comparison and a threefold contrast between the first and last Adams in verses 15-17. Both are sources of radical influence—"abounded *unto* many" (v. 15); both are conveyors of a judicial sentence—condemnation, justification (v. 16); both introduce a sovereign regime—"death reigned," "reign in life" (v. 17). But by Adam we lost, whereas in Christ we gain; we were charged with the one offence, but are cleared from many; we were the subjects of death, but are made co-heirs with Christ. By Adam we were ruined; by Christ we are more than restored. In Adam we occupied a position a little lower than the angels; in Christ we are instated far above all principality and power.

"Therefore as by the offence of one judgment came all men to condemnation; even so by the righteousness of one the free gift came upon all men unto justification of life" (Rom. 5:18). In verse 12 only the first member of the contrast was given (vv. 13-17 interrupting the extension by a necessary parenthesis), but here the case is stated in full. Throughout the whole passage Paul contrasts a state of Divine wrath and Divine favour, and not the states of depravity and holiness. Here it is plainly asserted that all are condemned for Adam's sin. Infants are therefore included, for they would not be punished if innocent—if Adam's sin were not legally theirs. In precisely the same way all for whom Christ transacted as their covenant Head are justified by His merits being legally reckoned to their account. As something *outside of ourselves* is the judicial ground of our falling under the Divine curse, so something outside of ourselves is the judicial ground of our being under the blessing of God. The second half of this verse speaks not of something which is provided for all mankind, but that which God actually imputes to all believers (cf. 4:20-24).

"For as by one man's disobedience many were made sinners, so by the obedience of one shall many be made righteous" (v. 19). This goes farther than the preceding verse. There it was the *causes* of condemnation and justification which were stated; here it is their actual issue or *results*. From verse 11 onwards the Apostle has shown that God's sentence is grounded upon the legally constituted unity of all with their covenant heads. By his breaking of the Divine Law, all who were federally one with the first Adam were made sinners, and all who were federally one with the last Adam are made righteous. The Greek word for "made" (*kathistemi*) never signifies to effect any change to a person or thing, but means to "ordain, appoint," to "constitute" legally or officially, as a reference to Matthew 24:45, 47; Luke 12:14; Acts 7:10, 27, clearly shows. Note well that it is *not* here said that Adam's disobedience makes us unholy: Paul goes farther back and explains why such should follow, namely because we are first constituted sinners by imputation.

Romans 5:12-21, is one of the most important passages in the bible. In it the fundamental doctrine of federal representation is openly stated, and the fact of imputation is emphatically affirmed. Here is revealed the basic principle according to which God deals with men. Here we behold the old and the new races receiving from their respective heads. Here are set before us the two central figures and facts of all history—the first Adam and his disobedience, the last Adam and His obedience. Upon those two things the Apostle hammered again and again with almost monotonous repetition. Why such unusual reiteration? Because of the great doctrinal importance of what is here treated of; because the purity of the Gospel and the glory of Christ's atonement turned thereon; because Paul was insisting upon that which is so repulsive to the proud heart of fallen man. Plain as is its language, this passage has been wrested and twisted to mean many things which it does not teach; and Socinians, Arminians and Universalists refuse to accept what is so plainly asserted.

Wherever this passage has been plainly expounded it has, in all generations encountered the fiercest opposition—not the least so from men professing to be Christians. The doctrine of imputation is as bitterly hated as those of unconditional election and eternal punishment. Those who teach it are accused of representing God as dealing *unjustly*. The only reply necessary is, What saith the Scriptures? As we have seen, Romans 5 declares that death has passed upon all men because all sinned in Adam (v. 12), that "through the offence of one many be dead" (v. 15), that "the judgment was by one to condemnation" (v. 16), that "by one man's offence death reigned" (v. 17), that "by one man's offence judgment came upon all men to condemnation" (v. 18), that "by one man's disobedience many were made sinners" (v. 19). "In Adam all die" (1 Cor. 15:22). God deals with men on the principle of *imputation*. "The sins of the fathers are visited upon the children" (Exo. 20:5). The curse of Canaan fell on all his posterity (Gen. 9:25). The Egyptians perished for Pharaoh's obduracy. His whole family died for Achan's crime (Josh. 7:24). All Israel suffered for David's sin (2 Samuel 24:15, 17). The leprosy visited upon Gehazi passed to "all his seed forever" (2 Kings 5:27). The blood of all the prophets was exacted of the members of Christ's generation (Luke 11:50).

If there be one word which fitly expresses what every man is by nature, it is "sinner." Waiving all theological systems, if we inquire what be the popular meaning of that term, the answer is, "one who has sinned" or one who makes a practice of sinning. But such a definition comes far short of the scriptural import of that word. "By the disobedience *of one* many were made sinners." They are such, legally made so, neither because of what they have done personally nor by what they are in the habit of doing; but rather by the action of their first parent. It is quite true that it is the nature of sinners to sin, but according to the unmistakable testimony of Romans 5 we are all sinners *antecedent to* and independent of any personal transgressing of God's Law. It was by the offence of Adam that we were legally constituted sinners. The universal reign of death is the *proof* of the universal power of sin, yet so far from representing death as the consequence of individual acts of disobedience, it is expressly insisted upon that death reigns over infants, who are incapable of acts of disobedience. Human probation ended with the original offence, and, in consequence, not only was human nature vitiated at its fountain-head, but all of Adam's descendants fell under the curse of God, the guilt of his transgression being imputed to them.

No finite creature, and still less a fallen and depraved one, is capable of measuring or even understanding the justice of the infinite God. Yet this we may ask: Which appears to be more consonant to human conceptions of justice—that we should suffer through Adam *because* we were legally connected with him and he transacted in our name; or that we should suffer solely because we derive our *nature* from him by generation, though we had *no part* in or connection with his sin? In the former we can perceive the ground on which his guilt is charged to our account; but by the latter we can discover no ground or cause that *any* share of the fatal effects of Adam's sin should be visited upon us. The latter alternative means that we are depraved and wretched without any sufficient reason, and in such an event our present condition is but a misfortune and in no wise criminal. Nor is God to be blamed: He made man upright, but man deliberately apostatized. Nor was God under any obligation to preserve man from falling. Finally, let it be remembered that our salvation depends upon the self-same principle and fact: if we were cursed and ruined by the first Adam's disobedience, we are redeemed and blessed by the last man's obedience.

THE DOCTRINE OF HUMAN DEPRAVITY
Its Consequences

The key which opens to us the mystery of human depravity is to be found in a right understanding of the relations which God appointed between the first man and his posterity. As the grand truth of redemption cannot be rightly and intelligently apprehended until we perceive the *federal connection* which God ordained between the Redeemer and the redeemed, neither can the tragedy of man's ruin be contemplated in its proper perspective unless we view it in the light of Adam's apostasy from his Creator. He was the prototype of all humanity. As he stood for the whole human race, so in him God dealt with all who should issue from him. Had not Adam been our covenant head and federal representative, the mere circumstance that he was our first parent would not have involved us in the legal consequences of his sin, nor would it have entitled us to the legal reward of his righteousness had he maintained his integrity and served his probation by rendering to his Maker and Lord that obedience which was His due and which he was fully capacitated to perform. It was the Divinely constituted *nexus* (connecting principle or tie) and *oneness* of the first man and all mankind in the sight of the Law which explains the latter's participation in the penalty visited upon the former.

In the previous chapters of this book we dwelt at some length upon the *origin* of human depravity, and the Divine *imputation* of the guilt of Adam's transgression unto all his descendants. We are now to consider the consequences entailed by the Fall. Abominable indeed is sin, fearful are the wages it receives, dreadful are the effects which it has produced. Therein we are shown the Holy One's estimate of sin—the severity of His punishment expressing its hatefulness unto Him. Conversely the dire doom of Adam makes evident the enormity of his offence. That offence is not to be measured by the external act of eating the fruit, but by the awful affront which was offered against God's majesty. In his single sin there was a complication of many crimes. There was base ingratitude against the One who had so richly endowed him, and discontent with the goodly heritage allotted him. There was disbelief of the holy veracity of God, a doubting of His word and a believing of the serpent's lie. There was a repudiation of the infinite obligations he was under to love and serve his Maker, a preferring of his own will and way. There was a contempt of God's high authority, a breaking of His covenant, a flying in the face of His solemn threat. The curse of Heaven fell upon him because he deliberately and presumptuously defied the Almighty.

Very much more was included and involved in Adam's transgression than is commonly supposed or recognized. Three hundred years ago that profound theologian James Usher pointed out that it had wrapped up in it "the breach of the whole Law of God." Summarizing in our own language what the Bishop of Armagh developed at length, Adam's violation of all the Ten Commandments of the moral Law may be set forth thus. The first commandment he broke by choosing him another "god" when he followed the counsel of Satan. The second, in idolizing his palate, making a god of his belly by eating the forbidden fruit. The third, by believing not God's threatening, therein taking His name in vain. The fourth, by breaking the sinless rest in which he had been placed. The fifth, thereby is dishonouring his Father in Heaven. The sixth, by slaying himself and all his posterity. The seventh, by committing spiritual adultery, and preferring the creature above the Creator. The eighth, by laying hands upon to which he had no right. The ninth, by accepting the serpent's false witness against God. The tenth, by coveting that which God had not given to him.

We by no means share the popular idea that the Lord *saved Adam* very soon after his fall, but rather take decided exception thereto. Negatively, we cannot find anything whatever in Holy Writ on which to base such a belief: positively, much to the contrary. First of all it is clear that his sin was not one of "infirmity," but instead a "presumptuous" one, pertaining to that class of willful sins and open defiance of God for which no sacrifice was provided (Exo. 21:14; Num. 15:30, 31; Deut. 17:12; Heb. 10:26-29), and therefore, an unpardonable sin. There is not the slightest sign that he ever repented his sin or record of his confessing it to God: on the contrary, when charged with it, he attempted to excuse and extenuate it. Genesis 3 closes with the awful statement: "So he *drove out* the man." Nothing whatever is mentioned to his credit afterwards: no offering of sacrifice, no acts of faith or obedience! Instead we are merely told that he knew his wife (4:1, 25), begat a son in his own likeness, and died (5:3-5). If the reader can see in those statements intimations or even indications that Adam was a regenerated man, then he has much better eyes than the writer—or, possibly, a more lively imagination.

Nor is there a single word in his favour in the later Scriptures: rather is everything to his condemnation. Job denied that he covered his transgression or hid his iniquity in his bosom "as Adam" did (31:33). The Psalmist declared that those who judged unjustly and the persons of the wicked should "die like men" (82:7), for the Hebrew word there "men" is *Adam*! In the New Testament he is contrasted in considerable detail with Christ (Rom. 5:12, 21; 1 Cor. 15:22, 45-47), and if he were saved, then the antithesis would fail at its principal point. Moreover, such a glaring anomaly is quite out of keeping with what is revealed of God's justice—that the great majority of those whom he represented should eternally perish, while the responsible head should be recovered. In 1 Timothy 2:14 specific mention is made of the fact that "Adam was not deceived," which emphasizes the enormity of his transgression. In Hebrews 11 the Holy Spirit has cited the faith of Old Testament saints, and though He mentions that of Able, Enoch, Abraham, Isaac, Jacob, etc., He says nothing about Adam's! His being *omitted* from that list is solemnly significant. Thus, after his being driven out of Eden, Scripture makes no mention of God having any further dealing with Adam!

Before taking up the consequences upon his descendants of Adam's defection, we will consider those which fell more immediately upon him and his guilty partner. These are recorded in Genesis 3. No sooner had he revolted from his gracious Maker and Benefactor than the evil effects thereof became apparent. His understanding, originally enlightened with heavenly wisdom, became darkened and overcast with crass ignorance. His heart, formally fired with holy veneration toward his Creator and warm with love to Him, now became alienated and filled with enmity against Him. His will, which had been in subjection to his rightful Governor, had cast off the yoke of obedience. His whole moral constitution was wrecked, had become unhinged, perverse. In a word, the life of God had departed from his soul. His aversion for the supremely excellent One appeared in his flight from Him as soon as he heard His approach. His crass ignorance and stupidity were evinced by his vain attempt to conceal himself from the eyes of Omniscience. His pride was displayed in refusing to acknowledge his guilt: his ingratitude when he indirectly upbraided God for giving him a wife. But, let us turn to the inspired account of these things.

"And the eyes of them both were opened. and they knew that they were naked" (Gen. 3:7). Very, very striking is this. We do not read of any change taking place when Eve partook of the forbidden fruit, but as soon as Adam did so, "the eyes of them *both* were opened." This furnishes definite confirmation of what we dwelt upon in the preceding chapters. Adam was the covenant head and legal representative of *his wife,* as well as of the future children which were to issue from them. Therefore, the penalty for disobedience was not inflicted by God until the one to whom the prohibition had been made violated the same—and then the consequences thereof began to be immediately felt by both of them. But what is meant by "the eyes of them both were opened"? Certainly not their physical eyes, for those had previously been open—thus we have here another intimation that we must not slavishly limit ourselves to the literal meaning of all the terms used in this chapter. The answer, then, must be the "eyes" of their understanding: or, more strictly, those of their *conscience*—which sees or perceives, as well as hears, speaks and chastises. In that expression, "the eyes of them both were opened," is to be found the key to what follows.

The result of eating the forbidden fruit was not the acquisition of supernatural wisdom, as they fondly hoped, but a discovery that they had reduced themselves to a condition of wretchedness. They knew that they were "naked," and that in a sense very different from that mentioned in Genesis 2:25. Though in their original state they wore no material clothing, yet we do not believe for a moment that they were without any covering at all. Rather do we agree with G. H. Bishop that they "were not without effulgence shining from them and around them, which wrapped them in a radiant and translucent robe—and in a certain lovely way obscured their outlines. It is contrary to nature and it is repugnant to us that anything should be unclothed absolutely bare. Each bird has its plumage and each animal its coat, and there is no beauty if the covering be removed. Strip the most beautiful bird of its feathers, and, though the form remain unchanged, we no longer admire it. We conceive, then, that artists are wholly at fault and grossly offend against purity when they paint the human form unclothed, and plead as an excuse the case of Adam in Eden. Could the animals in all their splendid covering coats have bowed down as to the vice-regents of God (Gen. 1:28) before beings wholly unclothed? Should Adam, the crown and king of creation, be the *only* living thing without a screen? Impossible. To the spiritual sense there certainly is a hint of something about our first parents that impressed and overawed the animal creation. What was that thing? What, but that shining forth like the sun, which describes the body of the resurrection (Daniel 12:3)? If the face of Moses so shone by reflection that the children of Israel were afraid to come near him, how much more must the (unimpeded) indwelling Spirit of God in Adam and Eve have flung around them a radiance which made all creation do them reverence at their approach—beholding in them the image and likeness of the Lord God Almighty—glorious in brightness—shining like a sun?

Supplementing the above, let it be pointed out that of the Lord God, it is said, "Thou art clothed with honour and majesty: who coverest Thyself with light as with a garment" (Psa. 104:1, 2), and man was made, originally, in His image! God "crowned him with glory and honour," and made him "to have dominion over the works of His hand" (Psa. 8:5, 6), and accordingly covered him with bright apparel, as will be the ultimate case of those recovered from the Fall and its consequences, for "they are equal unto the angels" (Luke 20:36)–compare "two men stood by them in shining garments" (Luke 24:4). Further, the implication of Romans 8:3, is irresistible: "God sending His own Son in the likeness of sinful flesh." Note how discriminating is that language: not merely in "the likeness of the flesh," but literally "sin's flesh." Upon those words R. Haldane rightly remarked, "If the flesh of Jesus Christ was the likeness of sinful flesh, there must be a difference between the *appearance* of sinful flesh and our nature or flesh in its original condition when Adam was created. Christ, then, was not made in the likeness of the flesh of man before sin entered the world, but in the likeness of his fallen flesh." And since Christ *restored* that which He took not away (Psa. 69:4), then its resurrected state shows us its primitive glory (Phil. 3:21).

Following the statement "the eyes of them both were opened," we would naturally expect the next clause to read "and they *saw* that they were naked," but instead it says, "they *knew* that they were naked"—something more than a discovery of their woeful physical plight being included therein. The Hebrew verb is rendered "know" in the vast majority of references, yet eighteen times it is translated "perceive" and three times "feel." As the opening of their eyes refers to those of their understanding, so we are informed of what they now discerned, namely the loss of their innocence. There is a nakedness of soul which is far worse than an unclothed body, for it unfits it for the presence of the Holy One. The nakedness of Adam and Eve was the loss of the image of God, the inherent righteousness and holiness in which He created them. Such is the awful condition in which all of their descendants are born. That is why Christ bids them buy of Him "white raiment, that thou mayest be clothed, and that the shame of thy nakedness do not appear" (Rev. 3:18). The "white raiment" is "the robe of righteousness" (Isa. 61:10), the "wedding garment" of Matthew 22:11-13, without which the soul is eternally lost.

"They knew that they were naked." As Bishop expressed it, "Their halo had vanished, and the Spirit of righteousness who had been to them a covering of light and purity withdrew, and they felt that they were stripped and bare. But more: they realized that their physical condition imaged their spiritual loss. They were made painfully conscious of sin and its dire consequences. This was the first result of their transgression: a guilty conscience condemned them, and *a sense of shame* possessed their souls. Their hearts smote them for what they had done. Now that the fearful deed of disobedience had been committed, they realized the happiness they had flung away and the misery into which they had plunged themselves. They knew that they were not only stripped of all the bliss and honours of the Paradise state, but were defiled and degraded, and a sense of wretchedness possessed them. They knew that they were naked of everything that is holy. They might now be rightly termed "Ichabod," for the glory of the Lord had departed from them. Such, my reader, is ever the effect of sin: it destroys our peace, robs of our joy, and brings in its train a consciousness of guilt and a sense of shame.

There is, we believe, a yet deeper meaning in those words, "they knew that they were naked," namely a realization that they were exposed to the wrath of an offended God. They perceived that *their defense* was gone. They were morally naked, without any protection against the broken Law! Very striking and solemn is this. *Before* the Lord appeared unto them, before He said a word or came near to them, Adam and Eve *knew* the dreadful state they were now in, and were ashamed! Oh, the power of conscience! Our first parents stood self-accused and self-condemned! Before their Judge appeared on the scene, man became, as it were, the judge of his own fallen and woeful condition. Yes, they knew of themselves that they were disgraced: their holiness defiled, their innocence gone, the image of God in their souls broken, their tranquillity disrupted, their protection against the Law removed. Stripped of their original righteousness, they stood defenseless. What a terrible discovery to make! Such is the state into which fallen man has come—one of which he is himself ashamed!

And what did the guilty pair do upon their painful discovery? How did they now conduct themselves? Cry unto God for mercy? Seek unto Him for a covering? No indeed. Not even an awakened conscience moves its tormented possessor to turn unto the Lord, though it *must* do its work ere the sinner flies to Him for refuge. A lost soul needs something more than an active conscience to draw him to Christ. That is very evident from the case of the scribes and Pharisees in His very presence, for "being convicted by their own conscience, they *went out*" (John 8:9). Instead of a convicted conscience causing them to cast themselves at the feet of the Saviour, it resulted in their leaving Him! Nothing short of the Holy Spirit's quickening, enmity-subduing, heart-melting, faith-bestowing operations brings anyone into saving contact with the Lord Jesus. He does indeed wound before He applies the balm of Gilead—makes use of the Law to prepare the way for the Gospel, break up the hard soil of the heart to make it receptive to the Seed. But even a conscience aroused by Him, accusing the soul with a voice which cannot be stilled, will never of itself bring one into "the way of peace."

No, instead of betaking themselves to God, Adam and Eve attempted by their own puny efforts to repair the damage they had wrought in themselves. "They sewed fig leaves together, and made themselves aprons." Here we see the second consequence of their sin: a worthless expedient, a futile attempt to *conceal their real character* and hide their shame from themselves. As others have pointed out, our first parents were more anxious to save their credit before each other than they were to seek the pardon of God. They sought to arm themselves against a feeling of shame and thereby quieten their accusing conscience. There was no concern at their unfitness to appear before *God* in such a plight, but only that they might stand unabashed before each other! And thus it is with their children to this day. They are more afraid of being *detected* in sin than of *committing* it, and more concerned about appearing well before their fellows than about obtaining the approbation of God. The chief object which the fallen sons of men propose unto themselves is to quieten their guilty conscience and to stand well with their neighbours. And hence it is that so many of the unregenerate assume the garb of religion.

"And they heard the voice of the LORD God walking in the garden in the cool of the day: and Adam and his wife hid themselves from the presence of the LORD God amongst the trees of the garden" (Gen. 3:8). Here was the third consequence of their fall: *a dread of God.* Up to this point they had been concerned only with their own selves and wretchedness, but now they had to reckon with Another. It was the approach of their Judge. Apparently they saw not His form at this moment, but heard only His voice. It was to *test* them. But instead of welcoming such a sound, they were horrified, and fled in terror. But where could they flee from *His* presence? "Can any hide himself in secret places that I shall not see him? saith the LORD" (Jer. 23:24). In the attempt of Adam and Eve to seclude themselves among the trees we behold how sin has turned man into an utter fool, for none but an imbecile would imagine that he could conceal himself from the eyes of Omniscience.

When Adam and Eve, by an act of willful transgression, broke the condition of the covenant under which they had been placed, they incurred the double guilt of disbelieving God's Word and defying His will. Thereby they forfeited the promise of life and brought upon themselves the penalty of death. That one act of theirs completely changed their relation to God and, at the same time, reversed their feelings toward Him. They were no longer the objects of His favour, but instead the subjects of His wrath. As the effect of their sinfulness and the result of their spiritual death, the Lord God ceased to be the object of their love and confidence, and became the object of their aversion and distrust. A sense of degradation and of God's displeasure filled them with fright and inspired them with an awful enmity against Him. So swift and so drastic was the change which sin produced in their relations and feelings toward their Maker that they were ashamed and afraid to appear before Him, and as soon as they heard His voice in the garden they fled in horror and terror, seeking to hide from Him among the trees. They dreaded to hear Him pronounce formal sentence of condemnation upon them, for they knew in themselves that they deserved it.

Each action of our first parents after the Fall was emblematic and prophetic, for it shadowed forth how their descendants would conduct themselves. First, upon the discovery of their nakedness, or loss of their original purity and glory, they sewed themselves aprons of fig leaves in an attempt to reserve their self-respect and make themselves presentable to one another. Thus it is with the natural man the world over: by a variety of efforts he seeks to conceal his spiritual wretchedness, yet at best his religious exercises and altruistic performances are but things of time, and will not endure the test of eternity. Second, Adam and Eve sought to hide from the One they now feared and hated. So it is with their children. They are fallen and depraved; God is holy and righteous: and despite their self-manufactured coverings of creature respectability and piety, the very thought of a face-to-face meeting with their Sovereign renders the unregenerate uneasy. That is why the Bible is so much neglected—because in it *God* is heard speaking. That is why the theatre is preferred to the prayer meeting. Proof is this that all shared in the first sin and died in Adam, for all inherit his nature and perpetuate his conduct.

How clearly did the actions of the guilty pair make evident the serpent's lie. The more closely verses 4 and 5 be scrutinized in the light of the immediate sequel, the more will their falsity appear. The serpent had assured them. "Ye shall not surely die," yet they had done so spiritually, and now fled in terror lest they lost their physical lives. He had declared that they should be advanced—for that was the evident force of his "your eyes shall be opened"; instead, they had been abased. He had promised that they should be increased in knowledge, whereas they had become so stupid as to entertain the idea that they could conceal themselves from the omniscient and omnipresent One. He had said they should "be as gods," but here we behold them as self-accused and trembling criminals. Well do we ever bear in mind the Lord's pronouncement concerning the Devil: "He is a liar, and the father of it" (John 8:44)—the perverter and denier of the Truth, the promoter and instigator of falsehood of every kind throughout the

Its Consequences

earth, ever employing dissimulation and treachery, subtlety and deception to further his evil interests.

Behold the terrible consequences of listening to the Devil's lies. See the awful ravage which sin works. Not only had Adam and Eve irreparably damaged themselves, but they had become fugitives from their all-glorious Creator. He is ineffably pure, and they were polluted, and therefore sought to avoid Him. How unbearable the thought to a guilty conscience that the unpardoned sinner will yet have to stand before the thrice Holy One! Yet he *must*. There is no possible way in which any of us can escape that awful meeting. Writer and reader must yet appear before Him and render an account of their stewardship, and unless we fled to Christ for refuge, and had our sins blotted out by His atoning blood, we shall hear His sentence of eternal doom. Then seek Him while He may be found in mercy; call upon Him while He is near in His gracious overtures of the Gospel, for "How shall we escape" the lake of fire if we neglect so great a salvation? Assume not that you are a Christian, but examine well your foundation; yea, beg God to search your heart and show you your real condition. Take the place of a Hell-deserving sinner and receive the sinner's Saviour.

In the verses that follow we may discover a solemn shadowing forth of the day to come. "And the LORD God called unto Adam, and said unto him, Where art thou?" (Gen. 3:9). It was the Divine Judge summoning him to an account of what he had done. It was a word designed to impress upon him the guilty distance from God to which sin had removed him. His offence had severed all communion between them, for "what fellowship hath righteousness with unrighteousness, and what communion hath light with darkness?" Observe well that the Lord ignored Eve and confined His address to the responsible head! God had plainly warned him about the forbidden fruit, "In the day that thou eatest thereof, thou shalt surely die." And *death*, my reader, is not annihilation, but alienation: as physical death is the separation of the soul from the body, so spiritual death is the separation of the soul from the Holy One—"Your iniquities have separated between you and your God, and your sins have hid His face from you" (Isa. 59:2). Such is the terrible plight of us all by nature—"far off" (Eph. 2:13)—and unless Divine grace saves us, we shall be "punished with everlasting destruction from the presence of the Lord" (2 Thess. 1:9).

"And he said, I heard Thy voice in the garden (which suggests that He was now seen in theophanic manifestation), and I was afraid, because I was naked; and I hid myself" (Gen. 3:10). Mark how utterly unable sinful man is to meet the Divine inquisition. He could offer no adequate defense. Hear his sorry admission, "I was afraid": his conscience condemned him. Such will be the woeful plight of every lost soul when, brought out from "the refuge of lies" in which he formerly sheltered, he now appears before his Maker—destitute of that righteousness and holiness which He inexorably requires, and which we can obtain only in and from Christ: filled with horror and terror. Weigh well those words, "I was afraid, because I was naked." His apron of fig leaves was of no avail! Thus it is even now when the Holy Spirit convicts a soul. The garb of religion is discovered to be naught but filthy rags when one is given to see light in God's light; the heart is filled with fear and shame as he realizes he has to do with One before whom all things are naked and opened. Have *you* passed through any such experience?—seen and felt yourself to be a spiritual bankrupt, a moral leper, a lost sinner? If not, you *will* in the day to come.

"And He said, Who told thee that thou wast naked?" (v. 11). To which inquiry Adam made no reply. Instead of humbling himself before his aggrieved Benefactor, the culprit failed to make answer. Whereupon the Lord said, "Hast thou eaten of the tree, whereof I commanded thee that thou shouldest not eat?" It is striking to notice that God made no reply to the idle and perverse excuses which Adam had at first proffered. They were unworthy of His notice. If the words of Adam in verse 10 be carefully pondered, a solemn and fatal *omission* from them will be observed: he said nothing about his sin, but mentioned only the painful *effects* which it had produced. As another has said, "this was the language of impenitent misery." God therefore directed him to the *cause* of those effects. Yet observe the manner in which He framed His words. The Lord did not directly charge the offender with his crime, but instead interrogated him: "Hast thou eaten?" That opened the way and made it much easier for Adam contritely to *acknowledge* his transgression. But alas, he failed to avail himself of the opportunity and declined making broken-hearted confession of his iniquity.

God did not put those questions to Adam because He desired to be informed, but rather to provide him with an occasion penitently to own what he had done; and in his refusal to do so we behold the fourth consequence of the Fall, namely *the hardening of the heart* by sin. There was no deep sorrow for his flagrant disobedience, and therefore no sincere owning of the same. To the second inquiry of God, the man said, "The woman whom Thou gavest to be with me, she gave me of the tree, and I did eat." Here was the fifth consequence of the fall: *self-justification* by an attempt to excuse sin. Instead of confessing his wickedness, Adam sought to mitigate and extenuate it, by throwing the onus upon another. The entrance of evil into man produced a dishonest and disingenuous heart: rather than take the blame upon himself, Adam sought to place it upon his wife. And thus it is with his descendants. They endeavour to shelve their responsibility and repudiate their culpability by attributing the wrongdoing to anyone or anything rather than themselves, ascribing their sins to the force of circumstances, an evil environment, temptations, or the Devil.

But in those words of Adam we may behold something still more heinous, and a sixth consequence of his fall, namely a blasphemous *impugning of God Himself*. Adam did not simply say, "my wife gave me of the tree, and I did eat," but "the woman whom *Thou* gavest me." Thus did he covertly reproach the Lord. It was as though he said, Hadst Thou not given me this woman, I had not eaten. Why didst Thou put such a snare upon me? Behold here the pride and hardheadedness which characterizes the Devil, whose kingdom has now been set up within man! So it is with his children to this day. That is why we are enjoined: "Let no man say when he is tempted, I am tempted of God: for God cannot be tempted with evil, neither tempteth He any man" (James 1:13). It is because the depraved mind of the fallen creature is so prone to think that very thing he seeks shelter therein. If God had not ordered His providences, I had never been so strongly tempted; if He had disposed things differently, I should not have been enticed, still less overcome. Thus do we, in our efforts at self-vindication, cast reflection on the ways of Him who cannot err.

"The foolishness of man perverteth his way: and his heart fretteth against the LORD" (Prov. 19:3). This is one of the vilest forms in which human depravity manifests itself: that after deliberately playing the fool, and discovering that the way of transgressors is hard, we murmur against God instead of meekly submitting to His rod. When we pervert our way—through self-will, carnal greed, rash conduct, hasty actions—let us not charge God with the bitter fruits thereof; since we are the authors of our misery, it is but reasonable that we should fret against *ourselves*. But such is the pride of our hearts, and unsubdued enmity against God, that we are fearfully apt to fret against Him, as though He were responsible for our troubles. We must not expect to gather grapes from thorns or figs from thistles! Charge not the unpleasant reaping on the severity of God, but upon your own perversity. Say not, God should not have endowed me with such strong passions if I may not indulge them. Ask not, Why did He not give grace so that I would have resisted the temptation? Impeach not His sovereignty, question not His dispensations, harbour no doubts about His goodness. If you *do*, you are but repeating the wickedness of your first father.

"And the man said, The woman whom Thou gavest to be with me, she gave me of the tree, and I did eat." He indeed recited the facts of the case, yet in so doing made it worse rather than better. He was the woman's head and protector, and therefore should have taken more care to prevent her falling into evil. When she had succumbed to the serpent's wiles, so far from following her example, he should have rebuked her and refused her offer. To plead we were allured by others is no valid excuse; yet it is one commonly offered. When Aaron was charged with making the golden calf, he admitted the fact, but sought to extenuate the fault by blaming the congregation (Exo. 32:22-24). In like manner, the disobedient Saul sought to transfer the onus unto "the people" (1 Sam. 15:21). So too Pilate gave orders for the crucifixion of Christ, and then charged the crime upon the Jews (Matt. 27:24). Finally, we behold here yet another consequence of the Fall: it produced *a breach of affection* between man and his neighbour—in this case his wife, whom he now loved so little as to thrust her forth to receive the stroke of Divine vengeance.

"And the LORD God said unto the woman, What is this that thou hast done?" Behold here both the infinite condescension of the Most High and His fairness as Judge. He acted not in high sovereignty, disdaining to parley with the creature; nor did He condemn the transgressors unheard, but gave them opportunity to defend themselves or confess their crime. So it will be at the Great Assize: it will be conducted in such a manner as to make it transparently evident that every transgressor receives "the due reward of his iniquities," and that God is clear when He judges" (Psa. 51:4). "And the woman said, The serpent beguiled me, and I did eat" (Gen. 3:13). Eve followed the same course and manifested the same evil spirit as her husband. She humbled not herself before the Lord, gave no sign of repentance, made no broken-hearted confession. Instead, there was a vain attempt to vindicate herself by casting the blame upon the serpent. Idle excuse was that, for God had capacitated her to perceive his lies and rectitude of nature to reject them with horror. Equally useless for her children to plead, "I had no intention of sinning, but the Devil tempted me," for he can force none, nor prevail without our consent.

Standing before their Judge self-accused and self-condemned, He now proceeded to pronounce sentence upon the guilty pair. But before so doing He dealt with the one who had been instrumental in their fall. "And the LORD God said unto the serpent, Because thou hast done this, thou art cursed above all cattle, and above every beast of the field; upon thy belly shalt thou go, and dust shalt thou eat all the days of thy life. And I will put enmity between thee and the woman, and between thy seed and her Seed: It shall bruise thy head, and thou shalt bruise His heel" (Gen. 3:14, 15). Observe that no question was put to the serpent: rather did the Lord treat with him as an avowed enemy. His sentence is to be taken literally in its application to the serpent, mystically in relation to Satan. "The words may imply a visible punishment to be executed on the serpent, as the instrument in this temptation; but the curse was directed against the invisible tempter, whose abject, degraded condition, and base endeavours to find satisfaction in rendering others wicked and miserable, might be figuratively intimated by the serpent's moving on his belly, and feeding on the dust" (Thomas Scott).

The Lord began His denunciations where sin began—with the serpent. Each part of the sentence expresses the fearful degradation which should henceforth be his portion. First, he was "cursed *above all cattle*"—the curse has extended to the whole creation, as Romans 8:20-23 makes clear. Second, hereafter it would crawl in the dust: from which it is to be inferred that originally it stood erect—compare our remarks on Genesis 3:1. Third, God Himself now put an enmity between it and the female, so that where there had been intimate converse there should now be mutual aversion. Fourth, passing from the literal snake to "that old serpent, the devil," God announced that he should ultimately be crushed—not by His hand dealing immediately with him, but by One in human nature, and what would be yet more humiliating, by the *woman's* Seed. Satan had made use of the weaker vessel, and God would defeat him through the same medium! Wrapped up in that pronouncement was a prophecy and a promise, yet let it be carefully noted that it was in the form of a sentence of doom on Satan, and *not* a gracious declaration made unto Adam and Eve—intimating that *they* had no personal interest therein!

The sentences pronounced upon our first parents need not detain us, for their language is so plain and simple that they call for neither explanation nor comment. Since Eve was the first in the transgression, and had tempted Adam, she was the next to receive sentence. "Unto the woman He said, I will greatly multiply thy sorrow and thy conception: in sorrow thou shalt bring forth children; and thy desire shall be to thy husband, and he shall rule over thee" (Gen. 3:16). Thus was she condemned to a state of sorrow, suffering and servitude. "And unto Adam He said, Because thou hast hearkened unto the voice of thy wife, and hast eaten of the tree, of which I commanded thee, saying, Thou shalt not eat of it: cursed is the ground for thy sake; in sorrow shalt Thou eat of it *all* the days of thy life (definitely precluding the idea that, later, God saved him!); thorns also and thistles shall it bring forth to thee. . . . In the sweat of thy face shalt thou eat bread" (vv. 17-19). Sorrow, toil and sweat were to be the burden to fall most heavily upon the male. Here we behold the eighth consequence of the Fall: *physical suffering* and death—"unto dust shalt thou return."

"And Adam called his wife's name Eve (that is "living"); because she was the mother of all living" (v. 20). This is manifestly a detail communicated by God to Moses the historian, for Eve gave birth to no children until after she and her husband had been expelled from Eden. It seems to be introduced here for the purpose of illustrating and exemplifying the concluding portion of the sentence passed upon the woman in verse 16. As Adam had made proof of his dominion over all the lower creatures (1:28) by giving names to them (2:19), so in token of his rule over his wife he bestowed a name upon her. "Unto Adam also and to his wife, did the LORD God make coats of skins and clothed them" (Gen. 3:21). With what design we are *not told*: so that each reader is free to form his own opinion. In the face of everything that makes directly against any such theory, many have supposed these words intimate that God now dealt (typically at least) in mercy with the fallen pair, and that emblematically they were robed in Christ's righteousness and covered with the garments of salvation. To the contrary, this writer sees therein the ninth consequence of the Fall: that man had thereby *descended to the level of the animal*—observe how in Daniel 7 and Revelation 17, where God sets before us the character of the leading kingdoms of the world (as *He* sees them), He employs the symbol of *beasts*!

"And the LORD God said, Behold, the man is become as one of Us, to know good and evil" (v. 22), which is obviously the language of *sarcasm* and *irony*—"See the one who vainly imagined that by defying Us he should "be as gods" (3:5), now degraded to the level of the beasts!" "Therefore the LORD God sent him forth from the garden of Eden, to till the ground from whence he was taken," i.e., bade him leave the garden. But as Matthew Henry intimates, such an order did not at all appeal to the apostate rebel. "So He *drove out* the man: and He placed at the east of the garden of Eden, Cherubims, and a flaming sword which turned every way, to keep the way of the tree of life" (Gen. 3:24), thereby effectually preventing his return. Therein we behold the tenth consequence of the Fall: man *an outcast from God,* estranged from His favour and fellowship—banished from the place of delight, sent forth a fugitive into the world. Observe how the closing verse corroborates our interpretation of verse 21. The Lord does not drive from Him any child of His! And this is the *finally recorded* act of God in connection with Adam! As He cast out of Heaven the angels that sinned, so He drove Adam and Eve out of the earthly paradise, in proof of their abhorrence to Him and alienation from Him.

Having considered those consequences which fell more immediately upon our first parents for their original offense, we shall now look at those they entailed upon their descendants. Nor do we have to go outside of Genesis 3 to find proof that the penal consequences of their transgression are visited upon their posterity. What God said to them was said to the whole of mankind, for the sin was common to all, so was the penalty too. "Unto the woman He said, I will greatly multiply thy sorrow and thy conception; in sorrow thou shalt bring forth children" (Gen. 3:16), and such has been the lot of all Eve's daughters. "Cursed is the ground for thy sake: in sorrow shalt thou eat of it all the days of thy life . . . . In the sweat of thy face shalt thou eat bread, till thou return unto the ground. . . .for dust thou art, and unto dust shalt thou return" (vv. 17, 19), and such has been the portion of Adam's sons—in every generation and in all parts of the earth. The calamity or evil which then descended upon the world continues unto this hour: all of Adam's and Eve's children are equally involved in the sentence of the pain of childbirth, the curse upon the ground, the obligation to live by toil and sweat, the decay and death of the body.

But let it be pointed out that the things just mentioned above, severe and painful though they be, are trivial in comparison with the Divine judgment which has been visited upon man's *soul*, that they are but the external and visible marks of the moral and spiritual calamity which overtook Adam and his race. By his disobedience he forfeited the favour of his Maker, fell under His holy condemnation and curse, received the awful wages of his sin, came under the sentence of the Law, was alienated from the life of God, became totally depraved, and as such, an object of abhorrence to the Holy One—driven from His presence. Since the guilt of his offense was imputed or judicially charged unto all those he represented, it follows that they participate in all the misery that came upon him. Guilt consists of an obligation or liability to suffer punishment for an offense committed, and that in proportion to the aggravation of the same. In consequence thereof, every child is born into this world in a state of ante-natal disgrace and condemnation, and with an entire depravity of nature or disposition which inevitably leads to and produces actual transgression, and with a complete inability of soul to change its nature or do anything pleasing to God.

"The wicked are estranged from the womb: they go astray as soon as they be born, speaking lies" (Psa. 58:3). First, from the moment of birth every child is morally and spiritually cut off from the Lord—a lost sinner. "Estranged from God and all good: alienated from the Divine life, and its principles, powers, and blessings" (Matthew Henry). Adam lost not only the image of God, but His favour and fellowship too—being expelled from His presence: and each of his children was born *outside* Eden, born in a state of guilt. Second, in consequence thereof they are delinquents, perverts, from the beginning. Their very being is polluted, for evil is bred in the bone with them, their "nature" being inclined unto wickedness only: and if God leaves them unto themselves they will never return therefrom. Third, quickly do they supply evidence of their separation from God and the corruption of their hearts—as every godly parent perceives to his sorrow. While in the cradle itself they evince their opposition to truth, sincerity, integrity. "Foolishness is bound in the heart of a child" (Prov. 22:15): not "childishness" but "foolishness"—that positive propensity to evil, the entering into an ungodly course, the forming and following of bad habits: "bound in the heart"—held firmly there by chains invincible to human power.

But in all ages there have been those who sought to blunt the sharp edge of Psalm 58:3, by unwarrantably narrowing its scope, denying that it has a race-wide application: those who are determined at all costs to rid themselves of the unpalatable truth of the total depravity of all mankind. Pelagians and Socinians have insisted that that verse is speaking only of a particularly reprobate class, those who are flagrantly wayward from an early age. Rightly did John Owen point out: "It is to no purpose to say that he speaks of wicked men only: that is, such as are habitually and profligately so. For whatever any man may afterwards run into by a course of sin, all men are morally alike from the womb, and it is an aggravation of the wickedness of men that it begins so early and holds on in an uninterrupted course. Children are not able to speak from the womb, as soon as they be born. Yet here are they said to speak lies. It is therefore the perverse acting of depraved nature in infancy that is intended, for everything that is irregular, that answers not the law of our creation and rule of our obedience, is a *lie*."

"And were by nature the children of wrath, even as others" (Eph. 2:3). That statement is, if possible, even more awful and solemn than Psalm 58:3. It signifies much more than that we are born into the world with a defiled constitution, for it is not simply "children of corruption," but "of wrath"—obnoxious to God, criminals in His sight. Depravity of our natures is no mere misfortune: if it were, it would evoke pity, and not anger! The expression, "children of wrath" is a Hebraism, a very strong and emphatic one. In the margin of 1 Samuel 20:30, and 2 Samuel 12:5, we read of "the son of death," that is, one unto whom death is due. In Matthew 13:15, Christ used the fearful term "the child of Hell"—one whose sure portion is Hell; while in John 17:12, He designated Judas "the son of perdition"—Divinely appointed thereto. Thus "children of wrath" connotes those who are deserving of wrath, heirs thereto, meet for it. They are born unto wrath, and under it, as their heritage. Not only defiled and corrupt creatures, but the objects of God's judicial indignation. But why so? Because the sin of Adam is imputed unto them, and therefore they are regarded as guilty of having broken God's Law.

Equally forcible and explicit are the words "*by nature* the children of wrath," for it is in designed contrast with that which is artificially acquired. Many have insisted (contrary to the facts of common experience and observation) that children are corrupted by external contact with evil, that they *acquire* bad habits by imitation of others. We do not deny that environment has a measure of influence, yet if any baby could be placed in a perfect one and surrounded only by sinless beings it would soon be evident that he was corrupt. We are depraved not by a process of development, but by genesis. It is not "on account of nature," but "by nature," because of our nativity: it is innate, bred in us. As Goodwin solemnly pointed out, "They are children of wrath in the very womb, before they commit any actual sin." The depraved nature itself is a *penal evil*, and that is because of our federal union with Adam, as partaking of his transgression. We are the children of wrath because our federal head fell under the wrath of God: "there would be no truth in the assertion of Paul that all are by nature the children of wrath if they had not been already under the curse before their birth" (Calvin).

But a greater than Calvin has informed us: "For the children being not yet born, neither having done any good or evil, that the purpose of God according to election might stand, not of works, but of Him that calleth, it was said unto her, The elder shall serve the younger. As it is written, Jacob have I loved, but Esau have I hated" (Rom. 9:11-13). This goes back still farther: Esau was an object of God's hatred before he was born. Obviously, a righteous God could not abominate one who is pure and innocent. But how could Esau be guilty prior to doing any good or evil? Because he shared Adam's criminality, and for precisely the same reason all of us are by nature the children of wrath—obnoxious to Divine punishment—not only by virtue of our own personal transgressions, but first because of our constitution—it is coeval with our very being. We are members of a cursed head, branches of a condemned tree, streams of a polluted fountain—in a word, the guilt of Adam's sin lies hard upon us. No other explanation is possible; since our guilt and liability unto punishment be not, in the first place, due to our personal sins, they must be because of Adam's being imputed to us.

It is for the same reason that infants *die* naturally, for sin is not merely the occasion of physical dissolution, but the cause of it. Death is the wages of sin, tne sentence of the broken law, the penal infliction of a righteous God. Had Adam never sinned, neither he nor any of his descendants would have become subject to death. Death is altogether unnatural and abnormal to man, as the longevity of the patriarchs evidenced. Had not the guilt of Adam's offense been charged to his posterity, none would die in infancy. Yet it does not necessarily follow that any who expire in early childhood are eternally lost. That they are born into this world spiritually dead, alienated from the life of God, is clear; but whether they die eternally, or are saved by sovereign grace, is probably one of those secret things which belong unto the Lord. If they be saved, it must be because they are among the number elected by the Father, redeemed by the Son, and regenerated by the Spirit—without which none can enter Heaven; but concerning these things, Scripture appears to us to be silent. The Judge of all the earth will do right, and there we may submissively yet trustfully leave it. Parenthood is an unspeakably solemn matter!

In the opening verses of Ephesians 2, the Holy Spirit has described our fallen state. First, as being dead in trespasses and sins (v. 1): dead judicially, under sentence of the Law; dead experientially, without a spark of spiritual life. Second, the outward course of such is depicted (vv. 2, 3): as completely dominated by "the flesh," or evil principle, inspired unto an ungodly walk by Satan, so that our every action is sinful. Third, the resultant punishment (v. 3): obnoxious to the Divine Judge, born in such a condition, and remaining so while in a state of nature. Until the sinner believes, "the wrath of God abideth on him" (John 3:36). Though the sentence be not yet executed, it is suspended over him. The word "abideth" here denotes *perpetuity*: as Augustine said, "It hath been upon him from his birth, and remains to this day upon him." "The children of wrath, *even as others*": this is the case of *all* of Adam's descendants, and it is *equally* so. It is a common heritage: by nature no man is either better or worse than his fellows. The very fact that this awful visitation is *universal* can only be accounted for by our relation to the first man, as our covenant head and legal representative.

It would hardly be fair to conclude this chapter without taking some notice of those who attempt to dismiss all which has been pointed out above by dogmatically insisting that "Christ made atonement for original sin," so that the guilt of our first father's transgression rests not on his sons. But such an arbitrary assertion is manifestly contrary to those patent facts which confront us on every side. The judgment which God pronounced upon Adam and Eve is being as surely visited upon their children *today* as ever it was before the Son of God died upon the Cross. The curse upon the ground, the peculiar sufferings of females and all the pain of childbirth, the necessity to toil for our daily bread, the universal reign of death, including the demise of so many infants, are all just as evident and prevalent in the New Testament era as ever they were in the Old. But obviously such things could not be were the Arminian view sound, for if the *guilt* of original sin has been removed, the *effects* thereof could no longer continue. Such an affirmation is baseless, unconfirmed by a single clear statement in Scripture: though some do make a far-fetched attempt to substantiate it by appealing to John 1:29.

"The next day John seeth Jesus coming unto him, and saith, Behold the Lamb of God, which taketh away the sin of the world" (John 1:29). We wonder how many of our readers can perceive anything in those words which strikes them as relevant to the point. Men must surely be hard put to it when they have to press such a verse into service in order to bolster up their theory. Our Lord's forerunner was here presenting the Messiah unto the people in that sacrificial character which both type and prophecy had prepared them to look for Him, and not raising an abstruse question in theology, which is nowhere else mentioned in Scripture. Had those words occurred in one of Paul's profound doctrinal discussions, we should be ready to look for a deeper meaning in them, though we would require something very specific in the context obliging us to define "the sin of the world" as the sin of Adam! John was the herald of a new dispensation: one which would be radically different in its *scope* from the previous one, and one which should be inaugurated by breaking down the "middle wall of partition."

For two thousand years the grace of God had been restricted almost entirely unto a single nation; but now it was on the point of flowing out unto all. The Baptist was there announcing Christ as the Heaven-appointed sacrifice which was to expiate the sin not of believing Jews only, but of Gentiles also. Though "the world" be a general expression, it is not to be regarded as comprehending a universality of individuals, as synonymous with mankind. It is an *indefinite* expression, as "The glory of the LORD shall be revealed, and *all flesh* shall see it together" (Isa. 40:5) and "all flesh shall know that I the LORD am thy Saviour" (Isa. 49:26). "The *sin* of the whole world" signifies all the sins of all God's people as a collective whole, as one great and heavy burden—just as in Isaiah 53:6, "the Lord hath laid on Him *the iniquity* of us all." It was the entire penalty and punishment of sin which Christ took on Himself, and bore away from before the Divine Judge. As Hebrews 9:26, tells us, "But now once in the end of the world hath He appeared to put away sin by the sacrifice of Himself," and since that sacrifice was a *vicarious* one, it necessarily removed the guilt of all those in whose place it was made.

Not only is the theory we are here opposing without any scriptural evidence to support it, but it is refuted by very considerable evidence to the contrary. If attention be paid to *the relations* which Christ sustained to those in whose stead He obeyed and suffered, it at once appears that His work was no mere indefinite and general one, but with a particular and restricted design. He transacted as a Shepherd on behalf of His sheep (John 10:11, and contrast 10:26)—if He died also for the goats and the wolves, then there was no point in saying He laid down His life for the sheep. It was in the relation of a Husband He served (Eph. 5:25-27): *there* is singleness of affection, the exclusiveness of conjugal love! He sustained to His beneficiaries the relation of Head, there being a federal and legal unity between them (Heb. 2:11). The redemptive work of Christ was like His coat, "without seam," one complete and indivisible whole, so that what He did for one He did for all—and not merely took away the guilt of original sin.

If it were true that Christ atoned for Adam's offense, then it would necessarily follow that the government under which the human race is now placed is one which recognizes not the original curse. But such is far from being the case. From the Fall until now, all are born dead in sin, the objects of God's displeasure. That is very evident from the teaching of Romans 3, where, in unequivocal language, the whole world is pronounced to be under condemnation, brought in "guilty before God" (vv. 10-19)—not merely a possible condemnation, but an actual one; not one which may be incurred, but which has been incurred *already*, and under which all are now living; and the only way of deliverance therefrom is by faith in Christ. Precisely the same representation is given in the New Testament of the condition of all when first visited by the Gospel. They are addressed as those who are sinners, lost, living beneath the curse of a broken law, for the dark background of the Gospel is that "the wrath of God is revealed from Heaven against all ungodliness and unrighteousness" (Rom. 1:18), and until the terms of that Gospel are met, men have *no* hope (Eph. 2:12).

The very scene into which we are born confronts us with innumerable evidences that the earth is under the curse of its Maker. "The frowning aspect of Providence which so often darkens our world and appalls our minds, receives the only adequate solution in the fact that the Fall has fearfully changed the relations of God and the creature. We are manifestly treated as criminals under guard. We are dealt with as guilty, faithless, suspected beings that cannot be trusted for a moment. Our earth has been turned into a prison, and sentinels are posted around us to awe, rebuke, and check us. Still, there are traces of our ancient grandeur; there is so much consideration shown to us as to justify the impression that those prisoners were once kings, and that this dungeon was once a palace. To one unacquainted with the history of our race, the dealings of Providence in regard to us must appear inexplicably mysterious. But the whole subject is covered with light when the doctrine of the Fall is understood. The gravest theological errors with respect alike to the character of God and the character of man have arisen from the monstrous hypothesis that our present is our primitive condition, that we are now what God originally made us" (J. Thornwell).

THE DOCTRINE OF HUMAN DEPRAVITY
Its Transmission

In introducing this aspect of our subject we cannot do better than set before the reader what A. A. Hodge pointed out are "the self-evident moral principles which must ever be certainly presupposed in every inquiry into the dealings of God with His responsible creatures. (1) God cannot be the Author of sin. (2) We must not believe that He could consistently with His own perfections create a creature *de novo* (anew, originally) with a sinful nature. (3) The perfection of righteousness, not bare sovereignty, is the grand distinction of all God's dealings. (4) It is a heathen notion that the 'order of nature' or 'the nature of things' or 'natural law' is a real agent independent of God, limiting His freedom or acting with Him as an independent concause in producing effects. (5) We cannot believe that God would inflict either moral or physical evil upon any creature whose natural rights had not been previously forfeited.

"State the two distinct questions thence arising, which, though frequently confused, it is essential to keep separate. First, How does an innate sinful nature originate in each human being at the commencement of his existence, so that the Maker of the man is not the cause of his sin? If this corruption of nature originated in Adam, how is it transmitted to us? Second, *Why*, on what ground of justice, does God inflict this terrible evil, the root ground of all other evils, at the very commencement of personal existence? What fair probation have infants born in sin enjoyed? When, and why, were their rights as new created beings forfeited? It is self-evident that these questions are distinct and should be treated as such. The first may possibly be answered on physical grounds. The second question, however, concerns the moral government of God and inquires concerning the justice of His dispensations. In the history of theology, of all ages and in all schools, very much confusion has resulted from the failure to emphasize and preserve prominent this distinction" *(Outlines of Theology)*.

The "why" has been discussed by us at some length in preceding chapters: the guilt of Adam's offence was imputed to all his posterity because he served as their covenant head and federal representative. Since they were legally one with him, the punishment passed upon him falls on them too, involving them in all the dire consequences of his crime. One of the most terrible of those consequences is the receiving of a sinful nature, which brings us to consider the "how" of the great human tragedy. We do not propose to make any attempt to enter into a philosophical or metaphysical inquiry as to how God can be the Creator and Maker of our beings (Job 31:15), the "Father of spirits" (Heb. 12:9), and yet *not* be the Author of the sin now inherent in our natures. Rather shall we confine ourselves to an examination of the bare facts which Scripture presents thereon. Nowhere in the Word is the pollution of fallen man ascribed unto the Holy One, rather is it uniformly attributed unto human propagation, that by natural generation a corrupt offspring is begotten and conceived by corrupt parents.

It was a Divinely instituted law of the original creation that like should produce like, as plainly appears in that word "whose seed is in itself" (Gen. 1:11, 12), and that oft-repeated expression "after his kind" (vv. 21, 24, 25), and that law has never been revoked—as the biology of every department of nature demonstrates. Hence it follows that since the whole human race sinned in its covenant head, and since *every* member of it receives its nature from him, when the fountain itself became polluted all the streams issuing therefrom were polluted too. A corrupt tree can bring forth nothing but corrupt fruit: since the root became unholy, its branches must also be unholy. All of Adam's offspring do but perpetuate what began in him: from the first moment of their existence they become participants of his impurity. Though our immediate parents be the occasion of conveying a depraved nature unto their children, yet it is because that nature is derived originally from the first man. In other words, the present relation of sire and son is not that of cause and effect, but that of an instrument or channel, in transmitting the sinfulness of Adam and Eve.

In Genesis 5:3, we are told, "Adam lived an hundred and thirty years, and begat a son in his own likeness, after his image." That occurred after his fearful defection, and the statement is in designed and direct contrast with the declaration of verse 1: "In the day that God created man, in the likeness of God made He him." Adam communicated not to his descendants the pure nature which he had originally, by creation—but the polluted one which he acquired by the Fall. It is very striking to note the precise place where this statement is made in the sacred narrative: not at the beginning of Genesis 4 in connection with the begetting of Cain and Abel, but here as introducing a lengthy *obituary list*—showing that dying Adam could only beget mortals. The image of God included both holiness and immortality, but since Adam had lost them and become sinful and mortal, he could propagate none but those in his own fallen likeness, which had in it corruption and death (1 Cor. 15:49, 50, and cf. v. 22). The copy answered to the original. He could not beget in any other way than in his own image, for a clean thing will not issue from an unclean. A depraved parent could produce nothing but a depraved child.

Born in Adam's fallen likeness, not only in substance but in qualities also, all of his posterity are but a continuous repetition of himself. Remarkably is this intimated in the opening verse of that Psalm which has for its theme the awful depravity of the human race. As J. Owen pointed out, "there is a peculiar distinguishing mark put upon this Psalm, in that it is found twice in the Book of Psalms. The fourteenth and fifty-third Psalms are the same, with the alteration of one or two expressions at most. And there is another mark put upon its deep importance in that the Apostle transcribed a great part of it in Romans 3. That Psalm opens with the statement, "The fool hath said in his heart, *There is* no God." The careful reader will have noticed that the words "there is" have been supplied by the translators, and we consider unwarrantably so in this instance. The fool says not "in his head" there is no God, but rather "in his *heart*—no God" for me: I decline allegiance to Him. It is not intellectual unbelief denying the existence of Deity, but the enmity of a rebel who refuses to practically own or be in subjection to God.

"The fool hath said in *his* heart—no God. *They* are corrupt, they have done abominable works" (Psa. 14:1). Most significant and noticeable is that change of number in the pronouns, though for some strange reason it appears to have escaped the notice of the commentators—at any rate none whom we have consulted makes any reference thereto. As stated above, the verses which follow give a full description of the deplorable condition of all mankind, and that is prefaced with a statement about "the fool." Nor is there the slightest difficulty in identifying him. Were we to ask our readers carefully to ponder and answer the question, Who is *the fool* of all fools? we believe they would unanimously reply, *Adam*, for none has ever acted so madly and wickedly as he. This is confirmed by the fact that the Hebrew word for fool in Psalm 14:1, and 53:1 is nowhere else prefaced by the definite article—some render it "The apostate." Adam was the arch-fool: his heart had become not only devoid of wisdom, but filled with hatred against it. Such was now the father of our race, and what could his children be like? Our verse answers, "they are *corrupt*," and prove themselves to be so by doing abominable works.

"Behold, I was shapen in iniquity; and in sin did my mother conceive me" (Psa. 51:5). Such is the sad confession which every one of us makes. Born in the likeness of Adam as a fallen creature, all of his descendants are but replicas of himself, and since moral corruption be transmitted by him to them by a fixed constitution or law of heredity, then that corruption dates from the very beginning of their existence. Because by being Adam's children they are depraved, it necessarily follows that they must be so as soon as they *are* his children. David was the son of a lawful and honourable marriage, yet from his parents he received Adam's vitiated nature with all its evil dispositions. Note well that he was careful to intimate that it was not by Divine infusion, but by natural generation and human propagation. He mentioned it not to excuse his fearful fall, but to aggravate the same. "Had I duly considered this before, I should not have made so bold with the temptation, nor have ventured among the sparks with such tinder in my heart" (Matthew Henry). A realization that our being is horribly degenerated from its pristine purity and rectitude should make us thoroughly distrustful of self and cause us to walk most warily.

Because our very nature is contaminated, we enter the world a mass of potential wickedness, which is one reason why Job declared, "I have said to corruption, Thou art my father: to the worm, Thou art my mother, and my sister" (17:14). Hervey tells us the Hebrew word there for "worm" signifies a grub, which is bred by and feeds upon putrefaction. I commenced my existence with all sorts of impurity in my nature, with every cursed propensity to evil, with everything earthly, sensual, devilish in my mind. That depraved nature is the source of all our other miseries, the root from which proceed all evil actions. This solemn and sad fact is demonstrated by antithesis. Why was it necessary for Christ to be incarnated supernaturally, by the miracle of the Virgin birth? So that what was born of her should be "that *holy* thing" (Luke 1:35), which had not been the case if He had been begotten by natural generation from a man. Though this doctrine of original sin, of ante-natal defilement be purely a matter of Divine revelation, yet it explains what nothing else does, namely that "the imagination of man's heart is evil from his youth" (Gen. 8:21)—in every instance, Christ alone excepted.

"The wicked are estranged from the womb: they go astray as soon as they be born, speaking lies. Their poison is like the poison of a serpent" (Psa. 58:3, 4). There are three indictments here made against fallen human nature. First, that from the beginning of his existence man is alienated from God, divorced from His favour, cut off from fellowship with Him. Second, that he evidences his deplorable state as soon as he enters this world, manifesting his sinfulness in the cradle. But, third, why is it that everyone turns to his own way, and the very first steps he takes are in that broad road which leads to destruction? Because his very being is poisoned and poisonous, malicious: at ill will with God and goodness, and his fellows—"hateful, and hating one another" (Titus 3:3). Our poison "is like the poison of a serpent." The serpent does not acquire his venom, but is *generated* a poisonous creature. Poison, deadly poison, is its very nature from the outset, and when it bites it only acts out that with which it was born. Though its poison be hid, it is there lurking, ready for use as soon as the serpent be provoked.

"Antecedent to all trespasses and acts of sin, before any apprehension of good or evil has dawned upon our hearts, before any notion respecting God has been formed in our souls, before we have uttered a word or conceived a thought, sin—essential sin—is found to dwell within us. Bound up with our being, it enters into every sensation, lives in every thought, sways every faculty. If the senses, by means of which we communicate with the external world, had never acted—if our eye had never seen, and our ear had never heard; if our throat had never proved itself to be an open sepulchre, breathing forth corruption; if our tongue had never shown itself to be set on fire of Hell—still sin would have been the secret mistress of that world of thought and feeling which is found within us, and every hidden impulse there would have been enmity against God" (B. W. Newton). When therefore Scripture speaks of men as sinners, it refers not to their practice alone, but chiefly to their evil nature—a nature which is entailed by Adam and transmitted from parent to child in successive generations.

"Foolishness is bound in the heart of a child; but the rod of correction shall drive it from him" (Prov. 22:15). This foolishness is not merely intellectual ignorance, but a positive principle of evil, for in the book of Proverbs the "fool" is not the idiot, but the sinner. Deep-rooted is this corruption. It lies not on the surface, like some of the child's habits, which may easily be corrected. That moral madness, as Matthew Henry pointed out, "is not only *found* there, but *bound* there; it is annexed to the heart." It is rooted and riveted in him from the first breath he draws. This is the birthright of all Adam's progeny. "A little innocent" is but the miscalled name of fondness and fancy. Said John Bunyan "I do confess it is my opinion that children come polluted with sin into the world, and that oft-times the sins of youth, especially while they are very young, are rather by virtue of indwelling sin than by examples that are set before them by others; not but they may learn to sin by example too, but example is not the root, but rather the temptation to sin." The rod of correction (not of caprice or passion) is the means prescribed by God, and under His blessing it will prevent many an outburst of the flesh.

" 'The rod and reproof give wisdom; but a child left to himself bringeth his mother to shame' (Prov. 29:15). Discipline is the order of God's government. Parents are His dispensers of it to their children. The child must be broken in, to "bear the yoke in his youth" (Lam. 3:27). Let reproof be tried first; and if it succeed, let the rod be spared

(Prov. 17:10). If not, let it do its work" (C. Bridges). If parents fail to do their duty, sad will be the consequences—the "mother" only *is* mentioned as being brought to shame, because she is usually the most indulgent, and because she (normally) *feels* most keenly the affliction brought upon herself by her own neglect. But fathers, too, are disgraced. Eli gave reproof, but spared the rod (1 Sam. 2:22-25; 3:13), and paid dearly for his folly. What dishonour was brought upon David's name and what poignant grief must have filled him because his perverted fondness brought his sons to their ruin—one palliated in the most aggravated sin (2 Sam. 14:28-33; 15:6; 18:33), another having been not even corrected by a word (1 Kings 1:5-9). As E. Hopkins said, "Take this for certain, that as many deserved stripes as you spare from your children, you do but lay up for your own backs."

A child does not have to be taught to sin: remove all inhibitions and prohibitions and he will bring his parents to the grave in sorrow. If the child be humoured and no real efforts are made to counteract its evil propensities, it will assuredly grow more self-willed and intractable. How very far are the Scriptures from flattering us, my reader! A "transgressor from the womb" (Isa. 48:8) is one of the hereditary titles of everyone entering this world. We are transgressors by internal disposition before we are so in external acts. Because every parent is the channel of moral contagion to his offspring, they are by nature, "children of disobedience" (Eph. 2:2). Original sin is transmitted as leprosy is conveyed to the children of lepers (2 Kings 5:27). That is one reason why the corruption of nature is designated our "old man": it is coeval with our beings. Our very "heart," the center of our moral being, from which are "the issues (or "outgoings") of life," is deceitful above all things and desperately wicked from the first moment of its existence.

It is argued against what has been advanced above that if corruption be derived unto all men from their first parents, then all will be equally corrupt: and this is quite contrary to known fact, for we see some who are subject to no inordinate affections, respectable and law-abiding citizens. A number of answers may be given in reply to that objection, though all of them may be reduced into these two. First, though everything else being equal, such a conclusion is logical, yet even then it will not necessarily follow that all men will *manifest* the corruption in the same manner, nor even to the same extent. When we say "everything else being equal," we include such things as the watchful care of pious parents, the discipline of a good education, the demands and effects of a refined environment, the positions and circumstances in which one and another may be placed; for while none of these things, nor all of them combined, can produce any change in a person's nature, they are factors which exert an influence upon his outward conduct. Nevertheless, though one man may have less dissolute manners than another, yet his imaginations are not pure, and though his bodily lusts be under better control, he may yield more to the lusts of the mind. There are diversities in men's *lives*, but original sin has the same defiling effects upon all *hearts*.

Second, though all men be made in the likeness of fallen Adam, *God restrains*—in different ways and in varying degrees, the outbreakings of the corruption which has been transmitted to them. Nowhere is the sovereignty of God more evident than in His disposing of the lot of one, and another: denying to some the opportunity to satisfy their evil desires, hedging up their way by poverty, ill-health, or putting them in isolated places; whereas others are given up to their hearts' lusts and God so orders His providences that they fatten themselves as beasts for the slaughter. Some men's callings draw out their sins more than do those of their fellows, so that they are subject to frequent and fierce temptations. Various dispositions are excited to action by the conditions in which they are placed: as Jacob was induced to impose upon his father by an unscrupulous mother, or as a sight of the spoils of Jericho stirred up the cupidity of Achan. It was for this reason that holy Agar was moved to pray, "Remove far from me vanity and lies: give me neither poverty nor riches; feed me with food convenient for me: lest I be full, and deny Thee, and say, Who is the Lord? or lest I be poor, and steal, and take the name of my God in vain" (Prov. 30:8, 9).

THE DOCTRINE OF HUMAN DEPRAVITY
Its Nature

In our last chapter we showed how Scripture casts light upon the great moral problem of how an inherently corrupt nature originates in each child from the beginning of its existence *without* its Creator being the Author of sin. David declared, "Behold, I was shapen in iniquity; and in sin did my mother conceive me" (Psa. 51:5). Carefully did he describe his depravity as innate and not created, as derived from his mother and not his Maker, that defilement is transmitted directly from Adam through the channel of human propagation. The same fact was expressed by our Lord when He said, "That which is born of the flesh is flesh" (John 3:6). In the Old Testament the word "flesh" is used as a general term for human nature or mankind: "let *all flesh* bless His holy name" (Psa. 145:21)—that is, all men; "all flesh is grass" (Isa. 40:6)—the life of every member of our race is frail and fickle. The term occurs in the New Testament in the same sense: "except those days should be shortened, there should no flesh be saved" (Matt. 24:22); "by the deeds of the law there shall no flesh be justified in His sight" (Rom. 3:20)—i.e., by his own obedience no man can merit acceptance with God.

But since mankind be fallen and human nature is depraved, the term "flesh" becomes the expression of that fact, and every time it is used in Scripture in a moral sense has reference to *the corruption* of our entire beings, without any distinction between our visible and invisible parts—body and mind. This is evident from those passages where "the flesh" is contrasted with "the spirit" or the new nature: Romans 8:5, 6; 1 Corinthians 2:11; Galatians 5:17. When the Apostle declared, "For I know that in *me* (that is, in *my flesh*,) dwelleth no good thing" (Rom. 7:18), he had reference to far more than his body with its appetites, namely his entire natural man, with all its faculties, powers and propensities: the whole was polluted, and therefore nothing good could issue from him until Divine grace was imparted. Again, when we find included in that incomplete list of the horrible "works of the flesh" supplied by Galatians 5 such things as "hatred, emulations, wrath, and envyings," it is quite plain that the word takes in far more than the corporeal parts of our persons; the more so when we find that these works are set over against "the fruit of the spirit," each portion of which consists of the exercise of some *inward* quality or grace.

Thus it is clear that when Christ declared "that which is born of the flesh is flesh," He signified that that which is propagated by fallen man is depraved, that whatever comes into this world by ordinary generation is carnal and corrupt, causing the heart itself to be deceitful above all thing and desperately wicked. It is evident also from the immediate context (vv. 3-5), for what He affirmed in verse 6 was in order to demonstrate the absolute need of regeneration. Our Lord was there opposing the first birth to the new birth, and showing how imperative is the latter by the fact that we are radically tainted from the outset. All by nature are essentially evil, nothing but "flesh," everything in us contrary to holiness. Our very nature is vitiated, and by no process of education or culture can it be refined and made fit for the kingdom of God. The faculties which men receive at birth have a carnal bias, an earthly trend, a disrelish of the heavenly and Divine, and are inclined only to selfish aims and groveling pursuits. In the most polished or religious society, equally with the vulgar and profane, "that which is born of the flesh is flesh" and can never be anything better. Prune and trim a corrupt tree as much as you will, it can never be made to yield good fruit. Every man must be born again before he can be acceptable to a holy God.

Coming more directly to our present subject, we shall now attempt to supply an answer to the still more difficult question, In what does the vitiation of man by the Fall consist, precisely what is the nature of human depravity? That is far more than a question of academic interest which concerns none but teachers of theology: it is one of deep doctrinal and practical importance, and which it behooves all of us, especially preachers, to be quite clear upon, for a mistake at this point is very liable to lead to the most erroneous conclusions and serious consequences. Such has indeed proved to be the case, for not a few who were sound and Orthodox in many other respects have answered this question in such a way as inevitably led them seriously to weaken, if not altogether to repudiate, the *full responsibility* of fallen man, and caused them to become hyper-Calvinists and Antinomians. We shall therefore endeavour most carefully to define and describe the present condition of the natural man, beginning with the negative side, under which will be a number of things in which human depravity does not consist.

First, the Fall does not result in the extinguishment of that *spirit* which was a part of man's complex being when created by God: it did not either in the case of our first parents or in any of their descendants. It has, however, been argued from the Divine threat made to Adam, "in the day that thou eatest thereof thou shalt surely die," that such was the case, that since Adam did not immediately die physically, he must have done so spiritually. That is certainly a fact, yet it requires to be interpreted by Scripture. It is quite wrong to suppose that because Adam's body died not, his spirit did. It was not something in Adam which died, but Adam himself—in his relation to God.

The same is true of his offspring: they are indeed "dead *in* trespasses and sins" toward God, from the beginning of their existence, but nothing *within them* is positively dead in the ordinary meaning of that word. In the scriptural sense of the term, "death" never signifies annihilation, but separation. At physical death the soul is not extinguished but separated from the body: and the spiritual death of Adam was not the extinction of any part of his being but the severance of his fellowship with a holy God.

The same is true of all his children. The exact force of the solemn statement that they are "dead in trespasses and sins" is Divinely defined for us as "being *alienated from* the life of God through the ignorance that is in them, because of the blindness of their heart" (Eph. 4:18). When Christ represented the Father as saying, "this My son was dead, and is alive again" (Luke 15:21), He most certainly did not mean that he had ceased to exist, but that while the prodigal remained "in the far country" he was cut off from Him, and that he had now returned to Him. The lake of fire into which the wicked shall be cast is designated "the second death" (Rev. 20:14), not in order to signify that they shall then cease to be, but because they are "punished with everlasting destruction *from* the presence of the Lord and from the glory of His power" (2 Thess. 1:9). That fallen man *is* possessed of a spirit is clear from "the Lord, which . . . formeth the spirit of man within him" (Zech. 12:1), from "what man knoweth the things of a man save the spirit of man which is in him" (1 Cor. 2:11), and from "the spirit shall return unto God who gave it" (Eccl. 12:7). Man was created a tripartite being, consisting of spirit and soul and body (1 Thess. 5:23), and no part thereof ceased to exist when he fell.

Second, the Fall did not issue in the loss of any man's *faculties*. It did not divest man of reason, conscience, or moral taste—for that would have been to convert him into another species of being. As reason remained, he still had the power of distinguishing between truth and falsehood; conscience still enabled him to distinguish between what was right add wrong, between what was a duty and a crime; and moral taste capacitated him to perceive the contrasts in the sphere of the excellent and beautiful. It is most important that we should be quite clear at this point: the Fall has not touched the substance of the soul—that remains entire with all its original endowments of intellect, conscience and will. These are the characteristic elements of humanity, and to deprive him of them would be to unman man. They exist in the criminal as well as in the saint. They all have an essential unity in the unity of the human person: that is to say, they are co-ordinate faculties, though each has a sphere that is peculiar to itself. Collectively, they constitute the rational, moral, accountable being. It is not the mere possession of them which renders men evil or good, but the manner and motive of their exercise which makes their actions sinful or holy.

No, the Fall deprived man of no mental or moral faculty, but it took from him the power to use them aright. They were all brought under the malignant influence of sin, so that he was no longer capable of doing anything pleasing to God. Depravity is all-pervading, extending to the whole man. It was not, as different theorists have supposed, confined to one department of his being—to the will as contradistinguished from the understanding, or to the understanding as contradistinguished from the will. It was not restricted to the lower appetites, as contrasted with our higher principles of action—nor did it obtain in the heart alone, considered as the seat of the affections. On the contrary, it was a disease from which every organ has suffered. As found in the understanding, it consists of spiritual ignorance, blindness, darkness, folly. As found in the will, it is rebellion, perverseness, a spirit of disobedience. As found in the affections, it is hardness of heart, a total insensibility to and disrelish of spiritual and Divine things. The entrance of sin into the human constitution has not only affected all the faculties, so as to produce a complete disqualification for any spiritual exercise in any form, but it has crippled and enervated them in their exercise within the sphere of truth and holiness. They were vitiated in respect to everything wearing the image of God: of goodness and excellence.

Third, the Fall has not resulted in the loss of man's *freedom of will*, or his power of volition as a moral faculty. Admittedly this is a much harder point to treat of than either of the above: not because Scripture is ambiguous in its teaching, or even because it contains any seeming contradictions thereon, but because of the philosophical and metaphysical difficulties it raises in the minds of those who give careful thought thereto. Certain it is that the Fall did not reduce man to the condition of a stock or stone, or even into an irrational animal: he retained that rational power of volition which was a part of his original constitution, so that he was still able to choose spontaneously. Equally certain is it that man is not free to do as he pleases in any absolute sense, for then he would be a god, omnipotent. In his *unfallen* state Adam was made subservient to and dependent upon the Lord. So it is with his children: their wills are required to be fully subordinated to that of their Maker and Governor. Moreover, their freedom is strictly circumscribed by the supreme rule of Divine Providence, as it opens doors for or shuts doors against them.

As pointed out above, though each distinct faculty of the soul has a sphere that is peculiar to itself, yet are they co-ordinate, and therefore the will is not to be thought of as an independent, self-determining entity, standing apart from the other faculties and superior to them, capable of reversing the judgments of the mind or acting contrary to the desires of the heart—rather is the will influenced and determined by them. As G. S. Bishop most helpfully pointed out, "the true philosophy of moral action and its process is that of Genesis 3:6—'And when the woman saw that the tree was good for food (sense-perception, intelligence), and a tree to be desired (affections), she took and ate thereof (the will).' " Thus the freedom of the will is also limited by the bounds of human capabilities: it cannot, for example, go beyond the extent of knowledge possessed by the mind—it is impossible for me to cognize, love and choose any object I am totally unacquainted with. Thus it is the *understanding,* rather than the will, which is the dominant faculty and factor: hence, when Scripture delineates the condition of fallen men it attributes their alienation from God to "the ignorance that is in them" (Eph. 4:18), and makes regeneration to begin with "renewed in knowledge" (Col. 3:10).

The limitations of human freedom pointed out above pertain alike to man unfallen or fallen, but the entrance of sin into the human constitution has imposed much greater limitations. While it be true that man is as *truly free* now as Adam before his apostasy, yet he is not so *morally* free as he was. Fallen man is free in the sense that he is at liberty to act according to his own choice, without compulsion from without; yet, since his nature has been defiled and corrupted, he is no longer free unto that which is good and holy. Great care needs to be taken at this point, lest our definition of the freedom of fallen man clashes with such scriptures as Psalm 60:3, John 6:44, Romans 9:16, for he only wills now according to the desires and dictates of his evil heart. It has been well said that, "The will of the sinner is like to a manacled and fettered prisoner within a cell: his movements are hampered by his chains and circumscribed by the walls that confine him. He is indeed free to walk, but in a manner so constrained and within an area so bounded that his freedom is bondage"—bondage to sin.

Whether we understand by "the will," simply the faculty of volition by which the soul chooses or refuses, or whether we regard the "will" *as* the faculty of volition together with all else within us which affects the choice—reason, imagination, longing—yet fallen man is quite free in *exercising volition* according to his prevailing disposition and desire at the moment. Internal freedom is here used in contrast with external restraint or compulsion, and where such be absent, then the individual is at liberty to decide according to his pleasure. Where the Arminian errs so seriously on this point is to confound *power* with "will," insisting that the sinner is equally able to choose good as evil, for that is a repudiation of his total depravity or complete vassalage to evil. By the Fall man came under bondage to sin, and became the captive of the Devil: yet, even so, he first yields *voluntarily* to the enticements of his own lusts before he commits any act of sin, nor can Satan lead him into all wrongdoing without his own consent.

The natural man does as he pleases, but he pleases himself only in one direction—selfward and downward, never Godward and upward. As Romans 6:20 says of the saints while in their unregenerate state, "For when ye were the servants of sin, ye were free *from* righteousness." In all his sinning man acts as a free agent, for he is forced neither by God nor Satan. When he breaks the law he does so by his own option, and not by coercion from another: in so doing he is freely acting out his own fallen nature. Thus it is a mistake to say that a bias of the mind or propensity of heart is destructive of his volition. Both must be self-moved in order for there to be responsibility and guilt, and both *are* self-moved. The murderer is not compelled to hate his victim. Though he cannot prevent his inward hatred by any mere exercise of will, yet he *can* refrain from the outward act of murder by his own volition, and therefore is he blameworthy when he fails to do so. These are indisputable facts of our own consciousness!

Fourth, the Fall has not resulted in any reduction, still less the destruction, of *man's responsibility*. If all of the above be carefully pondered this should be quite evident. Human responsibility is the necessary corollary of Divine sovereignty. Since God be the Creator, since He is supreme Ruler over all, and since man be but a creature and a subject, there is no escape from his accountability unto his Maker and rightful Lord. If we be asked to define more distinctly—responsible *for* what?—we reply that man is obligated to answer unto the relationship which exists between him and his Creator: he occupies the place of creaturehood, subordination, utter dependency for every breath he draws, and therefore must he acknowledge God's dominion, submit to His authority, and love Him with all his strength and heart. The discharge of human responsibility is simply the recognition of God's rights and acting accordingly, a rendering to Him of His due. It is the practical acknowledgment of His ownership and government. We are justly required to be in constant subjection to His will, to employ in His service the faculties He has given us, to use the means He has appointed, to improve the opportunities and advantages He has vouchsafed us. Our whole duty is to glorify God.

From the above definition it should be crystal clear that the Fall did not, and could not to the slightest degree, cancel or impair human responsibility. The Fall did not change the fundamental relationship subsisting between the Creator and the creature. God is the Owner of sinful man as truly and as fully as He was of sinless man. God is still our sovereign, all we His subjects. Furthermore, as pointed out above, fallen man is still in possession of all those faculties which qualify for discharging his responsibility. Admittedly, the babe in arms and the poor idiot are not morally accountable for their actions, but, by parity of reason, those who have reached the age when they are capable of distinguishing between right and wrong *are* morally accountable for their deeds. Fallen man, though his understanding be spiritually darkened, is still possessed of rationality. Fallen man, though under the dominion of sin, has his power of volition, and is under binding obligation to make, every time, a right and good choice, to resist temptations and refrain from evil doing, as very human court of justice worthy of the name rightly insists.

Whatever difficulties may be theoretically involved by the fact that man's nature is now totally depraved and that he is in bondage to sin, yet God has not lost His right to command because man has lost his power to obey. While the Fall has cast us out of God's favour, it has not released us from His authority. It was not God who took from man his spiritual strength and deprived him of his ability to do that which is well pleasing in His sight. Man was originally endowed with power to meet the requirements of his Maker, and it was by his own madness and wickedness that he threw away his power. But as a human monarch does not forfeit his rights to allegiance from his subjects when they turn rebels, but rather maintains his prerogative by demanding that they cease their insurrection and return to their fealty: so has the King of kings an infinite right to demand that lawless rebels shall become loyal subjects. If God could justly require of us no more than we are able to render Him, it would follow that the more we enslave ourselves by evil habits, the less our liability—a palpable absurdity!

Not only is man's responsibility insisted upon throughout the Scripture, from Genesis to Revelation, but it is also asserted by man's own conscience! Whatever quibbles the individual raises from depravity, and however he argues from his moral impotency that his deeds are not criminal, he repudiates such reasoning where his fellow sinners are concerned. When others wrong him, he neither denies their accountability, nor offers excuse for them. If he be cruelly slandered, robbed of his possessions or maltreated in his body, instead of saying of the culprit, "Poor fellow, he could not help himself: Adam is to blame," he promptly applies to the police and seeks redress in the law courts. Moreover, when the sinner is quickened and awakened by the Holy Spirit, so far from complaining against God's righteous demands, he freely owns himself as deserving to be eternally damned for his vile rebellion, acknowledges that he was fully responsible for the same, that he is "without excuse," feels the burden of his guilt, and lies in the dust before God in sincere repentance.

Under this aspect of our subject we are endeavouring to supply an answer to the questions: What is connoted by the term "total depravity"? Wherein lies the essential difference or differences between man as unfallen and fallen? Precisely what is the nature of that awful malady which now afflicts us? In the last chapter we dwelt upon what it does *not* consist of, showing that man has not ceased to be a complete and tripartite being, that he is in possession of that spirit which is a necessary part of his constitution; that the Fall has not resulted in the loss of any faculties of his soul; that he has not been deprived of the freedom of his will or power of volition; and that there has been no lessening of his responsibility as an accountable creature unto God. Turning now to *what has* resulted from the Fall, it will be found that there is here both a privative and a positive side, that there were certain good things of which we were deprived, and that there were other evil things which we derived. Only as both of these are taken into consideration can we obtain a full answer to our question.

First, by the Fall man lost *the moral image of God*. As briefly pointed out in the second chapter of this book, the "image of God" in which he was originally created refers to his moral nature. It was that which constituted him a spiritual being, and, as Calvin expressed it, "It includes all the excellencies in which the nature of man surpasses all the other species of animals." More particularly what that "image" consisted of is intimated in Ephesians 4:24, and Colossians 3:10, where a detailed summary of the same is supplied, for our being "renewed" therein (at regeneration) clearly implies it to be the *same* Divine image in which man was made at the beginning. In those two passages it is described as consisting of "righteousness and true holiness" and the "knowledge of God." Let us now enlarge a little upon each of those component parts.

By "righteousness" we are to understand, as everywhere in Scripture, conformity to the Divine Law. Before the Fall there was an entire harmony between the whole moral nature of man and all the requirements of that Law which is "holy, and just, and good" (Rom. 7:12). This was very much more than a merely negative "innocence" or freedom from everything sinful, or even bias or tendency toward it, which is all that Socinians allow; namely something nobler, higher and more spiritual. There was perfect agreement and concord between the constitution of our first parents and the rule of conduct set before them, not only in their external actions, but also in the very springs of those actions, in the innermost parts of their beings—in their desires and motives, in all the tendencies and inclinations of their hearts and minds. As Ecclesiastes 7:29 declares, God "made man *upright*," which refers not to carriage of his body, except so far as that shadowed forth his moral excellence. That righteousness was lost at the Fall, but is, in principle, restored at regeneration, when God writes His laws in our hearts and puts them in our minds—imparts to us a love for and relish of them, makes us willingly subject to their authority.

By "holiness" we are to understand chastity and undefilement of being. As righteousness was that which made Adam *en rapport* with the Divine Law, so holiness was that which rendered him meet for fellowship with his Maker. There was in him that spotless purity of nature which fitted him for communion with the Holy One, for "holiness" is not only a relationship, but moral quality too—not only a separation from all that is evil, but the endowment and possession of that which is good. Jehovah is "glorious in holiness" (Exo. 15:11), and therefore those with whom He converses must be personally suited to Himself—none but the pure in heart shall see God (Matt. 5:8). It is inconceivable that God would, by an immediate act, have created any other kind of rational and responsible being than one that was pure and perfect, the more so since he was to be the archetype of mankind. As Thornwell so aptly expressed it, "Holiness was the inheritance of his nature—the birthright of his being. It was the state in which all his faculties received their form. "That holiness was lost when man fell, but by regeneration and sanctification it is restored to the elect who are made "partakers of His holiness" (Heb. 12:10)—a principle of holiness being communicated to them at the new birth, which develops as they grow in grace and in the knowledge of the Lord.

By "knowledge" we are to understand the cognition of Grid Himself. As Adam's holiness or purity of heart capacitated him to "see God" in the spiritual sense of the word, so also was he enabled thereto by the Holy Spirit's indwelling of him. As Goodwin pointed out, "Where holiness was, we may be sure the Spirit was too . . . the same Spirit (as in the regenerate) was in Adam's heart to assist his graces and to cause them to flow and bring forth, and to move him to live according to those principles of life given to him" (Vol. 6, p. 54).

It is clear from the nature of the case that since Adam was created in maturity of body he must have been created in maturity of mind, that there was then resident in him what we acquire only by slow experience. Adam was able to apprehend and appreciate God for what He is in Himself: he had a true and intuitive knowledge of the perfections of Deity, the heartfelt realization of their excellence. That knowledge of God was lost at the Fall, by Adam, and to his offspring, but it is restored to the elect at regeneration, when He shines "in our hearts to give the light of the knowledge of the glory of God in the face of Jesus Christ" (2 Cor. 4:6).

Second, by the Fall *man lost the life of God*. The soul was not only made by God but *for God*: fitted to know, enjoy, and commune with Him—and its life is in Him. But evil necessarily severs from the Holy One, and then instead of being alive in God, the soul is dead in sin. Not that the soul has ceased to be, for Scripture distinguishes sharply between life and existence, as in "But she that liveth in pleasure is dead while she liveth" (1 Tim. 5:6). It is a moral or spiritual death, not of being, but of *well-being*. "He that hath the Son hath life: and he that hath not the Son of God hath not life" (1 John 5:12). To have the Son of God for my very own is to have everything that is really worth having: to be without Him, no matter what temporal things I may momentarily possess, is to be an utter pauper. "Life," spiritual and eternal life, is a comprehensive expression to include all the blessedness which man is capable of enjoying here and hereafter. He that hath life is eternally saved, accepted in the Beloved, admitted into the Divine favour, made partaker of the Divine nature, is righteous and holy in the sight of God: he that is without "life" is destitute of all these things.

To be separated from God is necessarily to be deprived of everything which makes life worth living, for He is "the fountain of life" (Psa. 36:9), and therefore of light, of glory, of blessedness. No finite mind can conceive, still less can any human pen express, the fullness of those words "the fountain of life." We can but compare other passages of Scripture which make known something of their meaning. As we do so, we learn that there is at least a threefold life which His people receive from God. First, His benign approbation: "in His *favour* is life" (Psa. 30:5). In Leviticus 1:4, it is tendered "accepted" and in Deuteronomy 30:16, "the good will of Him that dwelt in the bush." But the verse which best enables us to understand its force is "O Naphtali, *satisfied with favour*, and full with the blessing of the Lord" (Deut 33:23)—those who are favourably regarded by Him need nothing more, can desire nothing better. To have the "good will" of the triune Jehovah is life indeed, the acme of blessedness: contrariwise, to be out of His favour is to be dead unto all that is worth while.

Second, *joy and blessedness of soul.* "O God, Thou art my God: early will I seek Thee . . . to see Thy power and Thy glory . . . because Thy lovingkindness is better than life" (Psa. 63:1-3). The life which His people receive from God is that which capacitates them to delight themselves in Him. Thus it was here. David had been rapt in adoration by the Divine attributes. It was the longing of his soul to have further communion with God, and this he was resolved to seek diligently, to have enlarged views of the Divine perfections and experiential discoveries of His excellence, as an anticipation of the felicity of Heaven. *That* he prized more than anything else. The natural man values his life above all else. Not so the spiritual: to him God's "lovingkindness" is better than all the comforts and luxuries of temporal life, better than the longest and most prosperous natural life. The lovingkindness of God is itself the present spiritual life of the saint, as it is also both an earnest and a foretaste of the life everlasting. It refreshes their hearts, strengthens their souls and sends them on their way rejoicing.

Thousands of his fellows are weary of life, but no Christian is ever weary of God's lovingkindness. The latter is infinitely better than the "life" of a king or a millionaire, for it has no sorrow added to it, no inconvenience in it, no evils attendant upon it. Physical death will put a period to the earthly existence of the most privileged, but it will not to God's lovingkindness, for that is from everlasting to everlasting. It is esteemed by the believer beyond everything else, for it is the spring from which every blessing proceeds. It was in God's lovingkindness that the Covenant of Grace originated. It was His lovingkindness which gave Christ unto His people and them unto Him. It is by His lovingkindness they are drawn to Him (Jer. 31:3), given a saving knowledge of Him, brought to know personally the love which He bears to them. Without God's lovingkindness life is but death. Well then may each believer exclaim, "Because Thy lovingkindness is better than life, my lips shall *praise Thee*"—I will revel in Thy perfections and exult in Thyself: I will seek to render somewhat of the homage which is Thy due.

Again, that life which His children receive from God consists not only in being the objects of His benign approbation, in the experiential enjoyment of His lovingkindness, but also in the reception of a principle of righteousness and holiness by which they are fitted to appreciate Him, and for want of which the unregenerate cannot enjoy Him, for they are "alienated from the life of God" (Eph. 4:18). It is clear, both from the immediate context and from the remainder of the verse, that the "life of God" there has a particular reference to holiness, for the contrary thereto appears in "that ye henceforth walk not as other Gentiles walk, in *the vanity* of their mind." The contrast is further pointed in "Having the understanding darkened, being alienated from the light of God through the ignorance that is in them, because of the blindness of their heart." The unconverted are wholly dominated by their depraved nature. Their minds are in a state of moral fatuity, engaged only with vain things: their understandings are devoid of spiritual intelligence, lacking any power to apprehend Truth or appreciate the beauties of virtue. Their souls are estranged from God, with an inveterate aversion from Him—their hearts are calloused, steeled against Him. Thus the corruption and depravity of the natural man are set over against the grace and holiness communicated at the new birth, here termed "the life of God."

Third, by the Fall, man has lost *his love for God.* There are two cardinal affections that influence unto action: love and hatred. The one cannot be without the other, for that which is contrary to what is desired will be repellent—"Ye that love the LORD, hate evil" (Psa. 97:10). Of the perfect Man the Father said, "Thou lovest righteousness, and hatest wickedness: therefore God, Thy God, hath anointed Thee with the oil of gladness above Thy fellows" (Psa. 45:7). So of the triune Jehovah, "Jacob have I loved, but Esau have I hated" (Rom. 9:13). It is the great work of grace in the redeemed to direct and fasten those affections upon their proper objects: when we put right our love and hatred, we prosper in the spiritual life. Fallen man differs from unfallen in this: they both have the same affections, but they are *misplaced* in fallen man, so that they now love what they should hate, and hate what they should love: their affections are like bodily members out of joint—as if the arms should hang down backward. To bestow their love and hatred aright is the very essence of true spirituality: to love all that is good and pure, to hate all that is evil and vile, for love moves us to seek union with and make our own, as hatred repels and makes us leave alone what is loathsome.

Now love was made *for God,* for He alone is its adequate and suited object: for all that is of Himself—His attributes, His Law, His ordinances, His dealings with us. But hatred was made for the serpent and sin. God is infinitely lovely in Himself, and if things are to be valued according to the greatness and excellence of them, then God supremely so, for every perfection centres and is found in its fullness in Him. To love Him above everything else is an act of homage due to Him, for who and what He is. There is everything in God to excite esteem, adoration and affection. Goodness is not an object of dread, but of attraction and delight. Now all that God required from Adam He freely furnished him with. Since he was created with perfect moral rectitude of heart and with a holy temper of mind, he was fully competent to love Him with all his being. He saw the Divine perfections shining forth. The heavens declared His glory, the firmament showed His handiwork, and His excellence was mirrored in everything around him. Thereby he realized what God deserved from him, and he was duly affected with His blessedness. His heart was filled with a sense of His ineffable beauty, and admiring and adoring thoughts of Him filled his mind, moving him to render unto Him that worship and submission to which He is infinitely entitled.

Love for God was what gave unity of action to all the faculties of Adam's soul, for since it was the dominant principle in him, it rendered all the exercises of them as so many expressions of devotion to Him. Hence, when love of God died within him, his faculties not only lost their original unity and orderliness, but *the power* to use them aright. All his faculties came under an evil and hostile influence, and were debased in their action. The natural man is without a single spark of true affection for God: "But I know you," said the omniscient Searcher of hearts to the religious Jews, "that ye have not the love of God in you" (John 5:42). Being without any love to God, all the outward acts of the natural man are worthless in His sight: "they that are in the flesh *cannot* please God" (Rom. 8:8), for they lack the root from which they must proceed in order for any fruit to be desirable unto Him. Love is that which animates the obedience which is agreeable to God: "If a man love Me, he will keep My words" (John 14:23). Love is the very life and substance of everything which is gratifying unto God.

As the principle of obedience, love takes the precedence, for faith works by love (Gal. 5:6): hence the order in that injunction "let us consider one another to provoke (1) unto love and (2) to good works" (Heb. 10:24)—stir up the affections and good works will follow, as a stirring up of the coals causes the flames to arise. It is love which makes all the Divine commandments to be "not grievous" (1 John 5:3). We heartily agree with Charnock's dictum, "In that one word *love* God hath wrapped up all the devotion He requires of us," and certainly our souls ought to be ravished with Him, for He is infinitely worthy of our choicest affections and strongest desires. Love is a thing acceptable in itself, but nothing can be acceptable to God without it. "They that worship Him must worship Him in spirit and in truth" (John 4:23)—the most decorous and punctilious forms of devotion are worthless if they lack vitality and sincerity. True worship proceeds from love, for it is the exercise of heavenly affections, the pouring out of its homage to Him who is "altogether lovely." Love is the best thing we can render God, and it is His right in every service. Without it we are an abomination unto Him: "If any man love not the Lord Jesus Christ, let him be Anathema Mararnatha" (1 Cor. 16:22).

Fourth, by the Fall our first parents and all mankind *lost communion* with God. This was enjoyed at the beginning, for God made man with faculties capable of this privilege, and designed them to have holy converse with Him. Indeed this was the paramount blessing of that covenant which Adam was placed under, and it was a foretaste of that more intimate communion which would have been his eternal portion had he survived his probation. But the apostasy of Adam and Eve could not but first deprive them and then all their posterity, of this inestimable privilege. This was the immediate and inevitable result of their revolt, whether we contemplate it from either the Divine or the human side, "for what fellowship hath righteousness with unrighteousness? And what communion hath light with darkness?" (2 Cor. 6:14). Two cannot walk together except they be agreed (Amos 3:3). The Holy One will not favourably manifest Himself unto rebels or admit them into His presence as friends. Nor had our first parents any longer the desire that He should do so, but rather very much to the contrary. Having lost all love to God, they had no relish for Him, but now hated and dreaded Him.

Here, then, my reader, is the terrible nature of human depravity. From the privative side, it consists of man's loss of the moral image of God—consciously felt by our first parents in the shameful sense they had of their nakedness. The loss of the life of God, so that they became alienated from His favour, devoid of joy, emptied of holiness—faintly perceived by them, as was evident from their attempt to make themselves more presentable by manufacturing aprons of fig leaves. The loss of their love to God, so that they no longer revered and adored Him, but were repelled by His perfections—manifested by their fleeing from Him as soon as they were conscious of His approach. The loss of communion with God, so that they were utterly unfit for His presence—adumbrated by His driving them from Eden. None but a regenerate can estimate how irreparable was man's forfeiture by the Fall, and how dreadful is the condition and case of the natural man: and *their* apprehension thereof is exceedingly meager in this life.

We have already pointed out a number of things in which the depravity of human nature *does not* consist: and, in the last chapter, some of the inestimable blessings of which man was *deprived* by the Fall. We now turn to the affirmative side, or a consideration of those evils which *have come* upon human nature as the result of our first parents' apostasy from God. We do not agree with those who teach that what is transmitted from Adam and Eve to their descendants, via the channel of natural generation and propagation, is a merely negative thing—the absence of good. Rather are we fully persuaded that something positive, an active principle of evil, is communicated from parents to their children. While we do not consider that sin is a substance or material thing, we are sure that it is very much more than a mere abstraction and nonentity. Man's very nature is corrupted: the virus of evil is in his blood. While there is privation in sin—a nonconformity to God's Law—there is also a real positive potency in it to mischief. Sin is a power, as holiness is a power, but a power working to disorder and death.

It has been said by some orthodox divines that "Men's natures are not now become sinful by putting anything in them to defile them, but by taking something from them which should have preserved them holy." But we much prefer the statement of the Westminster Catechism: "The sinfulness of that estate into which man fell consisteth in the guilt of Adam's first sin, the want of the righteousness wherein he was created, *and* the corruption of his nature, whereby he is utterly indisposed and disabled, and made opposite unto all that is spiritually good, and wholly inclined to evil, and that continually, which is commonly called original sin, and from which sin proceed all actual transgressions." That fallen human nature is not only devoid of all godliness, but also thoroughly impregnated with everything that is devilish, may surely be argued from the two different kinds of sin of which every man is guilty—those of omission, wherein there is failure to perform good works, and those of commission, or positive contumacy of the Law of God. Something answerable to *both* of those must exist in our sinful nature, or otherwise we should predicate a cause inadequate to produce the effect: while the absence of holiness explains the former, only the presence of positive evil accounts for the latter.

There are many names given in Scripture to original sin or the depravity of human nature which serve to cast light upon its nature. The following list makes no claim to being complete, though it probably contains the most significant ones. It is called the plague of the heart (1 Kings 8:38), "foolishness bound up in the heart" (Prov. 22:15), "the stony heart" (Ezek. 11:19), "the evil treasure" of the heart (Matt. 12:35). It is designated "the poison of asps" (Rom. 3:13), "the old man," because it is derived from the first man and is part and parcel of us since the beginning of our existence, and "the body of sin" (Rom. 6:6), for it is a whole assembly of evils, "sin that dwelleth in me" (Rom. 7:17). It is denominated "another law in my members" (Rom. 7:23), because of its unvarying nature and power, "the law of sin and death" (Rom. 8:2), "the carnal mind" which is "enmity against God" (Rom. 8:7). It is frequently spoken of as "the flesh" (Gal. 5:17), because conceived by natural generation, "the old man, which is corrupt" (Eph. 4:22), "the sin which doth so easily beset us" (Heb. 12:1), man's "own lust" (James 1:14), which inclines him to evil deeds.

It should be quite plain from the above definitions and descriptions of congenital sin that the human constitution is not merely negatively defective but positively depraved. There is not only in man's heart the lack of conformity unto the Divine Law, but a positive deformity. Not only is the natural man without any desire for holiness, he is born with a disposition which is now radically opposed thereto, and therefore not only has he no love for God, but he is full of enmity against Him. Sin is also likened to "leaven" (1 Cor. 5:6, 7), and that is far more than the negation of the right savour which should be in bread, namely a positive sourness which affects it in and makes it unsavoury. Sin is not only the absence of beauty, but the presence of horrid ugliness: not simply the unlovely, but the hateful; not only the want of order, but real disorder. As "righteousness" expresses objectively the qualities which constitute what is good, and "holiness" the subjective state which is the root of righteousness, so *sin* includes not only outward acts of transgression, but the evil and rotten state of the whole inner man which inclines to and animates those external iniquities. Very far from being only an "infirmity," indwelling sin is a loathsome disease.

In seeking to define and describe the nature of depravity from the positive side, we would say, first, that the Fall has brought man's soul *into subjection to death*. But it must be remembered that for the soul to be under the dominion of death is a very different thing from the body being so. When the body dies it becomes as inactive and insensible as a stone. Not so in the case of the soul, for it still retains its vitality and all its powers. Fallen man is a rational, moral, responsible agent: but his internal being is thoroughly deranged. Alienated from the life of God, he can neither think nor will, love nor hate, in conformity to the Divine Rule. All the faculties of the soul are in full operation, but they are all unholy, and consequently man can no more fulfill the design of his being than does a physical corpse. Dreadful and solemn are the analogies between the two. As a dead body is devoid of the principles which formerly vitalized it, so the soul has been abandoned by the Holy Spirit who once inhabited it. As a physical corpse rapidly becomes a mass of corruption and a repulsive object, such is the depraved soul of man unto the thrice holy God. As a lifeless body is incapable of renewing itself, so is the spiritually dead soul completely powerless to better itself.

"And you hath He quickened, who were dead in trespasses and sins" (Eph 2:1). "The design of the Apostle in this and some following verses is to show the exceeding sinfulness of sin, and to set forth the sad estate and condemnation of man by nature, and to magnify the riches of the grace of God, and represent the exceeding greatness of His power by conversion" (John Gill). More clearly and fully did Thomas Goodwin, the Puritan, expound the striking coherency of this passage with its context. In the nineteenth verse of the preceding chapter Paul had prayed that saints might duly apprehend and appreciate the greatness of that power which had been exercised by God in their salvation: that it was precisely the same as the Divine might put forth for the resurrection and exaltation of His Son, and which had now wrought an analogous change in them: the mighty power which had quickened Christ had also quickened them. Thus the blessed scope and end of the Holy Spirit here was to bring out *the answerable parallel* or show the analogous change which God had so wondrously wrought in them: that what had been effected for Christ, their Head, had been also in them, His members, the one being a glorious pattern for the other.

In connection with Christ's exaltation three things were conspicuous. First, the condition of humiliation and death from which He was delivered and raised. Second, the sublime state of life and honour unto which He was exalted. Third, the Author thereof: God, whose almighty power was eminently manifested by the vast difference there was between those two states. Corresponding to the glorious miracles described in the closing verses of Ephesians 1 is what is so graphically portrayed in the opening verses of chapter 2. First, the dreadful state in which God's elect were by nature, namely one of death in sin, and such a death as brought its subjects under complete bondage to sin and Satan, so that they walk not in conformity to the Divine Law, but according to the corrupt maxims and customs of the world: being guided not by the Holy Spirit, but energized and directed by the evil spirit, here denominated "the prince of the power of the air." Without any regard for God's will or concern for His glory, they gave free rein to the lusts of the flesh and the desires of their carnal minds. But second, notwithstanding their horrible condition, God, who is rich in mercy, had raised them from the grave of sin and made them one with Christ in the heavenlies, by a vital and indissoluble union. And third, this marvel had been effected solely by the invincible power and amazing grace of God, without any co-operation of theirs.

That death which has come upon man's soul is at least a threefold one. First, he is dead in law, like a murderer in the condemned cell awaiting execution. Second, he is dead vitally, without a single spark of spiritual life. Thus, he is totally dead unto God and holiness, cast out of His favour, without any power to recover it. He is dead in opposition to justification, and also dead in opposition to being regenerated and sanctified. And third, he is dead to all that is excellent. As "life" is not simply existence, but well-being, so "death" is not the negation of existence, but the absence of all the real pleasures of existence. In its scriptural sense life signifies happiness and blessedness; death, wretchedness and woe. As the utmost natural misery which can befall man is for him to die—for "a living dog is better than a dead lion" (Eccl. 9:4)—so spiritual death is the strongest expression which can be used to import our moral wretchedness. The former divests him of all those excellencies which are proper to him as man, but the latter makes him worse than a stone, for when he is dead he stinks, which a stone does not. So it is spiritually: the natural man is not only without any comeliness in the sight of God, but he is a stench in His nostrils.

In the first three verses of Ephesians 2 "there is an exact description of the state of man by nature, so complete and compendious a one as is nowhere together, that I know, in the whole Book of God" (Goodwin). The careful student will have observed that there is one detail in it upon which the Holy Spirit has placed special emphasis, namely the one we are here treating of, for in verse 5 He *repeats* the words "dead in sin." Three things are outstanding in sin, its guilt, its pollution, and its power, and in each of those respects man is in his natural estate—"dead in sin." "Thou art but a dead man," said God to Abimelech (Gen. 20:3): that is, thou art guilty of death by reason of this act of thine. It is said of Ephraim that "when he offended in Baal, he *died*—sentence of condemnation came upon him (Hosea 13:1). So of its pollution, for in Hebrews 6:1, we read of "repentance from *dead works*," because every deed the natural man performs issues from a principle of corruption. So too of its power, for every sin man commits disables him the more unto good: his very activity in sin *is* his death, and the more lively he be in sin the more dead will he become toward God.

That there *is* such a threefold death of which fallen man is the subject is further evident from the nature of the work of grace in the elect, for their spiritual death must needs answer to their spiritual quickening, and that is clearly threefold. There is a threefold life to which we are restored by Christ. There is, first, a life of justification from the guilt of sin and the condemnation and curse of the Law—termed by Christ "passing from death unto life" (John 5:24), and by the Apostle, "justification of life" (Rom. 5:18). This is entirely objective, having respect to our status or standing before God, and is a greater relative change than for a condemned murderer to receive pardon. Second, there is a life of regeneration from the power and dominion of sin, called by Christ a being "born again" (John 3:3), when a new nature or principle of holiness is communicated. This is wholly subjective, having respect to the change wrought in the soul when it is Divinely quickened. Third, there is a life of sanctification from the pollution of sin, promised by God through the prophet: "Then will I sprinkle clean water upon you, and you shall be clean: from all your filthiness, and from all your idols, will I cleanse you" (Ezek. 36:25). This is something experiential, consisting of a purifying of the heart from the love of sin, referred to as "the washing of regeneration" (Titus 3:5). The first is judicial, the second spiritual, and the third moral: the three comprising the principal parts of God's so-great salvation—the glorification of the saint is yet future.

Second, the Fall has brought man *into hopeless bondage to sin*. When the Holy Spirit assures the saints, "For sin shall not have dominion over you: for ye are not under the law, but under grace" (Rom. 6:14), He necessarily signifies that all those still under the covenant of works *are* beneath sin's dominion, that it holds sway over them. As the Lord Jesus declared, "Whoever committeth sin is the servant of sin" (John 8:34): that is to say, sin is his *master*. Nevertheless, he yields voluntary and ready submission to sin's orders: "Know ye not, that to whom ye yield yourselves to obey, his servants ye are to whom ye obey: whether of sin unto death, or of obedience unto righteousness" (Rom. 6:16). No one outside themselves coerces and compels them. The dominion of sin is not even an indwelling force against the will and endeavours of those who are under it, but it is connatural and congenial to them. Even though, occasionally, conscience feebly protests, it's voice is silenced by the clamourings of lust, to which the will freely complies. The dominion of sin over the natural man is entire, for it pervades the spirit with all its powers, the soul with all its faculties, the body with all its members, and it does so at all times and under all circumstances.

Sin is likened unto a monarch ruling over his subjects—"as sin hath *reigned* unto death" (Rom. 5:21). Its kingdom is world-wide, for all the children of Adam are its subjects. Sin occupies the throne of the human heart until almighty grace deposes it. Sin has taken possession of the complete soul, and under its direction and influence it constantly acts. The mind is in subjection to evil as a governing principle which determines all its volitions and acts, for sin's lustings are so many imperial and imperious edicts. Yet we say again, this rule of sin is not a force upon the mind to which it makes opposition, for the soul is a *subject*—as a king continues to occupy the throne only by the consent and free allegiance of *his* subjects. While the soul cannot but will evil because of the reign of sin, yet its volitions are spontaneous. The dominion of sin consists in its determining influence upon the will, and this sway it retains to the end, unless victorious grace makes a conquest of the soul by the implantation of a contrary principle, which opposes the influences of indwelling sin, and disposes the will to contrary acts. Let conscience remonstrate never so sharply against the fatal choice, sin ever regulates the decisions and deeds of the natural man.

This dominion of sin "is not a propensity to some particular evil, but an inclination to deviate from the rule of our duty taken in its *full compass*. Yet, as the mind is incapable of exerting itself in all manner of ways and about all sorts of objects at once and in an instant, it is sometimes acting in one manner and sometimes in another as it is variously affected by the different objects about which it is conversant: but all its actions are evil. And those who study their hearts most will best understand the surprising variety of ways wherein evil concupiscence acts its part in the soul. In the several stages of human life this sway of sin discovers itself. In childhood, by folly proper to that age. In youth it exerts itself in various ways: by a low ambition, pride, and a strange fondness for sinful pleasures. In the state of manhood, by a pursuit of the transitory things of this world, and this is often under specious pretences of more extensive usefulness: but, in fact, men are acted upon by a spirit of covetousness. In an advanced age, by impatience, etc" (Brine).

The dominion of sin is made to appear more plainly and openly in some than in others, by their following a course of gross and flagitious evil, though it is just as real and great in those whose wickedness is more confined to the mind and heart. Scripture speaks not only of the "filthiness of the flesh," but of "the spirit," too (2 Cor. 7:1), i.e., vile imaginations, envy and hatred of our fellows, inward rebellion, and ragings against God when His will crosses ours. A sovereign God permits and controls the direction and form it takes in each one. Our lot is cast in a day when the power and reign of sin is more manifest in the world than it has been for several generations. Nor is the reason for this far to seek. It is not because human nature has undergone any deterioration, for that is impossible—it has been rotten to the core since the time of Cain and Abel. No, rather is it because God would the more evidence the lie of evolutionism and men's proud boasts of "human progress" by increasingly removing His restraining hand, and thereby allowing the horrid corruptions of men's hearts to become more visible and obvious. There are indeed degrees of wickedness, but none in the root from which it proceeds: every man's nature is equally depraved, and everyone in an unregenerate state is wholly dominated by it.

So mighty is the power of sin that it has made all the sons of men its slaves. Few indeed realize that they are held fast by the cords of their sins (Prov. 5:22), and still fewer wherein its strength lies. Sin is a powerful thing in itself, for it has a will of its own (John 1:13), a mind of its own (Rom. 8:6, 7), passions (Rom. 7:5), yea, fiery ones (Rom. 1:27)—but as 1 Corinthians 15:56 informs us, "The sting of death is sin: and the strength of sin is the law." The first part of the statement is obvious, but the second calls for some explanation. Sin is manifestly what puts venom into the dart of death and gives it its power to hurt and slay. Sin places a painful sting in death from the fact that it was what brought death into the world: had there been no sin, there had been no death. But more: it is sin, unpardoned sin, which makes death so dreadful, for not only does the king of terrors put a final end to all the pleasures of sin, but it conducts its subject unto certain judgment. But wherein is the Law of God "the strength of sin"? The Law is holy . . . and just, and good" (Rom. 7:12): how, then, can it be the strength of that which is corrupt, evil, and abominable?

Most assuredly the Law does not give the slightest encouragement to sin: rather does it sternly forbid it. The Law is not the essential but the accidental strength of sin, because of sin's inherent depravity, as the pure rays of the sun result in the horrid steams and noxious stenches rising from a dunghill. As the presence of an enemy calls into exercise the malice which lies dormant in the heart, so the holy requirements of the Law presenting themselves before man's corrupt heart stir it unto active opposition. Thereby the exceeding sinfulness of sin is the more fully demonstrated, for its potency to evil is drawn forth by any restraint being laid upon it—the more a thing be forbidden, the more it is desired. Though fire and water be opposite elements, that is not so evident while there is distance between them, but let them meet together and great is the spluttering and striving betwixt them. If the heart of man were pure, the Law would be acceptable unto it: but since it be depraved, there is fierce resentment against its spiritual precepts.

As the Law makes no provision for pardon, the natural effect of guilt is to widen the breach between the sinner and God. Sensible (as in some measure the most degraded are) of the Divine displeasure, he is prone to withdraw farther and farther from the Divine presence. Every augmentation of guilt is an augmentation of his estrangement: the more the sinner sins, the wider becomes the gulf between himself and God. This it is which gives strength to sin. It provokes the malignity of the heart against the Law, against all holy order, against the Judge. It exasperates the spirit of rebellion to unwanted fierceness, and makes the sinner desperate in his sin, causing its subjects to become increasingly reckless, and, as they perceive the brevity of life, to plunge more eagerly into profligacy. As frosty weather causes the fire to burn more fiercely, so the Law renders man's enmity against God more violent. So Saul of Tarsus found it in his experience, for when the Divine prohibition "thou shalt not covet" was applied in power to his heart, he tells us that, "sin, taking occasion by the commandment, wrought in me all manner of concupiscence" (Rom. 7:7, 8).

Third, the Fall has resulted in *man's mind being enveloped in darkness*. As physical blindness is one of the greatest natural calamities, spiritual blindness is much more so. It consists not of universal ignorance, but a total incapacity to take in a real knowledge of Divine things. As it is said of the Jews, "blindness *in part* is happened to Israel" (Rom. 11:25). Men may become very learned in many things, and by exercising their minds upon the Scriptures they may acquire a considerable letter knowledge of its contents: but they are quite unable to obtain a vital and effectual knowledge thereof. "The natural man receiveth not the things of the Spirit of God: for they are foolishness unto him: neither can he know them, because they are spiritually discerned" (1 Cor. 2:14), and spiritual perception he has none. This darkness which is upon the mind renders the natural man incapable of receiving the excellence of God, the perfection of His Law, the real nature of sin, or his dire need of a Saviour. Should the Lord draw near and ask him, "What wilt thou that I should do unto thee?" his answer ought to be, "Lord, that I might receive my sight" (Mark 10:51).

This darkness is upon the noblest part of man's being, his soul; and upon the highest faculty of it, the mind, which performs the same office for it as the eye to the body. By means of our visive organ we cognize material objects, distinguish between them, recognize their beauty or repulsiveness. By the mind we think, reason, understand and are enabled to weigh and discern between the true and the false.

Since the mind occupies so high a place in the scale of our beings, and since it be the most active of our inward faculties, ever working, then what a fearful state the soul must be in for its very eye to be *blind*! It is "like a fiery, high-metalled horse whose eyes cannot see, furiously carrying his rider upon rocks, pits and dangerous precipices" (John Flavell). Or, as the Son of God declared, "The light of the body is the eye: if therefore thine eye be single, thy whole body shall be full of light. But if thine eye be evil, thy whole body shall be full of darkness. If therefore the light that is in thee be darkness, how great is that darkness!" (Matt. 6:22, 23).

Much is said in the Scriptures about this terrible affliction. Men are represented as groping at noonday (Deut. 28:29), yea, "they meet with darkness in the daytime, and grope in the noonday as in the night" (Job 5:14). "They know not, neither will they understand." And why? "They walk on in darkness" (Psa. 82:5) It cannot be otherwise: alienated from Him who is light, they must be in total spiritual darkness. "The way of the wicked is as darkness: they know not at what they stumble" (Prov. 4:19)—insensible of the very things which are leading to everlasting woe. Moral depravity inevitably results in moral darkness. As a physically blind eye of the soul excludes all spiritual light, it renders the Scriptures profitless to them, for in this respect the case of the Gentiles is identical with that of the Jews: "But their minds were blinded: for until this day remaineth the same veil untaken away in the reading of the Old Testament" (2 Cor. 3:14). Consequently, the highest wisdom they count folly, and objects which are in themselves the most glorious and attractive are despised and rejected.

It is a great mistake to suppose that depravity is confined to the heart or to any one of the faculties which is more immediately conversant with the distinctions of right and wrong. As a radical disease extends its influence to all the functions of the body, so depravity extends to all the powers of the soul. Sin is as really blindness to the mind as it is hardness to the heart, and therefore has it departed from its original tendencies. Its actions, however intense, are only in the wrong direction. This it is which alone affords a satisfactory explanation of the mental aberrations of men and the immoral conceptions they have formed of Deity. As we attempt to contemplate the manifold forms of religious error, both ancient and modern, the various superstitions, the disgusting rites of worship, the monstrous and hideous symbols of the Godhead, the cruel flagellations and obscenities which prevail in heathen lands: when we consider all the abominations which have long passed and still pass under the sacred name of

Divine worship, and ask *how* such delusions originated and have been propagated, it is not sufficient to trace them to sin in general: rather must they be attributed to a deranged mind. Only a debased and darkened understanding adequately accounts for the horrible lies which have taken the name of truth, and the fearful blasphemies which have been styled worship.

This moral darkness which is upon the mind appears in the speculations about Deity by philosophers and metaphysicians, for they are ever erroneous, defective and degrading, when not corrected by Divine revelation. All such speculations are necessarily vain when they attempt to deal with things which transcend the scope of our faculties—which undertake to carry knowledge beyond its first principles, and essay to comprehend the incomprehensible. The creature being dependent and finite can never hope to compass an absolute knowledge of anything. "Intelligence begins with principles that must be accepted and not explained: and in applying those principles to the phenomena of existence, apparent contradictions constantly emerge that require patience and further knowledge to resolve them. But the mind, anxious to know all and restless under doubts and uncertainty, is tempted to renounce the first principles of reason and to contradict the facts which it daily observes. It seeks consistency of thought, and rather than any gaps should be left unfilled it plunges everything into hopeless confusion. Instead of accepting the laws of intelligence and patiently following the light of reason, and submitting to ignorance where ignorance is the lot of his nature as limited and finite, and joyfully receiving the partial knowledge which is his earthly inheritance, man, under the impulse of curiosity, had rather make a world that he does understand than admit one which he cannot comprehend. When he cannot stretch himself to the infinite dimensions of truth, he contracts truth to his own little measure. This is what the Apostle means by *vanity of mind*" (J. H. Thornwell).

The only way of escape for fallen man from such vanity of mind is for him to reject the serpent's poison. "Ye shall be as gods, knowing good and evil," and submit unreservedly to Divine revelation, according to our Lord's word in Matthew 9:25, "I thank Thee, O Father, Lord of Heaven and earth, because Thou hast hid these things from the wise and prudent, and hast revealed them unto babes"—to renounce all such self-acquired knowledge, forsake all our own erroneous conclusions and fancies, and take the place of a little child before Him. But that is just what the pride of the depraved creature refuses to do. Sin has not only counteracted the normal development of reason; it has so thoroughly deranged the mind that, as Christ declared, "men loved *darkness* rather than light" (John 3:19). They are so infatuated with their delusions that they prefer error to the Truth. That which may be known of God is clearly manifested on every hand, but man refuses to see. But though they be carried away with the darkness of their corruptions, the light still shines all around them. As created, all men may and ought to know God; but, as fallen, practical atheism is their sad heritage.

But if the acutest intellects of men, in their fallen and degenerate condition, could not of themselves form any accurate or just speculative knowledge of God and His government, there is yet a more profound ignorance which requires to be noticed, namely that theoretical knowledge of God which there is in those countries that have been favoured with the Gospel. By the light of the Christian revelation many a humble peasant has been made familiar with truths of which Plato and Aristotle knew nothing. Thousands are notionally sound upon questions which perplexed and confounded the understandings of presumptuous sophists. They believe that God is Spirit: personal, eternal, and independent; that He made the heavens and the earth, and controls all His creatures and all their actions. They are persuaded that He is as infinitely good as He is infinitely great; yet despite this knowledge they glorify Him not as God. They *lack* that loving light which warms as well as convinces. They have no communion with Him: they neither love nor adore Him. In order to a spiritual, vital and transforming knowledge of God their dead hearts must be quickened, and their blind eyes opened, and in order to *that* there must be an atonement, redemption, reconciliation with God. The Cross is the only place where men find God, and the incarnate Son, the only One in whom God can be adequately known.

If man's mind were not enveloped by darkness, he would not be deceived by Satan's lies or allured by his baits. If man were not in total spiritual darkness, he would never cherish the delusion that the filthy rags of his own righteousness could render him acceptable to the Holy One. If he were not blind, he would perceive that his very prayers are an abomination unto the Lord (Prov. 15:8). Though this incapability of understanding heavenly things be common to all the unregenerate, it is more heightened in some than in others. As all are equally under the dominion of sin yet some forge themselves additional fetters of evil habits by drinking in iniquity like water, so many of the sons of men immerse themselves in greater darkness by the strong prejudices of their own contracting, through pride and self-will. Others are still further incapacitated to take in spiritual things, even theoretically, by a judicial act of God, giving them over wholly to follow the dictates of their own minds. "He hath blinded their eyes, and hardened their heart; that they should not see with their eyes, nor understand with their heart, and be converted" (John 12:40, and cf. 2 Thess. 2:10-12).

Fourth, the Fall has issued in man's becoming *the bondslave of Satan*. That is another mysterious but very real thing, about which we can know nothing except what is revealed thereon in Holy Writ: but its teaching leaves us in no doubt upon the fact. It reveals that men are, morally, the Devil's children (Acts 13:10; 1 John 3:10), that they are his captives (2 Tim. 2:26), under his power (Acts 26:1; Col. 1:13), that his lusts they are determined to do (John 8:44). He is described as the strong man armed, who holds undisputed possession of the sinner's soul, until a stronger than he dispossesses him (Luke 11:21, 22). It speaks of men being "oppressed of the devil" (Acts 10:38), and declares, "The god of this world (the inspirer and director of its false religions) hath blinded the minds of them which believe not, lest the light of the glorious Gospel of Christ, who is the image (Revealer) of God, should shine unto them" (2 Cor. 4:4). The heart of fallen man is the throne on which he reigns, and all the sons of Adam are naturally inclined to yield themselves slaves to him, The awful reality of his indwelling sin was authenticated beyond the possibility of doubt by the cases of demoniacal possession of Christ's day.

Their corrupt nature gives Satan the greatest advantage against men, for they are as ready to comply as he is to tempt. No age or condition of life is exempted from his assaults and suiting his evil solicitations according to their varied temperaments and tempers they are easily overcome. The longer he rules over men, the more guilt they contract, and the more do they come under his dominion. To be his bondslave is a state of abject misery, for he purposes nothing but the eternal ruin of his victims, and every step they take in that direction furthers his evil designs and increases their wretchedness. He is as ready to laugh at and mock them for the pangs and pains which their folly brings upon them as he was to tempt and solicit their service. Yet he has *no right* to their subjection. Though God permits him to rule over the children of disobedience, He has given him no grant or warrant which renders it *lawful* for him to do so. Thus he is an usurper, the declared enemy of God, and though sinners are suffered by Him to yield themselves up to the Devil's control, that is far from being by Divine approbation.

Ephesians 2:2, 3 contains the clearest and most concise description of this awful subject, and to it we now turn. "Wherein (a status and state of being dead in trespasses and sin) in times past ye walked according to the course of this world, according to the prince of the power of the air, the spirit that now worketh in the children of disobedience." The first thing we would observe about this verse is that the world and the prince of the power of the air are definitely linked together, for the dead in sin are said to "walk according to" the one equally as the other—the only difference being that the second statement is amplified by the clauses which follow, wherein we are shown *why* they so walked. The identifying of the world with Satan is easily understood. Three times our Lord denominated him "the prince of this world," and 1 John 5:19 declares "the whole world lieth in wickedness." The world is distinguished from the Church of Christ—the children of God. The two opposing companies and the radical difference between them was intimated at the beginning, in the word of Jehovah unto the serpent, when He made mention of "thy seed" and "her seed." Those two seeds were referred to by Christ in His parable of the parable of the Tares, and designated by Him, "the children of the kingdom" and "the children of the wicked one" (Matt. 13:38).

Our Lord also spoke of the "kingdom" of Satan (Matt. 12:26), by which He referred not only to his power and dominion, but to his subjects and officers being an *organized* company—in opposition to the "kingdom of God's dear Son" (Col. 1:1, 3). Thus, by the world, "the world of the ungodly" (2 Peter 2:5) is meant: not only the sum total of the children of the Devil, in contradiction from the children of God, but more especially the *joining together* of all the unregenerate, which greatly augments their strength and malignity.

"As in coals, though each coal hath fire in it, yet lay all those coals together and the fire is strengthened: so there is an intensification from this union of all the parts, from the *connecting* of this world. The collection of all carnal men in one and the same principles, practices and ways, are meant by 'the world' " (Goodwin). By its "course" is connoted, first, its "age" or time, each generation having a more or less distinct dress or character, but ever essentially the same "evil world" (Gal. 1:4). Second, its mold or manner, its custom or way of life—its "spirit" (1 Cor. 2:12) and "fashion" (1 Cor. 7:31). The unregenerate walk according to the same maxims and morals, and do as the generality of their fellows do, because in each is the same depraved nature.

"According to the prince of the power of the air." The world is what it is because it is under the dominion of Satan. The mass of the unregenerate are likened unto the sea (Isa. 57:20), for being bound by a common nature they all move together as the waters of the sea follow the tide. But as Goodwin said, "If the wind comes and blows upon the sea, how it rageth, how strong are the streams then! There is a breath, a spirit, the spirit of the power of the air, namely the Devil sendeth forth an influence whereby, as the wind that bloweth upon the trees which way it bloweth, so he bloweth and swayeth the hearts of the multitude one way . . . when all the coals lie together, they make a great fire, but if the bellows be used they make the fire more intense." Thus, the Holy Spirit has here given the double explanation of *why* the unregenerate follow the course which they do: as each one enters and grows up in the world, being a social creature, he naturally goes with the drove of his fellows, and being possessed of the same evil lusts he finds their ways agreeable to him. The world, then, is the *exemplary* cause according to which men shape their lives, but the Devil is the *impelling* cause.

Since the Fall this malignant spirit has entered into human nature in a manner somewhat analogous to that in which the Holy Spirit dwells in the hearts of believers. He has in intimate access to our faculties, and though he cannot, like God's Spirit, work at the roots so as to change and transform their tendencies, yet he can ply them with representations and delusions without effectually incline them to fulfill his behests. He can cheat the understanding with appearances of truth, fascinate the fancy with pretences of beauty, and deceive the heart with semblances of good. By a whisper, a touch, a secret suggestion, he can give an impulse to our thoughts and turn them into channels which exactly subserve his evil designs. Men not only do what he desires, but he has a *commanding power* over them, as his being termed a prince plainly implies, and therefore are they said to be "taken captive . . . at his will" (2 Tim. 2:26), and when converted they are delivered from his power (Col. 1:13). Yet he does not work *immediately in all hearts*, as the Spirit in the regenerate, for he is not omnipresent, but employs a host of demons as his agents therein.

One man can influence another (only from without by external means), but Satan can also affect from within. He is able not only to take thoughts out of men's minds (Luke 8:12), but to place thoughts in them, as we are told he "put into the heart of Judas" to betray Christ (John 13:2), and he works thus *indiscernibly* as a spirit—as he sowed his tares secretly in the night. As men yield to and comply with the Devil's insinuations, he gains increasing control over them, and God permits him to enter and indwell them, as Matthew 12:29 shows. So too, when Satan would move anyone unto some particularly awful sin, he takes possession of him, as we read that after Judas had consented to the vile insinuation which the Devil had put into his heart he "entered into" him (Luke 22:3) in order to ensure the carrying out of his design by strengthening the traitor to do his will, for the word for "entered" there is the same as in Mark 5:13 where the unclean spirits entered into the herd of swine, which brought about their destruction. He is able to "fill the heart" (Acts 5:3), giving an additional impulse to evil as a person filled with wine is abnormally fired. But let it be pointed out, there is no record in Scripture of either the Devil or a demon ever taking possession of a *regenerate* person.

But though the Devil works thus in men, and works effectually, yet all their sins are *their own*, for the Spirit is careful to add "worketh in the children of disobedience." Man consents first, and then the Devil strengthens his resolution. That appears again in Peter's reproaching of Ananias for yielding to temptation—"*Why* hath Satan filled thine heart to lie to the Holy Spirit." He does no violence either to the liberty or the faculties of men, disturbing neither the spontaneity of the understanding nor the freedom of the will. As the work of God's Spirit in His elect is by no means inconsistent with their full responsibility and their entire moral agency, so the work of the Devil in the reprobate makes it none the less *their* work, and therefore the dupes of his craft are without excuse for their sins. Unlike the Holy Spirit, the Devil has no creative power. He can impart no new nature, but can only avail himself of what is already there for him to work upon. He avails himself of the constitution of man's nature, especially of his depravity as a fallen being. He gives an impetus and direction to man's free but evil tendencies. Rightly did Goodwin point out that "as no man doth sin because God decrees him to sin, therefore none can excuse himself with that: so no man can excuse himself with this, that Satan worketh in him."

Here then, my reader, is the nature of human depravity as seen from the positive side. The Fall has brought man into subjection to the power of death, into hopeless bondage to sin, has completely enveloped his mind in darkness, and has issued in his being the bondslave of Satan. From that dreadful state he possesses not a particle of power to deliver himself or even to mitigate his wretchedness. In addition, it has filled him with enmity against God, but that aspect we reserve for our next chapter, when (D.V.) we shall consider the *vileness* of human depravity.

THE DOCTRINE OF HUMAN DEPRAVITY
Its Enormity

The theology of the last century has failed lamentably at two essential points, namely its teaching concerning God and its teaching concerning fallen man. As an Australian writer recently expressed it, "On the one hand, they have not ascended high enough . . . on the other hand, they do not descend low enough." God is infinitely greater and His dominion far more absolute and extensive, and man has sunk much lower and is far more depraved than they will allow. Consequently a man's conduct unto his Maker is vastly more evil than is commonly supposed. Its horrible hideousness cannot really be seen except in the light supplied by Holy Writ. Sin is infinitely more vile in its nature than any of us realize. Men may acknowledge that they sin, but it *appears sin* to very, very few. Sin was the original evil. Before it entered the universe there was no evil: "God saw everything that He had made, and, behold, it was very good" (Gen. 1:31). Sin is the greatest of all evils. There is nothing in it but evil, nor can it produce anything but evil—now, in the future, or forever. As soon as sin was conceived, all other evils followed in its train.

We may take a survey of everything in and on the earth, and we cannot find anything so vile as sin. The basest and most contemptible thing in this world has some degree of worth in it, as being the workmanship of God. But sin and its foul streams have not the least part of worth in them. Sin is wholly evil, without the least mixture of good—vileness in the abstract. Its heinousness appears in the author of it: "He that committeth sin is of the devil: for the devil sinneth from the beginning" (1 John 3:8)—sin is his trade, and he is the incessant practitioner of it. Sin's enormity is seen in what it has done to man: it has completely ruined his nature and brought him under the curse of God. Sin is the source of all our miseries: all unrighteousness and wretchedness being its fruits. There is no distress of the mind, no anguish of the heart, no pain of the body, but it is due to sin. All the miseries which mankind groan under today are to be ascribed to sin. It is the cause of all penal evils: "Thy way and thy doings have procured these things unto thee: this is thy wickedness, because it is bitter, because it reacheth unto thine heart" (Jer. 4:18). Had there been no sin, there had been no wars, no national calamities, no prisons, no hospitals, no insane asylums, no cemeteries! Yet who lays these things to heart?

Sin assumes many garbs, but when it appears in its nakedness it is seen as a black and misshapen monster. How God Himself views it may be learned from the various similitudes used by the Holy Spirit to set forth its ugliness and loathsomeness. He has compared it with

The Doctrine of Human Depravity

the greatest deformities and the most filthy and repulsive objects to be met with in this world. Sin is likened to the scum of a seething pot, wherein a detestable carcass is being destroyed (Ezek. 24:11, 12); to the blood and pollution of a newly born child, before it is washed, salted and swaddled (Ezek. 16:4, 6); to a dead and rotting body (Rom. 7:24); to the noisome stench and poisonous exhalations which issue from the mouth of an open sepulchre (Rom. 3:13); to the image of the Devil (John 8:44); to putrefying sores (Isa. 1:5, 6). To a menstruous cloth (Isa. 30:22), (Lam. 1:17); to a canker or gangrene (2 Tim. 2:17); to the dung of filthy creatures (Phil. 3:8); to the vomit of a dog and the wallowing of a sow in the stinking mire (2 Peter 2:22). Such comparisons show us something of the vileness and horribleness of sin, yet in reality it is beyond all comparison.

There is a far greater malignity in sin than is commonly supposed, even by the great majority of church members. Men regard it as an infirmity, and term it a "human frailty" or "hereditary weakness." But Scripture calls it "an evil thing and bitter" (Jer. 2:19), an abominable thing which God hates (Jer. 44:4). Few people think it to be so: rather do the great majority regard it as a mere trifle, as a matter of so little moment that they have but to cry in the hour of death, "Lord, pardon me; Lord, bless me," and all will be eternally well with them. They judge sin by the opinion of the world. But what can the world which "lieth in wickedness" (1 John 5:19) know about God's hatred of sin! It matters nothing what the world thinks, but it matters everything what God says thereon. Others measure the guilt of sin by what conscience tells them—or fails to! But conscience needs informing by the Bible. Many of the heathen put their female children and old folk to death, and conscience chided them not. A deadened conscience has accompanied multitudes to Hell without any voice of warning. So little filth do they see in sin that tens of thousands of religionists imagine that a few tears will wash away its stain. So little criminality do they perceive in it that they persuade themselves that a few good works will make full reparation for it.

That all comparisons fail to set forth the horrible malignity which there is in that abominable thing which God hates appears in the fact that we can say nothing more evil of sin than to term it what it is: "but sin, that it might appear *sin*" (Rom. 7:13). "Who is like unto Thee, O LORD?" (Exo. 15:11). When we say of God that He is *God* we say all that can be said of Him. "Who is a God like unto Thee" (Micah 7:18). We cannot say more good of Him than to call Him *God*. So we cannot say more evil of sin than to say it is *sin*. When we have called it that, we have said all that can be said of it. When the Apostle would put a descriptive epithet to sin, he invested it with its own name: "that sin by the commandment might become *exceeding sinful*" (Rom. 7:13). That was the worst he could say of it, the ugliest name he could give it—just as when Hosea denounced the Ephraimites for their idolatry: "so shall Bethel do unto you because of the evil of your evil" (10:15 margin). The Prophet could not paint their wickedness in any blacker colour than to double the expression.

The hideousness of sin can be set forth no more impressively than in the terms used by the Apostle in Romans 7:13. "That sin . . . might become exceeding sinful" is a very forcible expression. It reminds us of similar words used by him when magnifying that glory which is yet to be revealed in the saints, and with which the sufferings of this present time are not worthy to be compared, namely "a far more exceeding and eternal weight of glory." No viler name can be found for sin than its own. "If we speak of a treacherous person, we call him a Judas: if of Judas, we call him a *devil*; but if of Satan, we want a comparison, because we can find none that is worse than himself: we must therefore say, as Christ did, 'when he speaketh a lie, he speaketh of his own.' It was thus with the Apostle when speaking of the evil of his own heart: 'that sin by the commandment might become"—what? He wanted a name worse than its own: he could find none: he therefore unites a strong epithet to the thing itself, calling it 'exceeding sinful' " (Andrew Fuller).

There are four great evils in sin: the total absence of the moral image of God, the transgression of His just Law, obnoxiousness to His holiness, separation from Him—entailing the presence of positive evil, guilt which cannot be measured by any human standard, defilement the most repulsive, and misery inexpressible. Sin contains within it an *infinite* evil, for it is committed against a Being of infinite glory, unto whom we are under infinite obligations. Its odiousness appears in that fearful description, "filthiness and superfluity of naughtiness" (James 1:21), which is an allusion to the brook Kidron, into which the garbage of the temple sacrifices and other vile things were cast (2 Chron. 29:16). Its hatefulness to God is seen in His awful curse upon the workmanship of His own hands, for He would not anathematize man for a trifle. If He does not afflict willingly, then most certainly He would not curse without great provocation. The virulence and vileness of sin can only be gauged at Calvary, where it rose to the terrible commission of Deicide: at the Cross it "abounded" to the greatest possible degree. The demerits of sin are seen in the eternal damnation of sinners in Hell, for the indescribable sufferings which Divine vengeance will then inflict upon them are its righteous wages.

The Doctrine of Human Depravity

Sin is a species of *atheism,* for it is the virtual repudiation of God; to make of God no God, to set up our wills against His: "Who is the LORD, that I should obey His voice?" (Exo. 5:2). It is a malignant spirit of independence: whether imperceptibly influencing the mind or consciously present, it lies at the root of all evil and human depravity. Man would be lord of himself, hence his ready reception, at the beginning, of the Devil's lie, "Ye shall be as gods," and his credence thereof was the dissolution of that tie which bound the creature in willing subjection to the Author of his being. Thus sin is really the denial of our creaturehood, and in consequence, a rejection of the rights of the Creator. Its language is, "I am: I am my own, and therefore have I the right to live unto myself." As Thornwell pointed out, "Considered as the renunciation of dependence upon God, it may be called unbelief; as the exaltation of itself to the place of God, it may he called pride: as the transferring to another object the homage due to the Supreme, it may be called idolatry; but in all these aspects the central principle is one and the same."

An atheist is not only one who denies the existence of God, but also one who fails to render unto God that honour and subjection which are His due. Thus there is a *practical* atheism as well as a theoretical one. The former obtains wherever there is no genuine respect for God's authority and no concern for His glory. There are many who entertain theoretical notions in their heads of the Divine existence, yet whose hearts are devoid of any affection to Him. And *that* is now the natural condition of all the fallen descendants of Adam. Since there be "none that seeketh after God" (Rom. 3:11), it follows that there are none with any practical sense of His excellency or His claims. The natural man has no desire for communion with God, for he places his happiness in the creature. He prefers everything before Him and glorifies everything above Him. He loves his own pleasures more than God. His wisdom being "earthly, sensual, devilish" (James 3:15), the celestial and Divine are outside of his consideration. This appears in man's works, for actions speak louder than words. Our hearts are to be gauged by what we do, and not by what we say. Our tongues may be great liars, but our deeds tell the truth, showing what we really are.

How little is it recognized and realized that all outward impieties are the manifestations of an inward atheism! Yet such is indeed the case. As all bodily sores are evidences of the impurity of our blood, so our actions demonstrate the corruption of our natures. Therefore is sin so often termed ungodliness: "Behold, the Lord cometh with ten thousands of His saints, to execute judgment upon all, and to convince all that are ungodly among them of all their ungodly deeds which they have ungodly committed, and of all their hard speeches which ungodly sinners have spoken against Him" (Jude 14, 15). How vain it is, then, to deny atheism in the heart when there is so much of it in this life! Here too the tree is known by its fruits. As an active and operative principle in the soul, sin is the virtual assertion not only of self-sufficiency, but also of self-supremacy. Rightly did Stephen Charnock point out, "Those therefore, are more deserving of being termed atheists who acknowledge a God and walk as if there were none, than those (if there can be any such) that deny God, and walk as if there were one." To the writings of that eminent Puritan we are also indebted for part of what precedes and part of what follows.

As all virtuous actions spring from a due acknowledgment of God, so all vicious actions take their rise from a lurking denial of Him. He who makes no conscience of sin has no regard to the honour of God: and consequently none to His being. This is clear from that declaration, "By the fear of the LORD men depart from evil" (Prov. 16:6), for it clearly follows that it is in the absence of any awe of Him that they rush into evil. Every sin is all invading of the rights of God. When we transgress His laws we repudiate His sovereignty. When we lean unto our own understanding and set up reason as the guide of our actions, we despise His wisdom. When we think to find happiness in gratifying our lusts, we slight His excellence and deem His goodness insufficient to satisfy our hearts. When we commit those sins in secret which we would be ashamed to do in public, we virtually deny both His omniscience and omnipresence. When we lean upon the arm of flesh or put our trust in the means, we disbelieve His power. Sin is called a turning the back upon God (Jer. 32:33), a kicking against Him (Deut. 32:15), i.e., a treating of Him with the utmost contempt.

People do not like to regard themselves as practical atheists. No, they entertain a much better opinion of themselves than that. They pride themselves on possessing far too much intelligence to harbour so degrading an idea that there is no God. Instead they are persuaded that creation clearly evidences a Creator. But no matter what their intellectual beliefs may be, the fact remains that they are secret atheists. He who disowns the authority of God disowns His Godhead. It is the unquestionable prerogative of the Most High to have dominion over His creatures, to make known His will unto them, and to demand their subjection thereto. But their breaking of His bands and their casting away of His cords from them (Psa. 2:3) are a practical rejection of His rule over them. Practical atheism, my reader, consists of an utter contempt of God, a conducting of ourselves as though there were none infinitely above us, who has an absolute right to govern us—to whom we must yet render a full account of all that we have done and left undone, and who will then pronounce sentence of eternal judgment upon us.

The natural man renders that homage to himself which is due alone unto God. When he obtains something which makes him glitter in the eyes of the world, how happy is he, for they "receive honour one of another, and seek not the honour that cometh from God only" (John 5:44). They dote upon their own accomplishments and acquisitions, but delight not in the Divine perfections. They think highly of themselves, but contemptuously of others. They compare themselves with those lower than themselves, instead of with those above. He who deems himself worthy of his own supreme affection regards himself as being entitled to the supreme regard of his neighbours. Yet it is nothing but self-idolatry to magnify ourselves to the virtual forgetfulness of the Creator. When self-love wholly possesses us, we usurp God's prerogative by making self our chief end. This consuming egotism appears again in man's proneness to ascribe his achievements unto his own virtue, strength and skill, instead of unto Him from whom cometh every good and perfect gift: "Is not this great Babylon, that I have built?" (Dan. 4:30). God smote Herod for not giving Him the glory when instead of rebuking the people he accepted their impious adulations.

The same profane spirit is evidenced by man's envying the endowments and prosperity of others. Cain was angry with God, and hated and slew Abel, because his brother's offering was received and his own refused. Since it be God who assigns unto each his portion, to look with such a grudging eye upon that enjoyed by our fellows has much of practical atheism in it. It is an unwillingness for God to be the proprietor and distributor of His favours as He pleases. It is assuming the right to direct the Creator what He shall bestow upon His creatures, and a denial of His sovereignty to give more unto one than to another. God disposes of His benefits according to the counsel of His own will, but vain man thinks he could make a better distribution of them. This sin is to imitate that of Satan's, who was dissatisfied with the station which the Most High had allotted him (Isa. 14:12-14). It is a desiring to assume unto ourselves that right which the Devil lyingly asserted was his—to give the kingdoms of this world to whom he would. Thus would man have the Almighty degrade Himself to the satisfying of *his* whims, rather than His own mind.

There is in fallen man a disinclination unto any acquaintance with God's rule. He hates instruction and casts His words behind his back (Psa. 50:17). God has revealed unto man the great things of His Law, but they are counted as a strange thing (Hosea 8:12). What He accounts valuable they despise. The very purity of the Divine Rule renders it obnoxious to an impure heart. "Water and fire may as well kiss each other, and live together without quarreling and hissing, as the holy will of God and the unregenerate heart of a fallen creature" (Charnock). Not only is man's darkened understanding incapable of perceiving the excellency of God's commandments, but there is a disposition in his will which rises up against it. When any part of God's revealed will is made known to men, they endeavour to banish it from their thoughts: they like not to retain God in their knowledge (Rom. 1:28), and therefore do they resist the strivings of the Spirit unto an obedient compliance (Acts 7:51). How can a fleshly mind relish a spiritual Law? Since the palate of man be corrupted, Divine things are unsavoury to him, and forever remain so until his taste be restored by Divine grace.

The same atheistic spirit is seen again in man's denials of Divine providence. They will not allow that God presides over this scene, directing all its affairs, shaping the circumstances of each of our lives. Rather do they ascribe their lot to fortune or fate, to good or ill "luck." Even where intellectually convinced to the contrary, they continually quarrel with God's governing of this world, and particularly with His dealings with them. Whenever His will crosses theirs, they rebel and rave. Yes, if our plans be thwarted, how fretful are we! Men appraise themselves highly, and are angry if God appears not to value them at the same rate—as if *their* estimation of themselves were more accurate than His. What an evidence of practical atheism is this, that, instead of meekly submitting to God's will and adoring His righteousness, we proclaim Him as an unjust Governor, and demand that His wisdom be guided by our folly, and asperse Him rather than ourselves!

What proof is the whole of the foregoing of the fearful enormity of human depravity!

We have shown that the heart of the natural man is filled with a secret and unsuspected, yet a real and practical, spirit of atheism: that whatever theological notions he may hold, by his attitude and conduct he repudiates the very being of God. Even that fearful aspect of man's state does not fully express the desperate and deplorable condition to which the Fall has reduced him. Not only is he living in this world "without God" (Eph. 2:12)—without any due acknowledgment of or practical subjection to Him—but he has a disposition which is directly contrary to Him. With no desire for communion with the true God, he devises false gods and is devoted to them—mammon, pleasures, his belly. Fallen man has cast off all allegiance to God and set up himself in open and undisguised opposition to Him. Not only has he no love for God, but his very nature is wholly averse to Him. Sin has wrought in the whole of his being a radical antipathy to God: to His will and ways, for Divine things are holy and heavenly, and therefore bitter to his corrupt taste. He is alienated from God—inveterately opposed to Him.

As an operative principle in the soul, sin is virtually the assertion of self-sufficiency and self-supremacy, and thus it cannot but produce opposition to God. Sin is not only the negation but the positive contrary of holiness, and therefore it can bear naught but antagonism to the Holy One. He who affirms and asserts himself must deny and resist God. The Divine claims are regarded as those of its rival: God is looked upon as an enemy, and the carnal mind is enmity against Him; and enmity is not simply the absence of love—a condition of mere indifference—but is a principle of repugnance and virulent resistance. Hence as Owen said (*Indwelling Sin*, chapter 4): "Sin's proper formal object is *God*. It hath, as it were, that command from Satan which the Assyrians had from their king: 'fight neither with small nor great, save only with the king of Israel.' It is neither great nor small, but God Himself, the King of Israel, that sin sets itself against. There lies the secret, the formal reason of all opposition to good, even because it relates unto God . . . The law of sin makes not opposition to any duty, but to God in every duty." Thus sin is nothing less than high treason against the absolute sovereignty of God.

Terrible beyond words is it that any creature of His hands should harbour enmity against such a glorious being as the great God. He is the sum of all excellency, the source of all good, the spiritual and moral Sun of the universe. And yet fallen man is not only His enemy, but his very mind is "enmity against God" (Rom. 8:7). Enemies may be reconciled, but *enmity* cannot be; yea, the only way to reconcile enemies is to destroy their enmity. In Romans 5:10, the Apostle spoke of enemies being reconciled to God by the death of His Son, but when he makes reference to enmity he says, "having *abolished* in His flesh the enmity" (Eph. 2:15): there is no other way of getting rid of enmity except by its abolition or destruction. Now enmity operates along two lines: aversion and opposition—God is detested and resisted. Sin brings us into God's debt (Matt. 6:12) and this produces aversion of Him. As debtors hate the sight of their creditors and are loath to meet them, so do they who are unable to meet the just claims of God—exemplified at the beginning, when fallen Adam fled as soon as he heard the voice of his Maker.

Sin is a disease which has ravaged the whole of man's being, rendering God obnoxious to him. As in inflamed eye cannot endure the light, the depraved heart of man cannot endure to look upon God. He has a deeply rooted and inveterate detestation for Him, and therefore against everything that is of Him. The more spirituality there is in anything, the more it is disliked by the natural man. That which has most of God in it is the most unpalatable to him. Concerning those in whom enmity is most dominant, God says, "Ye have set at nought *all* My counsel, and would *none* of My reproof" (Prov. 1:25)—not simply this or that part of His revealed will was unacceptable to them, but the whole thereof. This enmity is universal in its manifestations. Not only is the unregenerate heart indisposed to all holy duties, finding them irksome and burdensome, but it hates God's Law and rejects His Christ. It abuses His mercies, despises the riches of His goodness and longsuffering. It mocks His messengers, resists His Spirit, flouts His Word, and persecutes those who bear His image. Those at enmity with God serve His adversary the Devil, and are heartily in love with that world of which he is prince.

Enmity is a principle which ever expresses itself by opposition against its object. It contends with what it loathes: as in the regenerate the flesh lusts against the spirit, so in the unregenerate it fights against God. Enmity is the energy behind every sinful act. Though the interests of particular sins may be contrary to one another, yet they all conspire in a joint league against God Himself. As an able expositor expressed it, "Sins are in conflict with one another: covetousness and profligacy, covetousness and intemperance agree not. But they are one in combining against the interest of God. In betraying Christ, Judas was actuated by covetousness; the high priest by envy, Pilate by popularity: but all shook hands together in the murdering of Christ. And those varied iniquities were blended together to make up one lump of enmity" (Part 2, p. 522, by W. Jenkyn on Jude, 1665). Though there be not in all sins an express hatred of God, nevertheless, in every sin there is an implicit and virtual hatred against Him. So deeply rooted is man's enmity that neither the most tender expostulations nor the direst threats will allay it. God may entreat, but men will not heed: He may chastise, but as soon as He lifts His rod they, like Pharaoh, are as defiant as ever.

The language of men's hearts and lives unto God is, "Depart from us; for we desire not the knowledge of Thy ways" (Job 21:14). Hence man is compared to a wild ass in the wilderness, that "snuffeth up the wind at her pleasure," rather than come under the yoke of God (Jer. 2:24). Fearfully was that fact exemplified all through the long history of Israel, and the carriage of *that* people was but a reflection and manifestation of the nature of all mankind, for "as in water face answereth to face, so the heart of man to man" (Prov. 27:19). The exercise of this enmity is continued without interruption from the very beginning of man's days to the end of his unregenerate life (Gen.

6:5). It varies not at all, ever being consistent with itself. Never does sin call a truce or lay down the weapons of its rebellion, but persists in its active hostility to God. Then if Divine grace works not a miracle in subduing such enmity and planting in the heart a contrary principle which opposes the same, what must be the doom of such creatures? "Thinkest thou this, O man . . . that thou shalt escape the judgment of God?" (Rom. 2:3). Vain imagination. Christ will yet say, "Those Mine enemies, which would not that I should reign over them, bring hither, and slay them before Me" (Luke 19:27).

But so far from owning that they hate God, the vast majority will not only vehemently deny it, but affirm that they respect and love Him. Yet if their fancied love be analyzed, it will be found to have respect only to their own interests. While one concludes that God is favourable and lenient with him, he entertains no hard thoughts against Him. So long as he deems God to be prospering him, he bears Him no ill will. He hates not God as One who confers benefits, but as a Sovereign, Lawgiver, Judge. He will not yield to His government or take His Law as the rule of his life, and therefore does he dread His tribunal. The only God against whom the natural man is not at enmity is one of his own imagination. The deity whom he professes to worship is not the living God, for He is truth and faithfulness, holiness and justice, as well as being gracious and merciful. The soul of man is a complete stranger to holiness, even when his head be bowed in the house of prayer. But God is not deceived by any verbal acknowledgments or external homage: "This people draweth nigh unto Me with their mouth, and honoureth Me with their lips; but their heart is far from Me" (Matt. 15:8). It is a god of their own devising and not the God of Holy Writ they believe in. It is an awful delusion to fancy they admire God's character while refusing His Son to reign over them.

This enmity against God is seen in man's insubordination to the Divine Law. That is the particular indictment which is made against him in Romans 8, for in proof of the statement that "to be carnally inclined is death," the Apostle declared, "Because the carnal mind is enmity against God," and then added by way of demonstration, "for it is not subject to the law of God, neither indeed can be." It should be quite evident that that final clause was not brought in by way of extenuation (for that had greatly weakened his argument), but instead to give added force unto the awful fact just affirmed. A servant who performs not his master's bidding may or may not be guilty of revolt. He cannot be so charged if the task assigned be altogether beyond his physical powers (the absence of eyesight, or the loss of a limb, or the infirmities of old age); but if nothing but moral perversity (a spirit of malice and defiance) prevents the discharge of his duty, then he is most certainly guilty of open revolt. When we are told that the brethren of Joseph "hated him, and could not speak peaceably unto him" (Gen. 37:4, 5), so far from excusing their evil conduct, that only intensified it—they bore him so much ill will as to be morally incapable of treating him amicably.

Such is the inability of fallen man to be in subjection to God's Law. Originally made upright, created in the Divine image, given a nature in perfect harmony with God's statutes, endowed with faculties both mental and moral which fully capacitated him to meet their requirements, he is now so hostile to his Maker as to be thoroughly averse to His government, so that he cannot but cherish what He abominates. Our respect for God is judged by our conformity to His Law. As love unto God is to be gauged by obedience (John 14:21), so is hatred of Him both measured and manifested by disobedience (Deut. 5:9, 10). The natural man knows that God opposes the gratification of his corrupt desires, and because His Law prohibits the indulging of his lusts with that freedom and security which he covets, he hates Him. God commands that which he loathes, and forbids what he longs after. Consequently, man's warfare against God is a double one: defensive and offensive. Defensively, he slights His Word, perverts His gifts, resists the motions of His Spirit (Acts 7:51). Offensively, he employs all his members and faculties as weapons of unrighteousness against God (Rom. 6:13). To slight and resist the Divine Law is to hold God Himself in contempt, for the Law is an expression of His goodness, the transcript of His righteousness, the image of His holiness.

Here, then, is the ground of the enmity of the carnal mind: it is not subject to the Law of God. "The secret is now revealed. God is the moral Governor of the universe. Oh, this is the *casus belli* between Him and the sinner! This constitutes the real secret of his fall, inveterate hostility to the Divine being. The question at issue is: who shall govern—God or the sinner? The non-subjection of the carnal heart to God's Law—its rebellion against the Divine government—clearly indicates the side of this question which the carnal mind takes. You may, my reader, succeed in reasoning yourself into the belief that you admire, adore, and love God as your Creator and Benefactor, and only feel a repugnance, and manifest an opposition to Him as a Lawgiver. But this is impossible in fact, however specious it may be in theory . . . God's nature and His office, His person and His throne, are one and inseparable. No individual can possibly be a friend to the being of God, who is not equally friendly to His government. Why is the oral Law offensive to the carnal mind? Because of the holiness of its nature and the strictness of its requirements. It not only takes cognizance of external actions, but it touches the very springs of action, the motives that lie concealed in the human heart and regulate the life. It demands supreme affection and universal obedience. To this the carnal mind demures" (O. Winslow).

Alas, there are multitudes today, even in so-called Christian countries, who are almost totally ignorant of even *the terms* of God's Law—so intense is the darkness that has settled upon us. The majority of those who have been brought up under a knowledge of the Law, so far from valuing such a privilege, despise the same. The language of their hearts against God's faithful servants is that which Israel used of old unto His Prophet: "As for the word that thou hast spoken unto us in the name of the LORD, we will not hearken unto thee" (Jer. 44:16). They "refused to walk in His law" (Psa. 78:10). They had rather be their own rulers than God's subjects, and thereby guide themselves to destruction, than be directed by Him to blessedness. They desire unbridled liberty and will not tolerate the restraints of a command which checks them. Whatever compliance there may be—for the sake of respectability—to any Divine precept which forbids a gross outward sin, the heart still rises up against the more spiritual part of the law which requires inward purity. The more man's inward corruptions be curbed and condemned, the more is he enraged. Therefore not only does God charge him with despising His judgments (precepts), but says that his soul *abhors* His statutes (Lev. 26:43).

The contrariety there is between man and God appears in an unwillingness that His Law should be observed by any. Not satisfied with being a rebel himself, he would have God left without any loyal subjects in the world, and therefore does he employ both temptations and threats to induce his fellows to follow his evil example: now painting the pleasures of sin in glowing colours, then sneering at and boycotting those who have any scruples. Ordinarily the workers of iniquity consider such as walk with God to be freaks and fools, and take delight in railing at them (1 Peter 4:4). Yet it is not because the righteous have wronged them in any way, but that the wicked hate them because they refuse to have fellowship with them in defying God. What proof is this of their awful enmity: not only are they themselves angry at God's laws, but they cannot bear to see anyone else respecting them. Thus the Apostle, after enumerating some of the vilest abominations, brought this indictment against the Gentiles, that they "not only do the same, but have pleasure in them that do them" (Rom. 1:32)—delighting in accomplishing the downfall of their fellows.

Another form taken by man's enmity is his manufacturing of false gods. Though this act be not so palpably committed by some, yet none is entirely clear of the setting up of something in the place of God, for this sin is common to all mankind, as history clearly shows. From the days of Nimrod until the appearing of Christ, the whole Gentile world was abandoned to this impiety: having "changed the glory of the incorruptible God into an image made like to corruptible man, and to birds, and fourfooted beasts, and creeping things" (Rom. 1:23). Even Abraham originally, as well as his parents, were guilty of the same (Josh. 24:2). From the making of the golden calf at Sinai until they were carried captives into Babylon, the Israelites repeatedly committed this crime. Even today the whole of heathendom abounds with hideous idols, and those parts of Christendom now under the accursed dominion of the Papacy are given up to the worship of idols and the adoration of a woman who acknowledged her own need of a Saviour (Luke 1:47). Yet the awfulness of idolatry is perceived by but a few. Satan himself cannot invent a more absolutely degrading and vilifying of the Most High, for it is a calling Him by the names of those senseless objects and repulsive creatures which men erect as representations of Him. The giving to an image that homage which belongs to God is making it equal to Him, if not above Him. It portrays the Glorious One as though He had no more excellency than a block of stone or piece of carved wood.

Man's enmity against God is a practical repudiation of His *holiness*, for it cherishes what is directly contrary thereto: "Thou art of purer eyes than to behold evil, and canst not look on iniquity" (Hab. 1:3). Since God be infinitely good, He has an infinite detestation of evil. But sin is the very element in which man lives, and therefore does he hate everything opposed thereto. Nothing is more distasteful to him than the company of the godly, and the stricter they be in performing the duties of piety, and the more the image of God is seen shining in and through them, the greater the longing of the unregenerate to be free from their presence. So much is man in love with sin that he seeks to justify himself in the very commission of it; yea, he goes farther and charges it upon the Holy One. Thus it was at the beginning. When arraigned by his Maker, instead of confessing the enormity of his offence, Adam sought to excuse himself by blaming it upon God: "The woman whom Thou gavest to be with me, she gave me of the tree, and I did eat." John Gill and others thought (and probably rightly so) that when Cain was charged with the murder of Abel, and answered, "Am I my brother's keeper?" he blatantly threw the onus on the Lord—*Thou* art the One who should have preserved him from harm. Holy David unholy charged the crime he had contrived upon Divine providence (2 Sam. 11:25). And man still blames God by attributing his sins to his constitution or his circumstances.

This fearful hostility is exercised against the very *being of God.* That was clearly demonstrated when He became incarnate. The Son of God was not wanted here, but was despised and rejected of men. They provided no better accommodation than a manger for His cradle. Before He reached the age of two such a determined effort was made to slay Him that Joseph and Mary had to flee with Him into Egypt. Though constantly engaged in going about doing good, both to the souls and bodies of men, He had to declare, "The foxes have holes, and the birds of the air have nests, but the Son of man hath not where to lay His head" (Matt. 8:20). They called Him the vilest names they could think of: a glutton and winebibber, a Samaritan, a devil. Again and again they took up stones to cast at Him. His miracles of mercy allayed not their enmity: "This is the Heir; come, let us kill Him," and no ordinary death would satisfy them. After heaping the worst possible indignities upon His sacred Person and inflicting most barbarous suffering, they nailed Him to a convict's gibbet, and then mocked and reviled Him while He was fastened hand and foot to the Cross. And as the Lord Jesus declared, "He that hateth Me, hateth My Father also" (John 15:23).

Now such an attitude against God inevitably recoils upon ourselves. Alienated from the Source of all real good and purity, what can the consequence be but to be polluted in every part of our beings—a mass of putrefaction? Fearful indeed is the havoc that sin has wrought in the human constitution. Man's very nature is abased. No creature is so degraded as man, for he alone has erased the image of God from his soul. Man that was once the glory of creation has become the vilest of all creatures. He who was given dominion over the beasts is now sunk lower, for *they* are not guilty of mad and wicked intemperance, they are not without natural affection toward their offspring (as so many of the human species now are), nor do any of them commit suicide. Man's apostasy from His Maker could not result in anything less than the complete mutilation of his soul, depriving it of that perfect harmony and balance of its faculties (with which it was originally endowed), robbing them of their primitive excellence and beauty. The whole of our inner man has been seized by a loathsome disease, so that there is now no soundness in it.

Oh, what a mass of villainy is there in fallen man's heart! No wonder that the Scriptures ask, "Who *can* know it?" (Jer. 27:9). None but the very One against whom it lifts its vile head. What an awful spectacle is this: to behold the finite in deadly opposition to the Infinite! The creature and the Creator are at direct odds, for while a serpentine nature and a devilish disposition remain unsubdued within him, fallen man will no more seek to glorify the Lord than will Satan himself. The unregenerate detest Him who is light and love. The ox knows its owner, and the ass his master's crib, but the one who has been endowed with rationality and immortality deigns not to "consider" the hand that daily ministers in mercy throughout his life. With what longsuffering does He bear with those who treat Him so basely! What abundant cause has the Christian to abhor himself and hang his head in shame as he contemplates the sinfulness of all the sin that still indwells him!

THE DOCTRINE OF HUMAN DEPRAVITY
Its Extent

Neither the scientist, the philosopher, nor the psychologist can correctly diagnose the fatal malady which has seized upon all mankind, and still less is any of them able to gauge the full extent thereof. For a right and true knowledge of the latter, as much as of the former, we are shut up to what the Holy Spirit has revealed in Holy Writ. There we are shown that man has become not only a fallen and corrupt creature, but a totally depraved one: that he is not only a criminal before the Divine Law, but a foul and repulsive object in the eyes of his Maker. There are two inseparable properties or effects in connection with sin: pollution and guilt, for neither of them can be detached from its being. Where there is sin, there is a stain. Uncleanness, ugliness, filthiness, and such-like expressions, indicate not only a property of sin objectively considered, but also the effect which it produces in its subjects. It defiles, leaving the imprint of its odious features behind it, making the soul the reflection of its own hideousness. Wherever it touches, it leaves its filthy slime, rendering its subject hateful and abominable.

No representations of sin are more common in the Scriptures than those taken from its defiling effects: throughout it is portrayed as ugly and revolting, unclean and disgusting. It is figured by leprosy, the most loathsome disease which can attack the human frame. It is likened to wounds, bruises and putrefying sores. It is compared to a cage of unclean birds. The inseparable connection of the two notions of the beautiful and good and the ugly and sinful pervades the moral teaching of both Testaments. That connection is ethical and not aesthetical: to reverse the order would be to reduce righteousness to a matter of taste, and to make regulating authority dependent upon its appeal to our sentiments. As another has said, "The aesthetical sentiment should be regarded as a reflection from the moral sphere, a transfer to the sensitive world of those perceptions which are found in their purity only in the realm of the spiritual and Divine. Sin is the really and originally ugly, and nothing else is ugly except in consequence of its analogies to sin." The ugliness which it creates is its own blot. It has deranged the whole structure of the soul, and morally ulcerated man from head to foot.

"We are all as an unclean thing" (Isa. 64:6) is how God's Word describes us—foul and filthy. That pollution is a deep and unmistakable one: of a crimson dye (Isa. 1:18). It is likened unto the blackness of the Ethiopian (Jer. 13:23), which cannot be washed away by the nitre of repentance or the soap of reformation (Jer. 2:22). It is an indelible pollution, for it is "written with a pen of iron, and with the point of a diamond: it is graven upon the table of the heart" (Jer. 17:1). The great deluge did not remove it from the earth, nor did the fire that came down upon Sodom wash it out. It is ineradicable, for the fire of Hell to eternity will not take away the stain of sin in the souls that shall be there. It is spreading, like leaven and leprosy—yea, it is universal, for it has defiled all the faculties of the inner man, so that there is "*no* soundness in it" (Isa. 1:6). Soul and body are alike contaminated, for we read of the "filthiness of the flesh and spirit" (2 Cor. 7:1). It extends to the thoughts and imaginations, as well as to words and deeds. It is malignant and deadly—"the poison of asps" (Romans 3:13). "I said unto thee when thou wast in thy blood, Live; yea, I said unto thee when thou wast in thy blood, Live" (Ezek. 16:6)—the doubling of that expression shows the deadly nature of the pollution.

Sin is as loathsome as it is criminal, exhaling foul vapours which are a stench in the nostrils of the Lord. Hence, the very day that man corrupted himself, his Maker could no longer endure him, but drove him out of the Garden (Gen. 3:24). The Scriptures liken man to foxes for their subtlety, to wild bulls for their intractableness, to briars and thorns for their hurtfulness, to swine for their greediness and filthiness, to bears and lions for their cruelty and bloodthirstiness, to serpents for their hatefulness. However unpleasant and forbidding this subject, it is an integral part of "the counsel of God" which His servants are not at liberty to withhold. They are not free to pick and choose their themes, still less to tone them down: rather is each one bidden by his Master, "speak unto them *all* that I commanded thee be not dismayed at their faces" (Jer. 1:17). Insane asylums, prisons and cemeteries are depressing sights, yet they are painful facts of human history. Refusal to consider fallen man's condition helps no one. Until we are brought to believe and realize this truth, we shall never despair of self and look away to Another. This solemn side of the picture is indeed dark, yet it is the necessary background to redemption.

The effects of the Fall are not only more terrible, but much wider-reaching than are commonly supposed. Yet this would not be the case were our thoughts formed by the teaching of Holy Writ thereon. God's Word is plain enough. It declares that "God saw that the wickedness of man was great in the earth, and that every imagination of the thoughts of his heart was only evil continually" (Gen. 6:5). Those words are as impressive as they are solemn. In Genesis 1:31, we read, "And God saw everything that He had made, and, behold, it was very good" but here the Omniscient One is portrayed as taking a universal survey of the condition of mankind, and recording His righteous verdict unto their utter condemnation. They announce

His unerring diagnosis of their inward state in terms which fully explain their outward conduct. The spring of all their actions is thoroughly corrupt. It is to be duly noted that the translators of the Authorized Version have given a fuller rendering in the margin, informing us that the Hebrew word signified "the whole imagination," including the purposes and desires. The very fount of man's being was defiled, and a most offensive sight did it present unto the Holy One.

The heart is the moral center from which all the issues or outgoings of life proceed, and none but God knows *how* "evil" it is. The thoughts which are formed within such a heart are vain and sinful. The imagination or formation of them, their very first motions, are evil. The Hebrew word for "imagination of the heart" signifies *matrix*, the frame in which our thoughts are cast. Observe that "*every* imagination" is evil: no good ones are intermingled with them—they are unrelieved badness. It is not simply the outward acts, but the first movements of the soul unto an object. There we have the source from which all the wickedness of men proceeds: the corrupt humour within us are in a constant fermentation. Man's heart is such that, left to itself, it will always be producing inordinate affections and motions. They are "*only* evil" without exception, wholly so, not a single virtuous one among them. Furthermore, they are "evil *continually*," without intermission all the days of our lives. Such is the habitual state of every unregenerate soul, and therefore are all his works evil and dead ones.

"The imagination of man's heart is evil from his youth" (Gen. 8:21). The former verse described human nature and conduct as it was prior to the flood: this one shows what man still is after it. The great deluge had swept away the whole of that corrupt generation to which Enoch had prophesied and Noah had preached in vain, but it had not cleansed man's nature: that remained as vile as hitherto. Man continued to be conceived in iniquity and born in sin. and that which is bred in the bone ever comes out in the flesh. From the first moment of his existence, every descendant of Adam is a defiled creature, fit only for God's abhorrence. His very thoughts while in embryo are essentially evil: every one of them is so. The Hebrew word for "youth," (*neurim*), is rendered "childhood" in 1 Samuel 12:2, and both personal experience and observation sadly verify this solemn fact. As Charnock said, "not a moment of a man's life wherein our hereditary corruption doth not belch its froth."

"Behold, He putteth no trust in His saints (for they are but mutable creatures, in themselves); yea, the heavens are not clean in His sight. How much more abominable and filthy is man, which drinketh iniquity like water?" (Job 15:15, 16). What a description of human nature is this—obnoxious to God, corrupt in itself! Filthy indeed is man, for sin is of a defiling nature, polluting the soul with all its faculties and the body with all its members. Man is thoroughly unclean, as his life bears witness, his very righteousness being "as filthy rags"—so impure that nothing but the blood of Christ can cleanse him. With such a character man is never weary of sinning. Even when worn out by age, his lusts are still active within: as Peter expresses it, "they cannot cease from sin," for it is their very nature to be sinful. Possessed of a disposition which craves indulgence with a greedy appetite, seeking satisfaction thereof with as passionate an earnestness as parched throats in the burning desert long for the quenching of their thirst, man delights in iniquity and, so far as he is left to follow his inordinate propensities, he is continually seeking to take his fill thereof.

"Because sentence against an evil work is not executed speedily, therefore the heart of the sons of men is fully set in them to do evil" (Eccl. 8:11). Such is the perversity of corrupt human nature that it abuses the very patience and forbearance of God: since the Divine judgment is not visited at once upon evil-doers, they set themselves against the Lord and promise themselves immunity. Thus it was with those in the days of Noah: God deferred the flood for one hundred and twenty years, giving them ample "space for repentance," but instead of availing themselves thereof, they regarded His threats as idle ones, and became increasingly corrupt and violent. Thus it was with Pharaoh, who only hardened his heart when respite was granted him. And thus it is still: though the marks of the Divine displeasure against our generation are multiplied, they grow more and more daring and desperate in defying God's Law, sinning with a high hand and presuming on their security.

"The heart of the sons of men is full of evil, and madness is in their heart while they live, and after that they go to the dead" (Eccl. 9:3). As Christ was, and is, "full of grace and truth" (John 1:14), the natural man is filled with unrighteousness and wickedness. He is filled with such enmity against God that as his corruptions kindle the same, so Divine and spiritual things stimulate and stir it into action. That awful enmity comprises the sum of all evil. "Madness is in their heart": they are so infatuated as to seek their pleasures in the things which God hates. They cast off all the restraints of reason and conscience as their heady and violent passions press them forward into sin; and, as we have just seen above, the Divine delay in taking vengeance upon them but emboldens them unto more wickedness. Who but a madman would strengthen himself against the Almighty and rush into evil heedless of danger and disaster? Who but madmen would plan a "festival" of money-squandering and merriment when the clouds of war hang so darkly over the nation? They are maddened by their lusts, mad against piety. "After that they go to the dead" signifies more than the grave, namely, gathered to their own company—the dead in sin, and not "the spirits of just men made perfect."

The teaching of the Lord Jesus was, of course, in perfect harmony with that of the Old Testament. He never flattered human nature or extolled its excellencies: instead, He painted it in the darkest of colours, announcing that He had "come to seek and to save that which *was lost*" (Luke 19:10). For the benefit of young preachers, here is an outline. Fallen man has lost all likeness to God, all communion with God, all love for God, all true knowledge of God, all delight in God, all favour with God, all power toward God, and has thrown off all subjection to God. The Saviour was not deceived by religious pretences or fair profession. Even when many believed in His name as they saw the miracles which He did: "Jesus did not commit Himself unto them . . . for He knew what was in man" (John 2:23-25). By declaring, "I am not come to call the righteous, but sinners to repentance" (Matt. 9:13), He had not only intimated the needs-be for His mission—for there had been no occasion for His coming among men unless they were perishing—but imported there were *none righteous,* for He called upon all to repent (Mark 1:15; Luke 13:5).

When Christ asserted, "Except a man be born again, he cannot enter the kingdom of God," He showed how desperate is his plight, for the new birth is not a mere correcting of some defect—nor the righting of a single facility, but an entire renovation of the soul: the same Spirit which formed Christ in the virgin's womb must form Him in our hearts to fit us for the presence of God. When he averred that "men loved darkness rather than light" (John 3:19), He exposed their awful depravity: that they were not only in the darkness, but *delighted* therein, and that "because their deeds were evil." When He stated that "the wrath of God abideth on" the unbeliever, Christ testified to man's awful condition. When he said, "I know you, that ye have not the love of God in you" (John 5:42), He again revealed their fearful state, for since all goodness or virtue consists in love to God and our neighbour, then where love be wanting, goodness or virtue has no existence. His "No man can come to Me, except the Father which hath sent Me draw him," (John 6:44), plainly showed the moral impotency of every descendant of Adam—an impotency which consists of turpitude and baseness, namely an inveterate opposition to God, due to its bitter hatred of Him—none will seek unto one he loathes: before ever he does so he must be given an entire change of disposition.

"For from within, out of the heart of men, proceed evil thoughts, adulteries, fornications, murders, thefts, covetousness, wickedness, deceit, lasciviousness, an evil eye, blasphemy, pride, foolishness: all these evil things come from within, and defile the man" (Mark 7:21-23). Note well that Christ employed "heart" in the singular number, for such is the common and uniform one of all mankind. Here the Lord made known what a loathsome den is the center of man's being, and that out of the abundance of its evil issues all those horrible crimes—they take their rise from that fountain which is poisoned by sin, being the external expressions of corrupt nature. Man is vile and polluted. "If ye then, *being evil*" (Matt. 7:11). In those words, too, the Son of God expressed His estimate of fallen mankind; they not only *do* that which is evil, but *are so* in their very nature—as the Psalmist said, "their inward part is very wickedness" (5:9). It is to be duly noted that those words were spoken by Christ not unto open enemies but to His own disciples, and that His language affirmed that by birth they were defiled both root and branch. How they abase human pride! Those who prate about the dignity and nobility of human nature fly in the face of Christ's solemn verdict to the contrary.

The Spirit of truth; whom the world cannot receive, because it seeth Him not, neither knoweth Him" (John 14:17). O, my reader, what a truly dreadful condition this world is in! As Christ said to the auditors of His day, "Because I tell you the truth, ye believe Me not" (John 8:45), so now—men are so infatuated with lies, they cannot receive the Spirit of Truth. In those fearful words the Son of God represented the unregenerate as not having the least degree of spiritual discernment and knowledge, which is the same thing as being completely destitute of holiness. Nothing but total depravity can render men so wholly blind to spiritual things as to be thoroughly opposed to and blankly despise and reject them.

Let us now define our terms more closely, and thus prevent anyone arguing with us at cross purposes. Our English word "depraved" is taken from depravatus, which means twisted, wrenched from the straight line, and thus moral disturbance—its root being pravits, "crooked," "bad." Total depravity connotes that this distortedness has affected the whole of man's being to such an extent that he has no inherent power of recovery left to restore himself to harmony with God, and that this is the case with *every* member of the human race. Yet "total depravity" does not import that sin has reached its highest intensity in a person, so that it is incapable of augmentation, for men add unto their sins (1 Sam. 12:19); and over and above their native spiritual blindness, God judicially blinds some (John 12:40), and then their doom is irrevocably sealed. No, fallen man does not enter this world as bad as he can be, but he has "*no* good thing" in him (Rom. 7:18); instead, he is wholly corrupt, entirely vitiated throughout his constitution.

The children of Adam are possessed of no degree of moral rectitude, but have hearts that are desperately wicked. In so affirming, we are but saying that the effect corresponds to the cause: as the apostasy of the first man was total, so his descendants are wholly sinful. That this *is* the case with all mankind was clearly and abundantly proved from Scripture in the last chapter. The entire corruption of the whole human race could not be stated more strongly and decisively than in the passages there cited. The natural man has not one iota of holiness in him, rather is he born with the seeds of every form of evil, radically inclined to sin. In our nature we are vileness itself, black as Hell, and unless a miracle of grace be wrought upon us we must inevitably be damned for all eternity. It is not that man has a few imperfections, but that he is altogether polluted—"an unclean thing," with "*no* soundness" in him (Isa. 1:6). Not only has man no holiness, but his heart is inveterately averse thereto.

The solemn doctrine of total depravity does *not* mean that there are no parents with a genuine love for their children, and no children who respectfully obey their parents; that there are none imbued with a spirit of benevolence to the poor and kindly sympathy unto the suffering; that there are no conscientious employers or honest employees. But it *does* mean that, where the unregenerate are concerned, those duties are discharged *without* any love for God, any subjection to His authority, or any concern for His glory. Parents are required to bring up their children in the nurture and admonition of the Lord, and children to obey their parents in the Lord (Eph. 6:1, 4): while servants are bidden to serve their masters "in singleness of heart, as unto Christ." Do the unconverted so act and render compliance with those injunctions? They do not, and therefore their performances not only possess no spiritual value, but are polluted. Every act performed by the natural man is faulty: "the plowing of the wicked is sin" (Prov. 21:4)—because done for selfish ends. Then better not plow at all? Wrong, for slothfulness is equally sinful! There are different degrees of enormity, but *every* act of man is sinful.

The condition of the natural man is such that in the discharge of his first responsibility unto his Maker he is utterly *recreant*. His chief obligation is to live unto the glory of God and to love Him with all his heart, but while he remains unrenewed, he has not the least spiritual, holy true love unto Him. Whatever there may be in his domestic and social conduct which is admirable in the eyes of his fellows, it is not prompted by any respect for the Divine will. So far as man's self-recovery and self-recuperation be concerned, his depravity is total, in the sense of being decisive and final. "Man is fallen: every part and passion of his nature is perverted: he has gone astray altogether, is sick from the crown of his head to the soles of his feet; yea, is dead in trespasses and sins and corrupt before God. O pride of human nature, we plow right over thee! The hemlock standing in thy field must be cut up by the roots. Thy weeds seem like fair flowers, but the plowshare must go right through them, till all thy beauty is shown to be a painted Jezebel, and all human glorying a bursting bubble" (C. H. Spurgeon).

What makes this awful view of man's total depravity yet more solemn is the fact that there is no exception to it, for it is *universal*. Corrupt nature is the same in all. The hand that writes these lines is as capable of perpetrating the foulest crime on the calendar, and the heart of the reader of devising the worst deed committed by the vilest wretch who ever lived. The only distinction of character between man and man is that which the sovereign power and grace of God effects. "We are *all* as an unclean thing" (Isa. 64:6), our original purity gone. "There is no difference: for all have sinned, and come short of the glory of God." In his comments on Romans 3:10-18. Calvin said, "In this terrible manner the Apostle inveighs not against particular individuals, but against all the posterity of Adam. He does not declaim against the depraved manners of one or another age, but accuses the perpetual corruption of our nature. For his design in that passage is not simply to rebuke men in order that they may repent, but rather to teach us that all men are overwhelmed with an inevitable calamity, from which they can never emerge unless they are extricated by the mercy of God."

When the Lord Jesus called Paul, He informed him that He was about to send him to the Gentiles "to open their eyes, and to turn them from darkness to light, and from the power of Satan unto God" (Acts 26:18). In those words Christ indicated what was the character of the whole Gentile world: they were all as ignorant of God, and of the way of acceptance with Him, as blind men are of the true objects of sight. True, there were then, as now, devout religionists, esteemed poets and boastful philosophers who gloried in their wisdom, professing to teach what was the true happiness of man. There were renowned sages, with innumerable disciples, whose schools were engaged solely with the study of virtue, knowledge and felicity; nevertheless, "the world by wisdom knew not God," and He declared, "I will destroy the wisdom of the wise, and will bring to nothing the understanding of the prudent" (1 Cor. 1:19), for it deceived and deluded them. The schools themselves were darkness, and the minds of their authors—men like Pythagoras and Plato, Socrates and Aristotle—"blinded by the god of this world," completely under the control of the Devil.

"The LORD looked down from Heaven upon the children of men, to see if there were any that did understand, and seek God" (Psa. 14:2). "Behold the eyes of Omniscience ransacking the globe, and prying among every people and nation. He who is looking down knows the good, is quick to discern it, would be delighted to find it; but as He views all the unregenerate children of men His search is fruitless, for of all the race of Adam no unrenewed soul is other than an enemy to God and goodness. 'They are all gone out of the way.' Without exception, all men have apostatized from the Lord their Maker, from His laws, and from the eternal principles of right. Like stubborn heifers, they have sturdily refused to receive the yoke. The original speaks of the race as a totality, humanity as a whole has become depraved in heart and life. 'They have altogether become filthy.' As a whole they are spoiled and soured like corrupt leaven, or, as some put it, they have become putrid and even stinking. The only reason why we do not more clearly see this foulness is because we are accustomed to it, just as those who work daily among offensive odors at last cease to smell them" (*Treasury of David*).

That terrible indictment, "The carnal mind is enmity against God: for it is not subject to the law of God, neither indeed can be" (Rom. 8:7), is not restricted to particularly reprobate persons, but is an unqualified statement which applies to every individual. It is "*the* carnal mind": whatsoever mind may properly be designated "carnal," i.e., natural, unspiritual. The undeveloped mind of the infant is "enmity against God." Moreover, that description is true at all times, though it is not equally so evident. But though the wolf may sleep, he *is* a wolf still. The snake which lurks amid the flowers is just as deadly as when it lies among noxious weeds. Furthermore, that solemn declaration holds good of the whole mind, of all its facilities. It is true of the memory: nursery rhymes, silly jokes and foolish songs are retained without effort, whereas passages of Scripture and spiritual sermons are quickly forgotten. It is so with the affections: the creature is idolized and the Creator slighted. So of the judgment: what erroneous conceptions it forms of the Deity and how fearfully it wrests His Word! It is true even of the conscience, for there have been those who, while killing the saints, thought they did God a service (John 16:2)—witness Saul of Tarsus.

As might well be expected, fierce opposition has been made against this flesh-withering truth of the total depravity of man, and ever will be where it is faithfully preached. When men are informed that they are suffering from something far more serious than a defect in their characters or an unhappy bias of disposition, namely that their very *nature* is rotten to the core, it is more than human pride can endure. When told that the center of their moral being is corrupt, that their heart—the potent fountain from which issues their desires and thoughts—is desperately wicked, that it is inherently and radically evil from the first moment of their existence, hot resentment is at once aroused. It is indeed awful to contemplate that not only is sin the element in which the natural man lives, but the whole of his life is one unmixed course of evil: and it is scarcely surprising that those who are not subject to the Word of Truth should revolt at such a concept, especially as it is contrary to what appears in not a few characters who must be respected for many amiable qualities. Nevertheless, since all sin be a coming short of the glory of God, then every act of fallen man has in it the nature of sin.

Even with Christendom this doctrine has been strongly and steadily resisted. The great controversy between Augustine and Pelagius in the fifth century turned upon whether that moral corruption which pertains to all mankind be total or partial. If the latter, then of course it follows that man still has within him something which is good, something which is accordant to the Divine Law, something which enables him at least partly to discharge the obligations lying upon him as a creature of God. Ever since the days of Augustine there have been those posing as Christians who, while acknowledging that man is a fallen and depraved creature, have flatly denied that he is *totally* depraved. Those who repudiate the inward and invincible call of the Spirit realize not the actual state of man's soul, nor perceive that a miracle of grace is necessary before he is made willing to comply with the demands of the Gospel. Arminians acknowledge the *aid* of the Spirit, but at once negate their admission by affirming that He can be successfully resisted after He has put forth all His efforts to woo the sinner unto Christ.

It is important to recognize that the principles of faith and love are not produced by mere moral suasion, by the external presentation of Christ to a person. Rather are they wrought by a miracle of Divine power and grace in the soul. Such a glorious work must be done by an efficient cause, and not by an deficient one. The natural man is blind, yea, dead, to spiritual things, and what can make the blind to see or the dead to act! Suasion is so far from giving a faculty that it presupposes one: the use of it is not to confer a power, but to stir and move

Its Extent

it to act. God is far more than an Orator beseeching men, namely a mighty operator quickening. His word of power is a commanding one: as He said, "Let light be," and there was light, so He calls for a new heart and brings it into existence. God is no mere Helper, but a Creator. "We are His workmanship," and not our own. It is God who makes us new creatures, all not we ourselves: "born not . . . of the will of man, but of God" (John 1:13). To say that we are in part born of our own wills is to blaspheme the Author of our spiritual beings and to place the crown on nature instead of grace.

Likewise does the evolutionist emphatically deny the total depravity of man, for the only fall he believes in is an upward one. He is loud in insisting that there is a Divine spark of life in the soul of every human being, burning very feebly it may be in some, yet capable of being fanned into a flame if the right influences be brought to bear upon it. A Divine "seed" of goodness, others term it, a seed which only needs cultivating in order to the ultimate development of a noble and virtuous character—a blank repudiation of the teaching of Christ that the human tree is essentially "corrupt." Now since the whole system of redemption rests upon this basic fact of man's total depravity, and since every false system of religion originates in the repudiation thereof, it is incumbent upon us to expose the fallacy of those objections which are commonly made against it—the principal ones of which we will now consider.

The first is an attempt to show that we do not enter this world in a defiled condition. The engaging simplicity, dependence and harmlessness of little ones is dwelt upon, and reference is even made unto Scripture in support of the contention that they are born in a state of innocence. But this need not detain us very long, for it scarcely presents even an apparent force. Appeal is made to, "And shed *innocent* blood, even the blood of their sons and their daughters, whom they sacrificed unto the idols of Canaan" (Psa. 106:38), which simply means they sacrificed their little ones, who had *not* been active participants in their idolatry. "For the children being not yet born, neither having done any good or evil" (Rom. 9:11) is nothing to the point, for those words refer not to their nature, but to a time before they committed any deeds. While in contrast with adults, infants possess a relative innocence in that they are guiltless of personal transgressions, yet that they partake of original sin is clear from Psalms 51:5; 58:3; Proverbs 22:15. Scripture never contradicts itself.

In rebuttal of this doctrine it is insisted that there is some good in the very worst, that even the most confirmed villains, though it be but momentarily, turn away shudderingly from certain deeds of wickedness when temptation unto the same is first presented to them. From that the conclusion is drawn that, deeply buried under the ashes of a life of unbridled crime, the sparks of some power of goodness still remain. But that is to confound the faint motions of man's moral nature with potential spirituality. Moreover, it is nothing but confusion of thought which leads people to infer that because there are degrees of wickedness there must still he a modicum of good. Because one stage of depravity is lower than another, this does not warrant us to deny that the first stage is degraded. The development of wickedness is one thing, the presence of any measure of holiness or virtue is another. The absence of certain forms of sins does not imply any innate purity. It might as well be affirmed that a recent corpse, which is less loathsome, is therefore *less dead* than one which is far gone in decay and putrefaction.

Not a few have argued that the *strivings* of *conscience* in the unregenerate demonstrate that they are not totally depraved. It is pointed out that every man is possessed of that faculty which bears witness within him in countless instances of what is right and wrong: that this inward monitor exerts considerable influence even on wicked men, so as to impel them to the performance of actions which are relatively good, and to deter them from others which are evil. That is freely admitted, but it makes nothing whatever against the truth we are here contending for. In the first place, while conscience he necessary to the performance of both good and evil, it does not itself partake of either the one or the other, for it is that part of the mind which takes cognizance of the virtue or vice of our actions, but is itself quite distinct from both. It is that ethical instinct which passes judgment upon the lawfulness or unlawfulness of our desires and deeds. The conscience itself needs instructing, for its dictates go no farther than the knowledge it possesses. It does not *reveal* anything, but simply declares the character of what is presented to the mind's eye, and that according to the light it has.

It is important that we should be quite clear upon this point. The conscience is not in itself a standard of duty, for that of the heathen speaks very differently from that of a Christian who is taught by the Holy Spirit. It is an ear to hear, and the character of *what* it hears—whether true or false—is the measure of its intelligence. In proportion as this inward eye is tutored will be the truthfulness of its perception. The term defines itself: *conscience*, with knowledge—to know with oneself—informing and impressing us with the difference between good and evil. But, since all duty consists of and is contained in *love* (unto God and our neighbour), then good and evil must consist entirely in the *disposition of the* heart: and the mere dictates of conscience including no such dispositions, then neither good nor evil can, strictly speaking, be predicated of those dictates. Both men and demons will forever possess consciences witnessing to them what is good and evil, even in Hell itself—being "the worm that dieth not"—when, as all must allow, they will be utterly destitute of any virtue or goodness. We do indeed read in God's Word of a good conscience and an evil one; and so too we read of "an evil eye," yet there is neither good nor evil in the sight of the eye, only as it is under the influence of a holy or unholy disposition of the soul. So it is with the dictates of the conscience.

The conscience, then, bears solemn witness unto the loss of man's purity and the presence of depravity. But to regard the resistance which conscience makes to each successive stage of sin as an evidence of innate goodness asserting itself is to ignore the very real distinction there is between the authority of conscience and a soul's love for God. The conscience certainly remonstrates and enforces the right in the form of an unconditional and absolute imposition: it also threatens man with the destruction of his peace if he persists in his course of wrongdoing: but that remonstrance and threatening comes to him as a *restraint*, as a force, as something against which the current of his soul is set. There is no love for God in it, no respect to His will as declared by it, no reward for His honour. The struggle is not between good and evil (as *is* the case in a saint), but between sinful inclination and positive prohibition. To know duty and yet be reluctant to perform it is no evidence of any goodness of heart; even to find satisfaction in the performing of duty at the dictate of conscience argues no complacence whatever in God Himself.

Let it be clearly understood that the conflicts which the natural man experiences are most certainly not between any love he has for God and the inordinate desires of his fallen nature, but rather between his conscience and his lusts; and that any remorse which he may suffer is not sorrow for having offended his Maker, but a vexation under the sense of his degradation, which is naught but the injury done to his pride. There is no grief before God for having been a reproach unto Him. Nor does the wretchedness which dissipation produces in any wise dispose its subject unto a more favourable reception of the Gospel. The groaning under the chains which sinful habits forge and the sighing for deliverance therefrom are not longings to be freed from sin, but rather desires to escape from its painful consequences, both to the conscience and to the body. It is mental tranquillity and physical health that are coveted, and not the approbation of the Lord. Any misery suffered by the natural man is not from having offended God, but because he cannot defy Him with impunity and immunity.

None but the Holy Spirit can produce a hatred of sin *as sin*, for that is something the conscience never does.

While we do not wish to labour unduly any particular point in these pages, there are some aspects of the Truth which call for a greater emphasis and fuller treatment than do others. That is not because of any ambiguity in them, for our failure to apprehend the teaching of Holy Writ is not due to its indistinctness, but because of our unwillingness to receive God's Word at its face value, or the obscuring of the same by the clouds of dust raised by the opposition of men against the same. Noticeably is that the case with the one now before us, for though the evolutionists and even openly avowed infidels cannot get away from the fact that man, as yet, is a very imperfect creature, they are far from allowing that he is *totally* depraved—averse to all that is good, prone to all that is evil. Such a declaration is much too humbling and humiliating for any natural heart honestly to accept and be duly affected by it. Plain and insistent as is God's Word upon the subject, not a few professing Christians find it so distasteful that, if they do not repudiate it *in toto*, they go to a great many shifts in order to blunt its sharp edge and remove its most cutting features. The language of Hazael well expresses their resentment against the dark picture which the Divine Artist has drawn of them.

When the Syrian beheld Elijah weeping, and inquired what was the occasion of his distress, God's servant replied, "Because I know the evil that thou wilt do unto the children of Israel: their strong holds wilt thou set on fire, and their young men wilt thou slay with the sword, and wilt dash their children, and rip up their women with child" (2 Kings 8:12). So little was Hazael aware of the vileness of his nature that he became highly indignant, and answered, "But what, is thy servant a dog, that he should do this great thing?" He fondly imagined himself to be incapable of such foul deeds. Nevertheless the sad sequel fully vindicated the Prophet, for albeit Hazael supposed himself to be as gentle as a lamb, when he came into power he proved himself to be as fierce as a savage dog and as cruel as a tiger, for he not only murdered his royal master, usurped the throne of Syria, burnt the cities of Israel and slew their inhabitants with the sword, but barbarously conducted himself toward the women and children, until, as 2 Kings 13:7 states, he went on destroying Israel till he "had made them like the dust by threshing."

Every passage in the Word of Truth which declares the impossibility of the natural man doing anything acceptable to God (such as Jer. 13:23; Matt. 7:18; Rom. 8:8; Heb. 11:6) demonstrates man's total depravity. If men performed any part of their duty toward God it would be pleasing to Him, for He is not a capricious or hard Master, but delights in righteousness wherever He sees it. But as the Lord Jesus pointed out, men will gather grapes of thorns and figs of thistles before unrenewed nature will yield any fruit unto God. Every passage in the Bible which insists upon the necessity of the new birth imports the total depravity of man, for if there were any degree of virtue in the human heart it could be cultivated and increased, and in that case regeneration would be obviated, since the development and improvement of what is already in man would suffice. But our Lord informed a devout religionist, a master in Israel, that except he were born again he could not enter the kingdom of God. Likewise, every passage which calls on men to repent and believe the Gospel presupposes their present sinful and lost condition, for they that are whole need not a physician. "Except ye repent, ye shall all likewise perish" (Luke 13:5) was the decisive verdict of Christ.

We will now resume our notice of the different forms taken by the repudiation of this truth. They are varied and numerous, for unbelief is very fertile. That is but another way of saying that the carnal mind is enmity against God, and at no one point is that enmity more active and evident than in its antipathy to God's Word in general, and the opposition it makes more particularly unto those aspects of it which expose and condemn mankind. Thus, when we are told that all the actions of the unregenerate are not only mixed with sin, but are in their own nature sinful, many sneeringly reply that such is a palpable absurdity. They argue that there be many actions performed by men, such as eating and drinking in moderation, which, being merely *natural* actions, can have in them neither moral good nor moral evil. But that is a bare assertion rather than a logical argument, and is easily refuted.

When we affirm that all the actions of the unregenerate are sinful, we refer only to those which are performed voluntarily, and which are capable of being exercised unto a good end. Whatever falls into that category is not a merely natural but a moral action. That eating and drinking, and all other voluntary exercises, *are* moral actions is evident, for Scripture expressly exhorts us, "Whether therefore ye eat, or drink, or whatsoever ye do, do all to the glory of God" (1 Cor. 10:31). In an irrational being such actions would be merely natural ones, but in a moral agent it is otherwise—the manner in which he attends to them rendering the same good or evil. It is the motive which, largely, determines the quality of the act. Eating and drinking are virtuous when, from a gracious principle, the agent thankfully acknowledges God as the Giver, prayerfully seeks His blessing upon the food, and purposes to use the strength therefrom to His praise. But the unregenerate lack that gracious principle, eating and drinking out of no respect to God's authority, without any love to Him in their hearts, and with no concern for His glory: merely to satisfy their appetites and to provide fuel for the further gratification of their lusts.

If every act of the unregenerate be sinful, then, asks the objector, how is the fact to be accounted for that God Himself regards favourably and even rewards some of the performances of the wicked—such as the case of Ahab and the repentance of the Ninevites at the preaching of Jonah? The first answer is, We must distinguish between God's governmental ways in connection with this world, and that which He requires in order to admittance into Heaven. Though the Most High knows the secrets of all hearts, He does not always proceed accordingly in His administration of the affairs of earth. When God approves of any of the deeds of the wicked, it is not because He regards the same as *theirs,* but because those deeds tend to further His own wise counsels. "God rewarded Nebuchadnezzar for his long siege against Tyre, in giving him the land of Egypt, yet Nebuchadnezzar did nothing in that undertaking which in its own nature could approve itself unto God. The only reason why he was thus rewarded was that what he had done subserved the Divine purpose in punishing Tyre for her insulting treatment toward His people (Ezek. 26:1-7; 29:17-20). God rewarded Cyrus with the treasures of Babylon (Isa. 14:3), not because he did anything that was pleasing in His sight, for his motive was the lust of dominion: but because what he did effected the deliverance of Judah, and fulfilled the Divine predictions upon Babylon"(Andrew Fuller, to whom we are indebted for part of what follows).

In God's governmental dealings with men, actions which possess no appearance of having any intrinsic goodness in them may well be rewarded without any compromise of holiness and righteousness, yea, even those which *have* such an appearance though it be nothing but appearance. God does not always deal with men according to His omniscience, but rather does He generally treat with them in this life according to what they profess and appear to be. Thus, the Lord's design in punishing the wicked person and house of Ahab was to *make manifest His displeasure* against their idolatries. If, then, when Ahab humbled himself and rent his garments, God had proceeded toward him on the ground of His omniscience, knowing him to be destitute of godly sorrow, and made no difference in His treatment of him, that design would not have been answered. Whatever might be Ahab's motives, they were unknown to men, and had no difference appeared in the Divine treatment they would have concluded it was vain to repent and serve Him. It therefore seemed good unto Jehovah to deal with him in this life as though his reformation were sincere, leaving his insincerity to be called to account in the day to come.

As Fuller pointed out, there is a case much resembling that of Ahab in the history of Abijah, the son of Rehoboam. In 2 Chronicles 13 we read of his wars with Jeroboam, king of Israel, and how he addressed the apostate Israelites previous to the battle. Having reproached them for forsaking the God of their fathers and turning to idolatry, he added, "But as for us, the LORD is our God, and we have not forsaken Him; and the priests, which minister unto the Lord, are the sons of Aaron, and the Levites wait upon their business: and they burn unto the LORD every morning and every evening burnt sacrifices and sweet incense: the shewbread also set they in order upon the pure table: and the candlestick of gold with the lamps thereof, to burn every evening: for we keep the charge of the LORD our God: but ye have forsaken Him" (vv. 10, 11). To all appearance this prince was very zealous for the Lord, and one might conclude that the signal victory given him over Jeroboam was an expression of Divine approbation, but if we consult the account given of his reign in 1 Kings 15 (where he is called Abijam), we learn that he was a wicked king, and that he walked in all the sins of his father, and although God granted success to his arms, it was not out of regard to him, but *for David's sake,* and for the establishment of Jerusalem.

Much of what was said above about Ahab holds good of the Ninevites, and Pharaoh too. Concerning the former, there might have been sincere and spiritual penitents among them for all we know, but whether godly sorrow or slavish fear actuated them they professed and appeared to be humbled before God, displaying the external marks of contrition; and for God to treat with them on the ground of their repentance being apparently sincere was obviously an exemplification of Divine wisdom, for it magnified His righteous and merciful government in the sight of the surrounding nations. In like manner, the acknowledgments of Pharaoh's sins, and his requests for Moses to entreat the Lord on his behalf, were repeatedly followed by the removal of those judgments which so appalled his proud spirit; yet who would insist that there was any good or spirituality in Egypt's king? Not only God, but Moses himself, perceived his evident insincerity; nevertheless, it became the Most High to remove His rod when that guilty tyrant made confession, even though he might laugh to himself for having imposed upon Moses so far as to gain his point.

In their strictures upon the doctrine of man's total depravity some have appealed to Christ's words in Mark 13:28-34, where He assured the scribe who answered Him "discreetly" that "thou art not far from the kingdom of God"; arguing therefrom that though he was unsaved, yet our Lord found in his character which was praiseworthy. But if the passage be read attentively it will be found that Christ was not approving of his spirit or his conduct, but instead was simply commending his confession of faith. When this Jew acknowledged that the love of God and man was of more importance and value than whole burnt offerings—that the moral Law was more excellent than the ceremonial, which was soon to be abolished—he gave utterance to sound doctrine, and approximated so closely to the spirit of the Gospel dispensation that Christ very properly informed him he was not far from the kingdom of God, i.e., the principles which he had avowed, if truly embraced and duly pursued, would lead him into the very heart of Christianity, for it is by the Law that a knowledge of sin is obtained, and thereby our need of mercy is discovered. The things to which the scribe assented were the very ones Christ insisted upon in His teaching.

Dissenters against the Truth ask, If all men alike be totally depraved, then how is it that some lead less and others more vicious lives? This objection was briefly noticed by us in an earlier chapter of this book, but since it be the one most likely to occasion difficulty to our readers, we will offer a few more remarks thereon. In examining the same it is necessary to revert unto our definition of terms, and bear in mind that total depravity consists not, in the first place, of what a man *does,* but what he is in himself: and second, what is his relation and attitude *unto God.* Because particular persons are not swearers, morally unclean, drunkards or thieves, they are very apt to imagine that they are far from being wholly corrupt, yea, that they are good and respectable people. Such are included among those described in Proverbs 30:12, "There is a generation that are pure in their own eyes, and yet is not washed from their filthiness." However irreproachable be the walk of the natural man, his nature is polluted and his heart thoroughly defiled: and the very fact that he is quite unaware of his vileness is sad proof of the blinding power of indwelling sin.

The total depravity of human nature does not mean that it actually breaks forth into open acts of all kinds of evil in any man. It is freely granted that there are marked differences among the unregenerate in the eruption of sin in their conduct: some being more honest, sober and benevolent than their fellows, running into less excess of not than do others: nevertheless, the seeds of all evil are present in every human breast. "As in water face answereth to face, so the heart of man to man" (Prov. 27:19). It has been truly said of all that "If they were in Cain's circumstances, and God should suffer them, they would do as he did. If they were in Pharaoh's circumstances, and left of God, they would be as cruel, false, and hard-hearted as he. If they were in the like circumstances with Doeg, though they condemn him for his hypocrisy, flattery, and cruelty, they would do every whit as bad as he. If they were in like circumstances as Judas was, whatever indignation they feel against him, they would be as false and impudent, and as very traitors as he. If they were under the circumstances that the fallen angels are, they would be as very devils as they" (Mr. T. Stoddard, *The Nature* of *Conversion*, 1710).

It is indeed true that their fearful enmity against God and the hatred which is in their hearts against their fellows (Titus 3:3) are less openly displayed by some than others, yet that is not because they are any better in themselves than those who are flagrantly irreligious and who cast off all pretences of decency. Not at all: their moderation in wickedness must be attributed unto the greater restraints which the Governor of this world places upon them: either by the secret workings of His Spirit upon their hopes and fears or by His external providences, such as a godly home, early education, the subduing influence of pious companions. But none is born into this world with the smallest spark of love to God in him. Instead, "their poison is like the poison of a serpent" (Psa. 58:4), and the poison of a serpent is radically the same in all its species. God estimates us by what we are internally, though we shall yet be called to an account for all that we have done externally. It is ever to be borne in mind—for our humbling—that there is very much evil within each of us that God does not suffer to break forth into particular actings of sin, sovereignly preventing temptations and opportunities unto the same.

All men are equally depraved, but that depravity discovers itself in many different forms and ways: and it is a fatal delusion to suppose that, because Divine power and mercy keep me from certain crimes, I am less corrupt than my fellows, and less a criminal in His sight. God judges not as man: Capernaum was more obnoxious to Him than Sodom! Many who do not act a brutish part act a diabolical one: there is a filthiness of the spirit, as well as of the flesh (2 Cor. 8:1), and though some give not free rein to their sensual lusts, yet they are under the dominion of mental lusts—pride, covetousness, envy, contempt of others, malice, revenge. God restrains both the internal and external workings of sin as best serves the outworking of His eternal purpose, permitting different degrees of iniquity in different individuals, though all be "clay of the same lump." None by nature possesses the slightest degree of holiness. Different measures of wickedness issue from the same individual at different times: that I have been kept from certain sins in the past is no guarantee that I shall not be guilty of them in the future.

Finally, the demurrer is made, If man be so totally depraved as to be entirely incapable of doing anything that is pleasing to God, then there can be no ground for a ministerial address, no motives by which to exhort the unregenerate to cease from evil and do good, and certainly no encouragement left for them to comply. Our first reply is that no minister of the Gospel is warranted to entertain the slightest degree of hope of success from his endeavours on the ground of the pliability of the hearts of his hearers: rather must their corrupt state exclude any such expectation. Unless the preacher's confidence be based alone on the power and promise of God, his hopes are certain to be disappointed. But, second, if the objector means that in view of their total depravity it is *unreasonable* to exhort men to do good, this can by no means be admitted, for it would then follow that if a total depravity removes all ground for a rational address, then a *partial* one would take it away in part, and thus, in proportion as we perceive men to be disinclined unto good, we are to cease warning and expostulating with them—a self-evident absurdity!

While men be rational creatures they are justly accountable for all that they do, whatever be the disposition of their hearts: and, so long as they be not yet consigned to a hopeless perdition, their responsibility is to be enforced, and they are to be regarded as fit subjects of a Gospel address. Nor can it be truly asserted that there are no motives by which they may properly be exhorted to cease to do evil and learn to do well. The proper motives unto these things remain in all their original force, independently of the inclination or disinclination of men's hearts to comply. God's rights, His authority, His Law, abide unchanged, no matter what change has taken place in the creature. The example of Christ and His Apostles is too plain to be misunderstood. Neither the one nor the other toned down their demands upon fallen sinners. Repentance toward God and faith toward our Lord Jesus Christ were the grand duties upon which they ever insisted, and so far from hesitating to exhort their unregenerate hearers unto what was *spiritually good*, it may be safely affirmed that they never exhorted unto anything else. Nothing less than the heart is what God ever requires. Throw down the weapons of your rebellion and yield to Christ's sceptre must be the call of His servants.

The violent antagonism of men against this truth is precisely what might well be expected, so that instead of causing us to doubt it we should rather regard the same as a strong confirmation. Indeed it would be surprising if a doctrine so humbling and distasteful were not resisted. Nor need we be dismayed by its widespread repudiation by preachers and professing Christians. When the Lord Jesus averred, "I am come into this world, that they which see not might see: and that they which [pretend to] see might be made blind" (John 9:39), the Pharisees haughtily asked, "Are we blind also?" (John 9:40). When He declared that human nature is so in love with sin and possessed of such enmity against God, and insisted that "no man can come unto Me, except it were given unto him of My Father," we are told that "From that time many of His disciples went back, and walked no more with Him" (John 6:65, 66). The rejection which this doctrine meets with demonstrates how dense is that darkness which is not dispelled by so clear a light, and how great is the power of Satan when the testimony of Divine revelation does not carry conviction. Every effort to tone it down verifies the fact that "the heart" *is* deceitful above all things, and desperately wicked."

THE DOCTRINE OF HUMAN DEPRAVITY
Its Ramifications

While endeavouring to present a complete picture of fallen man as he is depicted by the Divine pencil in the Scriptures, it is very difficult to avoid a measure of overlapping as we turn from one aspect or feature of the same to another, or to prevent a certain amount of repetition when devoting a separate portrayal of each. Yet, seeing that this is the method which the Holy Spirit has largely taken, an apology is scarcely required from those who seek to follow His plan. In the preceding chapters we have shown in a more or less general way the terrible havoc which sin has wrought in the human constitution; now we shall consider the same more specifically. Having presented the broad outline, it remains for us to fill in the details. In other words, our immediate task is to ponder and describe *the several parts of* human depravity, according as it has vitiated the several sections of our inner man. Though the soul, like the body, is a unit, it also has a number of distinct members or faculties, and none of them has been exempted from the debasing effects of man's apostasy from his Maker.

This, we consider, was strikingly exemplified in the miracles of Christ. The various bodily disorders which the Divine Physician healed during His sojourn on earth were not only so many prefigurations of the marvels of grace that He performed in the spiritual realm in connection with the redeemed, but they were also many emblematical representations of the moral diseases which affect and afflict the soul of fallen man. The poor leper, covered with noisome sores, solemnly portrayed the horrible pollutions of the human heart. The man born blind, incapable of beholding the wonders and beauties of God's external works, expressed the benighted state of the human mind, which, because of the darkness that is upon it, is unable to discover or receive the things of the Spirit, no matter how simply and plainly they be explained to him. The paralytic's enervated limbs shadowed forth the impotency of the will Godwards, its being totally devoid of any power to turn us unto Christ. The woman lying sick of the fever, producing unnatural craving, delirium, etc., depicted the disordered state of our affections. The demon-possessed man, dwelling amid the tombs, incapable of being securely bound, crying and cutting himself, adumbrated the various activities of the conscience in the unregenerate.

Corruption has invaded every part of our nature, overspreading the whole of man's complex being. As physical disorders spare no members of the body, so man's very spirit has not escaped the ravages of depravity. Yet who is capable of comprehending the same in its awful breadth and depth, length and height? It is not simply the inferior powers of the soul which the plague of sin has seized, but the contagion has ascended into the higher regions of our persons, polluting the sublimest faculties. This is a part of God's punishment. It is a great mistake to suppose that the Divine judgment on man's defection is reserved for the next life. Mankind is heavily penalized in this world, both outwardly and inwardly, as they are subject to many adverse dispensations of providence therein. Outwardly, in their bodies, names, estates, relations and employments; finally, by physical death and dissolution. Inwardly, by blindness of mind, hardness of heart, turbulent passions, the gnawing of conscience. However little regarded, by reason of their stupidity and insensibility, yet the inward visitations of God's curse are far more dreadful than the outward ones, and are regarded as such by those who truly fear the Lord and see things in His light.

1. *Blindness* of *mind.* The mind is that faculty of the soul by which objects and things are first cognized and apprehended. In distinguishing the understanding from it, the latter is that which weighs, discriminates and determines—judging between the concepts formed in the former, being the guide of the soul, the selector and rejecter of those notions the mind has received. Both alike are deranged by sin, for we are told that "their minds were blinded" (2 Cor. 3:14), and we also read of "having the understanding darkened" (Eph. 4:18). As a derelict from God, the Fall has completely shuttered the windows of man's soul, yet he perceives it not; yea, emphatically denies it. Heathen philosophers and the schoolmen of medievalism both allowed that the affections, in the lower part of the soul, were somewhat defiled, but insisted that the intellectual faculty was pure, saying that reason still directed and advised us to the best things. When our Lord declared, "For judgment I am come into this world, that they which see not might see, and that they which see might be made blind," some of the Pharisees who heard Him indignantly asked, "Are we blind also?" (John 9:39, 40).

Now it is not strange that blind reason should think it sees, for while it judges everything else it is least capable of estimating itself because of its very nearness to itself. Though a man's eye can see the deformity of his hands or feet, it cannot see the bloodshot that is in itself, unless it has a glass by which to discern the same. In like manner, even corrupt nature, by its own light, recognizes the disorder in the sensual part of man, yet it cannot discern the defilement that is in the spirit itself. The glass of God's Word is required to discover that, and even that mirror is not sufficient—the light of Divine grace has to shine within, in order to expose and discover the imbecility of the reasoning faculty. And hence it is that Holy Writ throws the main emphasis on the depravity of this highest part of man's being. When the Apostle would show how impure are unbelievers, who nevertheless profess that they know God, he averred, "*even* their mind and conscience is defiled" (Titus 1:15). They least of all suspected that those parts were tainted, especially since they were illumined with some rays of the knowledge of God. Thus, in opposition to this conceit, the superior faculties alone are mentioned, and they stressed with an "even."

How weighty and full the testimony of Scripture is upon this solemn feature appears from the following. "When they knew God [traditionally], they glorified Him not as God, neither were thankful: but became vain in their imaginations, and their foolish heart was darkened. Professing themselves to be wise, they became fools" (Rom. 1:21, 22)—the reference is to the Gentiles after the flood. One of the fearful curses executed upon Israel, because they hearkened not unto the voice of the Lord their God and refused to do His commandments, was "The LORD shall smite thee with madness, and blindness, and astonishment of heart and thou shalt grope at noonday, as the blind gropeth in darkness" (Deut. 28:28, 29). Of all mankind it is said, "There is none that understandeth ... the way of peace have they not known" (Rom. 3:11, 17): so far from it that "there is a way which seemeth right unto a man, but the end thereof are the ways of death" (Prov. 14:12). "The world by wisdom knew not God" (1 Cor. 1:21): despite all their schools, they were ignorant of Him. "Desiring to be teachers of the law, understanding neither what they say, nor whereof they affirm" (1 Tim. 1:7). "Ever learning, and never able to come to the knowledge of the truth" (2 Tim. 2:7).

The natural darkness which blinds them from those regular operations that are directed by their outward senses is twofold: either external or internal. When night falls, unless there be the aid of artificial light, they can no longer perform their work. If they be blind, then it is one perpetual night to them. Such too is spiritual darkness: objective and subjective—a darkness that is both *on* men and *in* men. The first consists in a lack of those means whereby alone they may be enlightened in the knowledge of God and heavenly things. What the sun is to the earth unto natural things, that is the Word and the preaching of it as to things spiritual (Psa. 19:1-4: cf. Rom. 10:10, 11). This darkness is upon all unto whom the Gospel is not declared or by whom it is despised and rejected. Now it is the mission and work of the Holy Spirit to take away this objective darkness, and until it be done none can see or enter the kingdom of God. This He does by sending the Gospel into a country, nation, or town. It does not obtain

The Doctrine of Human Depravity   155

entrance there, nor is it restrained anywhere, by accident or by human effort: but it is dispensed according to the sovereign will of the Spirit of God. He it is who gifts, calls, and sends men forth to preach, determining the places where they shall minister, either by His secret impulses or by the operations of His providence (Acts 16:6-10).

But it is the *subjective* darkness upon the minds of the unregenerate, with the influences and consequences thereof, which is here more immediately to be considered. This is not a mere privative thing, but a positive, consisting not simply of ignorance, but of a foul disease, with a habitual evil disposition. "He is proud, knowing nothing; but sick about questions and strifes of words, whereof cometh envy, strife, railings, evil surmisings, perverse disputings of men of *corrupt minds,* and destitute of the truth" (1 Tim. 6:4, 5). Not only are their minds such as assent not to wholesome doctrine, but they are diseased and corrupt: "sick about questions"—longing for them as a diseased stomach does for any trash. This distemper of mind is also called an itch after fables (2 Tim. 4:3, 4). Still more solemnly, Scripture calls that contentious wisdom of which the learned of this world are so proud, "earthly, sensual, devilish" (James 3:15): both the verse before and the one following show that all the envy, malice, lying and dissembling, though in both the affections and the will, is rooted in the understanding. Hence it is that God must give "repentance" or a change of mind before there is an acknowledgment of the Truth and a recovery from the snare of the Devil (2 Tim. 2:25, 26).

This darkness of the understanding is the cause of that rebellion which is in the affections and will, for why do men seek so inordinately the pleasures of sin, but because their minds know not God, and are strangers to Him and can have no fellowship with Him?—For all friendship and fellowship is grounded upon knowledge. To have communion with God, the knowledge of Him is necessary, and accordingly the principal thing which God does when He gives admittance into the Covenant of Grace is to teach men to know Him (Jer. 31:33, 34): contrariwise, men are estranged from Him through ignorance (Eph. 4:17-19). The darkness of the mind is not only the root of all sin, but is the cause of most of the corruptions in men's lives. Hence we find that Paul mentions "fleshly wisdom" as the antithesis of the principle of grace (2 Cor. 1:12). For the same reason men are said to be "sottish children, and they have none understanding: they are wise to do evil, but to do good they have no knowledge" (Jer. 4:22). That this is the cause of the greatest part of wickedness which is in the world is clear from Isaiah 48:10, "Thy wisdom and thy knowledge, it hath perverted thee." Corrupt reasonings and false judgments of things are the chief movers in all our sinning. Pride has its chief place in the mind, as Colossians 2:18 shows.

That this darkness is forceful and influential—yea, dynamic—appears from that expression in Colossians 1:13, "delivered us from the *power* of darkness"—the word signifying that which sways or bears rule. It fills the mind with enmity against God and all His ways, and turns the will in a contrary direction, so that, instead of the affections being set upon things above, the unregenerate "mind earthly things" (Phil. 3:19). Such is its habitual inclination. It minds the things of the flesh (Rom. 8:5), setting itself to provide sensual objects for the gratification of the body. It fills the mind with strong prejudices against the spiritual things proposed in the Gospel. Those prejudices are called "strongholds" and "imaginations [or "reasonings"], and every high thing that exalteth itself against the knowledge of God" (2 Cor. 10:4, 5), which are pulled down and cast down in the day of God's power, when souls are brought into willing subjection to Him. The sins of the mind are of longest continuance, for when the body decays and its lusts wither, those of the mind are as vigorous and active in old age as in youth. As the understanding is the most excellent part of man, so its corruption is worse than that of the other faculties: "If . . . the light that is in thee be darkness, how great is that darkness!" (Matt. 6: 23).

Fearful indeed are the effects of this darkness. Its subjects are rendered incapable of discerning or receiving spiritual things, so that there is a total inability with respect unto God and the ways of pleasing Him. No matter how well endowed intellectually the unregenerate man may be, what the extent of his education and learning, how skilful in connection with natural things, in spiritual matters he is devoid of intelligence until he is renewed in the spirit of his mind. As a person who lacks the power of seeing is incapable of being impressed by the strongest rays of light reflected upon him, and cannot form any real ideas of the appearance of things, so the natural man, by reason of this blindness of mind, is unable to discern the nature of heavenly things. Said Christ to the Jews of His day, "If thou hadst known, even thou, at least in this thy day, the things which belong unto thy peace! but now they are *hid* from thine eyes" (Luke 19:42)—concealed from thy perception as effectually as things which are purposely hidden from prying eyes. Even though a man had the desire to discover them, he would search in vain for all eternity unless God was pleased to *reveal* them, as He did to Peter (Matt. 16:17).

The spiritual blindness which is upon the mind of the natural man not only disables him to make the first discovery of the things of God, but even when they are published and set before his eyes, as in the

Word of Truth they plainly are, he cannot discern them. Whatever notions he may form of them, they are dissonant to their nature, and the thoughts he has of them are the very reverse of what in fact they are: the highest wisdom they regard as folly, and objects most glorious in themselves are despised and rejected. "Behold, ye despisers, and wonder, and perish; for I work a work in your days, a work which ye shall in no wise believe, though a man declare it unto you" (Acts 13:41). The preceding verses show that Paul had clearly preached to them Christ and His Gospel, and then closed with a caution that they beware lest that came upon them which was spoken by the Prophet. Thus it is not the bare presentation of the Truth which will convince men. Though clearly propounded, it may still be obscure to them: "it is hid to them that are lost: in whom the god of this world hath blinded the minds of them which believe not" (2 Cor. 4:3, 4). Their understandings need to be Divinely opened in order to understand the Scriptures (Luke 24:45)!

The subjects of this darkness are spiritually insensible and stupid. This it is which prevents them from making a true inspection of their hearts. They see only the outward man, and feel not the deadly wound within. There is a sea of corruption, but it is unperceived. The holiness, beauty and rectitude of their nature have departed, but they are quite unconcerned. They are miserable and poor, blind and naked, yet totally unaware of it. This it is which causes the unregenerate to go on in a course of rebellion against the Lord, and at the same time conclude that all things are well with them. Thus they live securely and happily. As the goodness of God melts them not, neither do His sorest judgments move them to amend their ways. So far from it, they are like unto that wicked king Ahaz, of whom it is recorded, "And in the time of his distress did he trespass yet more against the LORD" (2 Chron. 28:22)—how madly and defiantly did the masses conduct themselves throughout the battle of Britain! So now, while the peace of the whole world is so seriously menaced "LORD, when Thy hand is lifted up, they will not see" (Isa. 26:11).

Space will allow us to mention only one other effect, and that is what Ephesians 4:17 terms "the vanity of their mind." Things in Scripture are said to be *vain* which are useless and fruitless: in Matthew 15:9, it signifies "to no purpose." Hence the idols of the heathen and the rites used in their worship are called vain things (Acts 15:15). In 1 Samuel 12:21, vain things are said to be those "which cannot profit nor deliver." It is also synonymous with folly, for in Proverbs 12:11, vain men are all one with "persons void of understanding." In Jeremiah 4:14, vain things are yoked with "wickedness," thus they are sinful ones—vain men and sons of Belial are synonymous (2

Chron. 13:7). This vanity of the mind induces the natural man to pursue shadows and miss the substance, to be engaged with figments instead of realities, to prefer lies to the truth. This it is which leads men to follow the fashions and revel in the pleasures of a vain world. This sinful vanity of mind is in all sorts of persons and ages, acting itself in foolish imaginations, whereby it makes provision for the flesh and its lusts. It appears in a loathness to think upon holy things, so that when under the preaching of the Word the mind wanders like a butterfly in the garden. It "feedeth on foolishness" (Prov. 15:14), and has an itching curiosity about the affairs of others.

2. *Hardness of heart.* The heart is the center of our moral being, out of which flow the issues of life (Prov. 4:23; cf. Matt. 12:35). The nature of it is at once indicated by its being designated a *stony* heart" (Ezek. 11:19). The figure is a very apt one. As a stone is nothing but a product of the earth, so it has the property of the earth—heaviness, a tendency to fall. Thus it is with the natural mind: men's affections are wholly set upon the world, and though God made man upright with his head erect, yet the soul is bowed down to the ground. The physical curse pronounced upon the serpent is also fulfilled in his seed, for the things upon which they feed turn to ashes, so that dust is their meat (Isa. 65:25). Sin has so calloused man's heart that, Godwards, it is loveless and lifeless, cold and insensible. That is one reason why the moral Law was written upon tables of stone: to represent emblematically the kind of hearts which men had, as is clearly implied by the contrast presented in 2 Corinthians 3:3—stupid, unyielding.

The heart of the unregenerate is also likened to "the rock" (Jer. 23:29), and to an "adamant stone" (Zech. 7:12), which is harder than a flint. The same thing is termed being "stout-hearted" (Isa. 46:12), and in Isaiah 48:4, God says, "thou art obstinate, and thy neck is an iron sinew, and thy brow brass." This hardness is often ascribed to the neck ("stiffnecked"), being a figure of man's obstinacy taken from refractory oxen which will not endure the yoke. This hardness evidences itself by a complete absence of spiritual sensibility, so that it is unmoved by God's goodness, has no awe of His authority and majesty, and no fear of His anger and vengeance, a presentation of the joys of Heaven or the horrors of Hell makes no impression upon it. As the Prophet of old lamented, they "put far away the evil day" (Amos 6:3), dismissing it from their thoughts as an unwelcome subject to dwell upon. They have no sense of guilt, no consciousness of having offended their Maker, no alarming realization of His wrath abiding on them, but are secure and at ease in their sins. So far from sin being a burden to them, it is their element and delight to enjoy its pleasures for a season.

That hardness of heart to which reference was made at the close of our last chapter is the perverseness and obstinacy of fallen man's nature, which makes him resolve to continue in sin no matter what be the consequences thereof. It renders him unwilling to be rebuked for his folly, and makes him refuse to be reclaimed from it, whatever methods are used in order thereunto. The Prophet made mention of this in his day, for referring to those who had been forewarned by sore judgments, and were at that very time under the most solemn rebukes of Providence, God had to say of them, "They will not hearken unto Me: for all the house of Israel are impudent and hardhearted" (Ezek. 3:7). So too the Lord Jesus complained, "We have piped unto you, and ye have not danced: we have mourned unto you, and ye have not lamented" (Matt. 11:17). The most pathetic entreaties and winsome expostulations will not move the unregenerate to close with what is absolutely necessary for their present peace and final felicity. "They are like the deaf adder that stoppeth her ear; which will not hearken to the voice of charmers, charming never so wisely" (Psa. 63:4, 5, and cf. Acts 8:57).

The hearts of the regenerate are ductile and pliable, easily bent to God's will, but the hearts of the wicked are so wedded to their lusts as to be impervious to all appeal. There is such an unyielding disposition against heavenly things that they respond not to the most alarming threatenings and thunderings. They will neither be convinced by the most cogent arguments nor won by the most tempting inducements. They are so addicted to self-pleasing that they cannot be persuaded to take Christ's yoke upon them. In Zechariah 7:11, 12, it is said, "But they refused to hearken, and pulled away the shoulder, and stopped their ears, that they should not hear. Yea, they made their hearts as an adamant stone, lest they should hear the Law, and the words which the LORD of hosts hath sent." They are less susceptible to be wrought upon by the preacher to receive any impressions of holiness than granite is to be engraved by the tool of the artificer. They scorn to be controlled and refuse to be admonished. They are "a stubborn and rebellious generation" (Psa. 78:8), being subject to neither the Law nor the Gospel. The doctrines of repentance, denying of self, walking with God, can find no entrance into their hearts.

3. *Disordered affections.* Some writers take in more and others less in the scope of the term "affections," and perhaps it is a moot point both theologically and psychologically whether the desire nature is to be included therein or to be considered separately. In the broadest meaning, the affections may be said to be the sensitive fac-

ulty of the soul. As the understanding is that power which discerns and judges things, so the affections allure and dispose the soul unto or against the objects contemplated. It is by the affections that the soul becomes pleased or displeased with what is cognized by the bodily senses or contemplated by the mind, and thus moved to approve or reject. As distinguished from both, the *will* is that faculty which executes the final decision of the mind or the strongest desire of the affections, carrying out the same into action. Since the affections pertain to the sensitive side of the soul, we are more conscious of *their stirrings* than we are of the actings of our minds or wills. In this chapter we shall employ the term in its widest latitude, including the desires, for what the appetites are to the body the affections are to the soul.

Goodwin likened the desire nature unto the stomach in the body. It is an empty void, fitted to receive from without, longing for a satisfying object. Its universal language is, "Who will show us any good?" (Psa. 4:6). Now God Himself is man's chief good, the only One who can afford him real, lasting and full satisfaction. At the beginning He created him in His own likeness; that as the needle touched by the landstone ever moves northward, so the soul being touched with the Divine image should carry the understanding, affections and will unto Himself. He also placed the soul in a material body, and that in this world, fitting each for the other, providing everything necessary for and suited to each part of man's complex being. The desire nature carried the soul unto the creature, but only as a means of enjoying God in and by them. The wonders of God's handiwork were meant to be admired, but chiefly as displaying His wisdom. Food was to be eaten and enjoyed, but in order to deepen gratitude unto the goodness of the Giver and to supply strength to serve Him. But alas, when man apostatized, his understanding, affections and will were divorced from God, and the exercise of them became directed only by self-love.

Originally the Lord sustained and directed the action of human affections unto Himself. Then He withheld that power, and left our first parents on their own creature footing, and in consequence their desires wandered after forbidden joys. They sought their happiness not in communion with their Maker, but in intercourse with the creature. Like their children ever since, they loved and served the creature more than the Creator. The result was disastrous to the last degree: they became separated from the Holy One. That was at once evidenced by their attempt to hide from Him—had their delight been in God as their chief good, the desire for concealment could not have possessed their minds. And as it was with Adam and Eve, so it has been with all their descendants. Many a proverb expresses that general truth. "The stream cannot rise higher than the fountain." "Men do not gather grapes of thorns, nor figs of thistles." "Like begets like." The parent stock of the human family must send forth scions of its own nature. "Depart from us; for we desire not the knowledge of Thy ways" (Job 21:14) is what the hearts and lives of all the unregenerate say unto the Almighty.

The natural center of unfallen man's soul, both for its rest and delight, was the One who gave him being, and therefore did David say, "Return unto thy rest, O my soul" (Psa. 116:7). But sin has caused men to "draw back" from Him, and to "depart from the living God" (Heb. 10:38; 3:12). God was not only to be the delightful portion of the one whom He had made in His image, but also the ultimate end of all his motions and actions, aiming to glorify and please Him in all things. But he forsook "the fountain of living waters" (Jer. 2:13)—the infinite and perpetual spring of comfort and joy. And now the inclinations and lustings of man's nature are wholly taken off from God, anything and everything being more agreeable to him than He who is the sum of all excellency: making the things of time and sense his chief good, and the pleasing of himself his supreme end. That is why their affections are termed "ungodly lusts" (Jude 18)— they are all turned *away from Him.* They have no relish for His holiness, no desire for fellowship with Him, no wish to retain Him in their thoughts.

But what has just been pointed out (the aversion of our affections from God) is only the privative part: the positive is their conversion to other things. Thus it was that God charged Israel, "My people have committed two evils; they have forsaken Me the fountain of living waters, and hewed them out cisterns, broken cisterns, that can hold no water"—betaking themselves to poor trifles which afford them no satisfaction. The creature is preferred before the Creator, for all the concern of the natural man is how to live at ease in the world, and not to honour and enjoy God. Thus do they observe "lying vanities" and "forsake their own mercy" (Jonah 2:8), for as to their emptiness they are vanities, and in regard to disappointing their expectations, "lying vanities." They are deceived by a vain show, and the outcome is vexation of spirit, because of a frustrating of their hopes. As the love of God shed abroad in the hearts of the redeemed seeks not its own (1 Cor. 13:5), so self-love does nothing else but that very thing: they all look to their own way, every one for his gain" (Isa. 56:11).

Not only are the lusts of the unregenerate carried away from God to the creature, but they are so greedily, excessively. Thus we read of "inordinate affections" (Col. 3:5), which signifies both immoderate and irregular, both a spirit of gluttony and a craving after things which are contrary to God: "lusting after evil things" (1 Cor. 10:6). The former is the sin of intemperance: the latter having "pleasure in unrighteousness" (2 Thess. 2:12). The body is esteemed above the soul, for all the efforts of the natural man are directed to making provision for the flesh to fulfill the lusts thereof, while his immortal spirit is little thought of and still less cared for. When providence smiles upon his labours, his language is, "Soul, thou hast much goods laid up for many years: take thine ease, eat, drink, and be merry" (Luke 12:19). Their thoughts rise not to a higher and future life. They are far more concerned with the clothing and adorning of the outward man than with the cultivation of a meek and quiet spirit, which in the sight of God is of great price (1 Peter 3:4). Earth is preferred before Heaven, things of time before eternity. Though death and the grave may put an end to all they had here much sooner than they imagine, yet their hearts are so set upon those things as their happiness that they will not be diverted from them.

Thus it is that the affections, which at the beginning were the servants of reason, now occupy the throne. That which is the glory of human nature—elevating it above the beasts of the field—is turned hither and thither by the rude rabble of our passions. God placed in man an instinct of happiness, to find the same in Himself, but now it creeps in the dust and pours itself out to every vanity. The counsels and contrivances of the mind are engaged in the accomplishment of man's carnal desires. Not only have his affections no relish for spiritual things, they are strongly prejudiced against them, for they run directly counter to the gratifying of his corrupt nature. His desires are set upon more wealth, more worldly honour and power, more fleshly merriment, and because the Gospel contains no promise of such things it is despised. Because it inculcates holiness, the mortifying of the flesh, separation from the world, resisting the Devil, the Gospel is most unwelcome to him. To turn the affections away from those material and temporal things which they have made their chief good, and to turn them unto unseen spiritual and eternal things, alienates the carnal mind against the Gospel, for it offers nothing attractive to the natural man in the place of those idols on which his heart centers. To renounce his own righteousness and be dependent upon that of Another is equally distasteful to his pride.

Not only are the affections alienated from and opposed to the holy *requirements* of the Gospel, but equally so unto its *mystery*. That mystery is what the Scriptures term the hidden wisdom of God, and the natural man not only fails to admire and adore it, but regards it with contempt and contumacy. He looks upon all the parts of its dec-

The Doctrine of Human Depravity

laration as empty and unintelligible notions. This prejudice has prevailed over the wise and learned of this world in all ages, and in none more effectual than in our evil day. The highest wisdom of God seems foolishness unto all who are puffed up by pride in their own intelligence, and what is foolishness unto them is despised and scorned. That which is addressed to faith rather than reason is unpalatable. To lean not unto their own understanding, but trust in the Lord with all their hearts, is a "hard saying" to those considered of towering intellect. To set aside their own ideas, forsake their thoughts (Isa. 55:7) and become as "little children," and be told they shall in no wise enter the kingdom of Heaven unless they do so, is most abhorrent unto them. No small part of man's depravity consists in its readiness to embrace those prejudices, to adhere perniciously unto them, with total lack of power to extricate themselves from them.

The disordered state of our affections is seen in the fact that the actions of the natural man are regulated far more by his senses than by his reason. His conduct consists principally in responding to the clamourings of his lusts rather than to the dictates of reason. The desires of children are swift to any corrupting diversion, but slow to any improving exercise: from the one they can scarcely be restrained, unto the other they have to be compelled. That the affections are turned away from God is made manifest every time His will crosses our desires. This disease appears too in the objects on which the several affections are placed. Instead of love being set upon God, it is centered on the world, and dotes upon idols. Instead of hatred being directed against sin, it is opposed to holiness. Instead of joy finding its delight in spiritual things, it wastes itself on those which soon pall. Instead of fear being actuated by displeasing the Lord, it dreads more the frowns of our fellows. If there be grief, it is for the thwarting of our pleasures and hopes, rather than because of our waywardness. If there be pity, it is exercised upon self, rather than upon the sufferings of others.

It now remains for us to point out that the very first stirring of our lusts is itself *evil*. The passions or lusts are those natural and unrestrained motions of the creature unto the advancement of its nature, by an inclination unto those objects which promote its good, and an aversion from those which are noxious. And thus they are to the soul what wings are to the bird and sails are to the ship. Desire is ever in pursuit of satisfaction, and if it is to be met must be regulated by right reason. But, alas, reason has been dethroned and man's passions and inclinations are lawless, and therefore their earliest risings after forbidden objects essentially evil. This was, as Matthew 5 shows, denied by the rabbins, who restricted sin to an open and outward transgression. But our Lord declared that unwarrantable anger against another was incipient murder, and that to look upon a woman so as to lust after her was a breach of the seventh commandment, that impure thoughts and wanton imaginations were nothing less than adultery. Hence it is that Scripture speaks of "deceitful lusts" (Eph. 4:22), "foolish and hurtful lusts" (1 Tim. 6:9), "worldly lusts" (Titus 2:12), "fleshly lusts, which war against the soul" (1 Peter 2:11), "ungodly lusts" (Jude 18).

The very first stirring of desire after anything evil, the slightest irregularity in the motions of the soul, is *sin*. This is clear from the universal command "Thou shalt not covet," or hanker after anything which God has prohibited. This irregular and evil longing is termed "concupiscence" in Romans 7:8, "in which the Apostle included mental as well as sensual desire" (Calvin). The Greek word is usually rendered "lust": in 1 Thessalonians 4:5, it is found in an intensified form: "the lust of concupiscence." These lustings of the soul are its initial motions, often unsuspected by ourselves, which precede the consent of the mind, and are designated "evil concupiscence" (Col. 3:5). They are the seeds from which spring our evil works, the original stirrings of our indwelling corruption. They are condemned by the Law of God, for the tenth commandment forbids the first outgoings of the affections after what belongs to another, so that the incipient longing, *before* the approbation of the mind be obtained, is sinful, and needs to be confessed unto God. Genesis 6:5 declares of fallen man that "every imagination of the thoughts of his heart" is evil, for sins while in their embryonic stage defile the soul, being contrary to that purity which the holiness of God requires.

What has been pointed out above is repudiated by Roman Catholics, for while they allow that the lusts of the flesh are the matter of sin or that in which sin originates, they will not admit the same to be essentially evil. The Council of Trent denied that the original movement of the soul tending to evil is itself sinful, stating that it only becomes so when the same is consented or yielded to. In like manner, the majority of Arminians (who in so many of their beliefs are one with papists) confine sin to an act of the will. Now it is freely confessed by all sound Calvinists that the mind's entertaining of the first evil desire is a further degree of sin, and that actual assenting thereto is yet more heinous; but they emphatically contend that *the original impulse is* also evil in the sight of God. If the original impulse be innocent (*per se*) how could its gratification be sinful? Motives and excitements do not undergo any change in their essential nature in consequence of their being humoured or encouraged. It cannot be wrong to heed innocent impulses. The Lord Jesus teaches us to judge

The Doctrine of Human Depravity

the tree by its fruits—if the fruit be corrupt, so too is the tree which bears it.

In Romans 8:7, the term is actually rendered sin: "I had not known *sin*, but by the Law: for I had not known *lust*, except the Law had said, Thou shalt not covet"—or "lust," for the Greek uses the same word. Here, then, sin and lust are used interchangeably: any inward nonconformity to the Law being sinful. Paul was made aware of that fact when the commandment was applied to him in power—as the sun shining on a dung-heap draws forth its stench. Men may deny that the very *desire after* forbidden objects is culpable, but Scripture affirms that even imaginations are evil—the buds of wickedness, for they are contrary to that rectitude of heart which the Law requires. Note how that terrible list of things which Christ enumerated as issuing from the heart of fallen man is headed with "evil thoughts" (Matt. 15:19). We cannot conceive of any inclination or proneness unto sin in an absolutely holy being. Certainly there was none in the Lord Jesus: "the prince of this world cometh, and hath nothing in Me" (John 14:30)—nothing that was capable of responding to his vile solicitations, no movement of His appetites or affections of which he could take advantage. Christ was inclined only unto what is good.

"For when we were in the flesh [i.e. while Christians were in their unregenerate state], the motions of sins [literally, the affections of sin, or the beginnings of our passions], which were [aggravated] by the Law, did work in our members [the faculties of the soul as well as of the body] to bring forth fruit unto death" (Rom. 7:5). Those "affections of sin" are the filthy streams which issue from the polluted fountain of our hearts. They are the first stirrings of our fallen nature, which precede the overt acts of transgression. They are the unlawful movements of our lusts prior to the studied and deliberate thoughts of the mind after sin. "But sin [indwelling corruption], taking occasion by the commandment, wrought in me all manner of concupiscence" or "evil lustings" (Rom. 7:8). Note well that word "wrought in me": there was a polluted disposition or evil propensity at work, distinct from and the spring of the deeds which it produced. Indwelling sin is a powerful principle, constantly exercising a bad influence, stimulating unholy affections, stirring unto avarice, enmity, malice, etc.

So important do we deem what was touched upon at the close of our last chapter, and so little is the same apprehended and understood today, that we are here adding a few words thereon. The popular idea which now prevails is that nothing is sinful save an open and outward transgression, but such a concept falls far short of the searching and humbling teaching of Holy Writ. It affirms that the source of all temptation lies within fallen man himself. It is the depravity of his own heart which induces him to listen to the Devil or be influenced by the profligacy of others. If this were not so, then no external solicitations unto wrongdoing would have any force, for there would be nothing within him for them to excite, nothing to which those solicitations correspond or over which they could exert any power. An evil example would be rejected with abhorrence if we were pure within. There must be an unsatisfied lust to which temptation from without appeals. Where there is no desire for food, a well-spread table allures not. If there be no love of acquisition, gold cannot attract the heart. In every instance the force of temptation lies in some propensity of our fallen nature.

Herein lies the uniqueness of the Bible; to wit, its exalted spirituality, insisting that any inward bias, the least gravitation of the soul from God and His will, is sinful and culpable, whether or not it be carried out into action. It reveals that the first stirring of sin itself is to draw away the soul from what it ought to be fixed upon, by an irregular craving for some foreign object which appears delightful. When our native corruptions are invited by something external which promises pleasure or profit, and the passions are attracted by the same, then temptation begins, and the heart is drawn out after it. Since fallen man is influenced most by his lusts, they sway both his mind and his will. So powerful are they that they rule his whole soul:

hence it was that the Apostle said, "I see another law in my members" (Rom. 7:23), for it is imperious, dominating the entire man. It is because their lusts are so violent that men are so mad upon sinning: "they weary themselves to commit iniquity" (Jer. 9:5). James 1:14, 15, traces out the origin of all our sinning, and to it we now turn.

"But every man is tempted, when he is drawn away of his own lust, and enticed. Then when lust hath conceived, it bringeth forth sin:

and sin, when it is finished, bringeth forth death." Those words show that sin encroaches upon the spirit by degrees, and describe the several stages before it be consummated in the outward act. They reveal that the procreating cause of all sin lies in every man's soul, namely his lusts: that he has within himself both the food and fuel of it. Rightly did Goodwin declare, "You can never come to see how deeply and how abominably corrupt creatures you are, until God opens your eyes to see your lusts." The old man is "corrupt *according to* the deceitful lusts " (Eph. 4:22).

Lust is both the womb and the root of all wickedness which there is upon earth. Says the Apostle to God's people, "having escaped the corruption that is in the world through lust" (2 Peter 1:4). The corruption": that wasting and destroying blight which is upon all mankind. "Which is in the world": like poison in the cup, like dry rot in wood, like a pestilence in the air—inherent, ineradicable. It taints every part of man's being—physi- cal, mental and moral; and all his relations of life, whether in the family, society. or the State.

"Every man is tempted when he is drawn away of his own lust." When men are tempted they usually seek to cast the onus upon God, the Devil, or their fellows; whereas the blame rests entirely upon themselves. First, their affections are removed from what is good and they are incited unto wrongful conduct by their corrupt inclinations, being attracted to a bait which Satan or the world dangles before them. "Lust" here signifies a yearning for or longing to obtain something, and it is so strong as to draw the soul after a forbidden object. The Greek word for "drawn away" means forcibly impelled: the impetuous violence of the desire which covets some sensual or worldly thing demands gratification. This is nothing but a species of self-will, a hankering after what God has not bestowed, arising from discontent with our present condition or portion. Even though that longing be a fleeting and involuntary one, yea, against our best judgment, nevertheless it is sinful, and when allowed produces yet deeper guilt.

"And enticed." The drawing away is by the irregularity and vehemence of the craving, the enticement is from the object contemplated. But that very allurement is something for which we are to blame. It is because we fail to resist, abominate and reject the first rising of unlawful desire, and instead entertain and encourage it, that the bait appears so attractive. The temptation promises pleasure or profit, which is "the deceitfulness of sin" (Heb. 3:13) at work, which beguiles us. Then wickedness is sweet in our mouth, and we hide it under our tongue (Job 20:12). "Then when lust hath conceived": anticipated delight is cherished, and in view thereof the mind fully consents. The sinful deed is now present in embryo, and the thoughts are engaged in contriving ways and means of gratification. "It bringeth forth sin" by a decree of the will: what was previously contemplated is now actually perpetrated. Rightly did Manton say, "Sin knows no mother but our own heart." "And sin, when it is finished, bringeth forth death": it is paid its wages and made to reap what was sown, damnation being the ultimate outcome. Such is the progress of sin within us, and such its several degrees of enormity.

4. Corrupted conscience. If there be one faculty of man's soul more than any other which may be thought to have retained the original image of God upon it, it is surely the conscience. Such a view has indeed been widely held. So decidedly were they of this opinion that not a few of the most renowned philosophers and moralists have contended that conscience is nothing less than the Divine voice itself speaking in the innermost chamber of our being. But without in any way minimizing the great importance and value of this internal monitor, either in its office or in its operations, it must be emphatically declared that such theorists err, that even this faculty has not escaped from the common ruin of our entire beings. This is evident from the plain teaching of God's Word thereon. Scripture speaks of a "weak conscience" (1 Cor. 8:12), of men "having their conscience seared with a hot iron" (1 Tim. 4:2), and says that their "conscience is defiled" (Titus 1:15), that they have "an evil conscience" (Heb. 10:22). Demonstration thereof is made in what follows.

They who affirm that there is something essentially good in the natural man insist that his conscience is an enemy to evil and a friend to holiness. They point out and stress the fact that the conscience produces an inward conviction against wrongdoing, a strife in the heart over sin, with a reluctance to it. They call attention to Pharaoh's acknowledgment of sin (Exo. 10:16), and that Darius was "sorely displeased with himself" for his unjust act in condemning Daniel to be cast into the lions' den (6:14). Some have even gone so far as to affirm that the opposition to greater and grosser crimes which is found at first in all men differs little or nothing from that conflict between the flesh and the spirit described in Romans 7:21-23. But such a sophistry is easily refuted. In the first place, while it be true that fallen man possesses a general notion of right and wrong, and is able in some instances to distinguish between good and evil, yet while he remains unregenerate that moral instinct never causes him to delight cordially in the former or really to abhor the latter; and in whatever measure he may approve of good or disapprove of evil, it is from no consideration for *God* therein.

Conscience is only able to work according to the light it has, and since the natural man cannot discern spiritual things (1 Cor. 2:14), it is useless in respect to them. How feeble is its light! It is more like that of a glimmering candle than the rays of the sun—merely sufficient to make the darkness visible. Owing to the benighted condition of the understanding, the conscience is fearfully ignorant. When it does discover that which is inimical, it does so feebly and ineffectually. Instead of directing, it mostly confuses. How manifest is this in the case of the heathen! Conscience gives them a sense of guilt and then puts them upon practicing the most abominable and often inhuman rites. It has induced them to invent and propagate the most impious misrepresentations of Deity. As a salve to their conscience, they often make the very objects of their worship the precedents and patrons of their favourite vices. The fact is that conscience is so sadly defective that it is unable to perform its duty until God enlightens, awakens, and renews it.

The Doctrine of Human Depravity

Its *operations* are equally faulty. Not only is conscience defective in vision, but its voice is very weak. How strongly it ought to upbraid us for our shocking ingratitude unto our great Benefactor! How loudly it should inveigh against the stupid neglect of our spiritual interests and eternal welfare. Yet it does neither the one nor the other. Though it offers some checks upon outward and gross sins, it makes no resistance to the subtler and secret workings of indwelling corruption. If it prompts to the performance of duty, it ignores the most important and spiritual part of the same. It may be uneasy if we fail to spend the usual amount of time each day in private prayer, but it is little concerned about our reverence, humility, faith and fervour therein. Those in the Prophet's day were guilty of offering unto God defective sacrifices, yet conscience never troubled them over the same (Mal. 1:7, 8). Conscience may be very scrupulous in carrying out the precepts of men or our personal predilections, and yet utterly neglect those things which the Lord has commanded: as the Pharisees would not eat food while their hands remained ceremonially unwashed, yet disregarded what God had enjoined (Mark 7:6-9).

Conscience is woefully *partial*: disregarding favourite sins and excusing those which most easily beset us. All such attempts to extenuate our faults are founded upon ignorance of God, of ourselves, of our duty; otherwise, conscience would bring in the verdict of guilty. Conscience often joins with our lusts to encourage a wicked deed. Saul's told him that he ought not to offer sacrifice till Samuel came, yet to please the people and prevent them from deserting him he did so. And when that servant of God reproved him, the king sought to justify his offence by saying that the Philistines were gathered together against Israel, and that he dared not assail them before making supplication to God, and added: "I forced myself therefore, and offered a burnt offering" (1 Sam. 13:8-12). Conscience will strain to find some consideration which will appease itself and then approve of the evil act. Even when rebuking certain sins, it will find motives and discover inducements thereunto. Thus, when Herod was about to commit the dastardly murder of John the Baptist, which was against his convictions, his very conscience came to his aid, and urged him forward by impressing on him that he must not violate the oath which he had taken before others (Mark 6:26).

Conscience often ignores great sins while condoning lesser ones, as Saul was hard upon the Israelites for a breach of the ceremonial law (1 Sam. 14:33) but made no scruple of slaying eighty-five of the Lord's priests. Conscience will even devise arguments which favour—yea, which warrant—the most outrageous acts, and thus it is not only a corrupt lawyer pleading an ill cause, but a corrupt judge which justifies the wicked. Thus those who clamoured for the crucifixion of Christ did so under the pretext of its being orderly and necessary: "We have a law, and by our law He ought to die, because He made Himself the Son of God" (John 19:7). Little wonder that the Lord says of men that they "call evil good, and good evil; . . . put darkness for light, and light for darkness" (Isa. 5:20). Conscience never moves the natural man to perform duties out of gratitude and thankfulness to God. It never convicts him of the heavy guilt of Adam's offence which is lying upon his soul, nor of lack of faith in Christ: suffering sinners to sleep in peace in the midst of their awful unbelief. But theirs is not a sound and solid peace, for there is no reason or ground for it: rather is it the false security of stupidity. Says God of them, "They consider not in their hearts that I remember all their wickedness" (Hosea 7:2).

Its accusations are ineffectual, for they produce no good fruit, yielding neither meekness, humility, nor genuine repentance, but rather a sensible dread of God as a harsh Judge or hatred of Him as an inexorable Enemy. Not only are its accusations ineffectual, but often they are quite erroneous. Because of the darkness which is upon the understanding, the moral perception of the natural man greatly errs. As Thomas Boston said of the corrupt conscience, "So it is often found like a mad and furious horse, which violently runs down himself, his rider, and all that come in his way." A fearful example of that appears in our Lord's prediction in John 16:2, which received repeated fulfillment in the Acts: "They shall put you out of the synagogues: yea, the time cometh, that whosoever killeth you will think he doeth God service." In like manner Saul of Tarsus, after his conversion, acknowledged: "I verily thought within myself, that I ought to do many things contrary to the name of Jesus of Nazareth" (Acts 26:9). What a putting of "bitter for sweet and sweet for bitter" were those cases! A most unreliable guide is the unrenewed conscience.

Even when the conscience of the unregenerate is awakened by the immediate hand of God and is smitten with deep and painful convictions of sin, so far from its moving the soul to seek the mercy of God through the Mediator, it fills him with shuddering and dismay. As Job 6:4, declares, when the arrows of the Almighty are within him, the poison thereof drinks up his spirit, and the terrors of God set themselves in array against him. Hitherto such a one had gone to great pains to stifle the accusations of his inward judge, and now he would fain do so, but cannot. Instead, conscience rages and roars, putting the whole man in a dreadful consternation, as he is terrified by a sense of the wrath of a holy God and is fearful of the fiery indignation which shall devour His adversaries. This fills him with such horror and despair that instead of turning to the Lord he endeavours to flee from Him. Thus it was in the case of Judas, who, when he was made to realize the awful gravity of his vile deed, went out and hanged himself. That the ragings of sin within the natural man cause him to turn from, rather than unto Christ, was demonstrated by the Pharisees in John 8:9, who, "being convicted by their own conscience, went out one by one"!

5. *Disabled will.* We have left this until the last because the will is not the lord but the servant of the other faculties, executing the strongest conviction of the mind or the most imperious behest of our lusts, for there can be but one dominating influence in the will at one and the same time. The excellency of man's will consisted, originally, in following the guidance of right reason and submitting to the influence of proper authority. But in Eden man's will rejected the former, and rebelled against the latter, and in consequence of the Fall his will has ever since been under the control of an understanding which prefers darkness to light and of affections which crave evil rather than good. And thus it is that the fleeting pleasures of sense and the puny interests of time excite our wishes, while the lasting delights of godliness and the riches of immortality receive little or no attention. The will of the natural man is biased by his corruptions, for his inclinations gravitate in the opposite direction to his duty, and therefore he is in complete bondage to sin, impelled by his lusts. It is not merely that the unregenerate are unwilling to seek after holiness—they inveterately hate the same.

Since the will turned traitor to God and entered the service of Satan, it has been completely paralyzed unto good. Said the Saviour, "No man can come unto Me, except the Father which hath sent Me draw him" (John 6:44). And why is it that he cannot come to Christ by his own natural powers? Because not only has he no inclination to do so, but the Saviour is an object that repels him: His yoke is unwelcome, His sceptre repulsive. In connection with spiritual things the condition of the will is like that of the woman in Luke 13:11—she "was bowed together, and could in no wise lift up herself." If such be the case, then how can man be said to act voluntarily? Because he freely chooses the evil, and that because "the soul of the wicked *desireth* evil" (Prov. 21:10), ever carrying out that desire except when prevented by the Divine government. Man is the slave of his corruptions, born like a wild ass's colt: from earliest childhood he is averse to restraint. The will of man is uniformly rebellious Godward: when Providence thwarts his endeavours, instead of bowing in humble resignation, he frets with disquietude and acts like a wild bull in a net.

Only the Son can make him "free" (John 8:36), and there is "liberty" only where His Spirit is (2 Cor. 3:17).

Here, then, are the ramifications of human depravity. The Fall has blinded man's mind, hardened his heart, disordered his affections, corrupted his conscience, disabled his will, so that there is "*no* soundness" in him (Isa. 1:6), "no good thing" dwelling in his flesh (Rom. 7:18).

THE DOCTRINE OF HUMAN DEPRAVITY
Its Evidences

After the ground we have already covered, it might be thought there was no need for us to devote a separate section to the furnishing of proof that man is a fallen and depraved creature, one who has departed far from his Maker and rightful Lord. Though the Word of God needs no confirming by anything outside itself, it is not without value or interest to find that the teaching of Genesis 3 is substantiated by the hard facts of history and observation. And since there is no point on which the world is so dark as concerning its own darkness, we deem it requisite to make demonstration of the same. All men by nature, unrenewed in their minds by the saving operations of the Holy Spirit, are in a state of darkness with respect to any vital knowledge of God. Be they in other things ever so learned and skilful, in spiritual matters they are blind and stupid. But that is something which they cannot endure to hear about, and when it be pressed upon their notice their ire is at once aroused. The proud intellectuals who deem themselves so much wiser than the humble and simple believer, regard it as but an empty conceit of illiterates when told that "the way of peace they have not known." Such infatuated souls are quite ignorant of their very ignorance.

Even in Christendom the average churchgoer is fully satisfied if he learns by rote a few of the elementary principles of religion. By so doing he comforts himself that he is not an infidel, and since he believes there is a God (though it be one which his own imagination has devised) he plumes himself that he is far from being an atheist. Yet as to having any living, spiritual, influential and practical knowledge of the Lord and His ways he is quite a stranger, altogether unenlightened. Nor does he feel in the least need of Divine illumination; nay, he has no relish of or desire for a closer acquaintance with God. Never having realized himself to be a lost sinner, he has never sought the Saviour, for it is only those who are sensible of sickness who value a physician—as none but those who are conscious of soul starvation yearn for the Bread of Life. Men may proudly boast that this twentieth century is an age of enlightenment, but however that may be so in a material and mechanical sense it is certainly very far from being the case spiritually. It is often averred by those who ought to know better that men today are more eager in their quest for Truth than in former days, but hard facts give the lie to such an assertion.

In Job 12:24, 25, we are told concerning "the chief people of the earth" that "they grope in the dark without light." How evident that is unto those whose eyes have been anointed with the Holy Spirit, yea, even to natural men who have not been given up to a strong delusion that they should believe a lie. Who but those blinded by prejudice and incapable of perceiving what is right before them would still believe in "the progress of man" and "the steady advance of the human race"? And yet such postulates are made daily by those who are regarded as being the best educated and the greatest thinkers. One had supposed that the idle dreams of idealists and theorizers would have been dispelled by the happenings of the past thirty years, when hundreds of millions of earth's inhabitants were engaged in a life and death struggle, in which the most barbarous inhumanities were perpetrated, tens of thousands of peaceful citizens killed in their homes, hundreds of thousands more maimed for the rest of their days, and incalculable material damage wrought. But so persistent is error, so widely accepted is this chimera of "evolution," and so radically is it opposed to that which we are here contending for, that no efforts are to be spared in exposing the one and establishing the other. It is with the desire to do so that we now present some of the abundant evidence which testifies clearly to the utterly ruined condition of fallen mankind.

These proofs may be drawn from the teaching of Holy Writ, the records of human historians, our own observations, and personal experience. The third chapter of Genesis describes the origin of human depravity. In the very next chapter the bitter fruits of the Fall quickly begin to be manifested. In the former we behold sin in our first parents, in the latter sin in their firstborn, who very soon supplied proof of his having received an evil nature from them. In Genesis 3 the sin was against God, in Genesis 4 it was both against Him and against a fellow man. That is ever the order: where there is no fear of God before the eyes, there will be no genuine respect for the rights of our neighbours. Yet even at that early date we behold the sovereign and distinguishing grace of God at work, for it was by a God-given faith that Abel presented unto the Lord an acceptable sacrifice (Heb. 11:4), whereas it was in blatant self-will and self-pleasing that Cain brought the fruit of the ground as an offering. Upon the Lord's rejection thereof we are told, "And Cain was very wroth" (Gen. 4:5), being angry because he could not approach and worship God according to the dictates of his own mind, and thereby displayed his native enmity against Him. Jealous of God's approval of Abel, Cain rose up and murdered his brother.

Like leprosy, sin contaminates, spreads, and produces death. Near the close of Genesis 4 we see sin corrupting family life, for Lamech was guilty of polygamy, murder, and a spirit of fierce revenge (v. 23). In Genesis 5 death is written in capital letters over the inspired record, for no less than eight times do we there read "and he died." But again we are shown grace superabounding in the midst of abounding sin, for Enoch, the seventh from Adam, died not, being translated without seeing death. That much of his time was spent in expostulating with and warning the wicked of his day is intimated in Jude 14, 15, where we are told that he prophesied. "Behold. the Lord cometh with ten thousands of His saints, to execute judgment upon all, and to convince all that are ungodly among them of all their ungodly deeds which they have ungodly committed, and of all their hard speeches which ungodly sinners have spoken *against* Him." Noah too was "a preacher of righteousness" (2 Peter 2:5) unto the antediluvians, but seemingly with little effect, for we read, "And God saw that the wickedness of men was great in the earth, and every imagination of the thoughts of his heart was only evil continually," that "all flesh had corrupted his way upon the earth," and that the earth was "filled with violence through them" (Gen. 6:5, 12, 13).

But though God sent a flood which swept away the whole of that wicked generation, sin was not eradicated from human man: instead, fresh evidence of the depravity of man was soon forthcoming. After such a merciful deliverance from the deluge, after witnessing such a fearful demonstration of God's holy wrath against sin, and after the Lord's making a gracious covenant with Noah, which contained most blessed promises and assurances, one had supposed that the human race would ever after adhere to the ways of virtue. But alas, the very next thing that we read of is that, "Noah began to be an husbandman, and he planted a vineyard: and he drank, of the wine, and was drunken; and he was uncovered within his tent" (Gen. 9:20, 21). Scholars tell us that the Hebrew word for "uncovered" clearly indicates a deliberate act, and not a mere unconscious effect of drunkenness—the sins of intemperance and impurity are twin sisters. The sad lapse of Noah gave occasion to his son to sin, for, instead of throwing the mantle of charity over his parent's infirmity, he dishonoured his father, manifesting a total disrespect for and subjection to him. In consequence he brought down upon his descendants a curse, the effects and results of which are apparent to this very day (v. 25).

As we pointed out over thirty years ago in an article on the subject, Genesis 9 brings before us the inauguration of a new beginning, and a pondering of the same causes our minds to turn back to the first beginning of the human race. A careful comparison of the two reveals a series of most remarkable parallels between the histories of Adam and Noah. Adam was placed upon an earth which came up out of "the great deep" (Gen. 1:2), so also did Noah come forth on to an earth which had just emerged from the waters of the great deluge. Adam was made lord of creation (1:28), and into the hand of Noah God also delivered all things (9:2). Adam was "blessed" of God and told to "be fruitful. and multiply, and replenish the earth" (1:28), and in like manner Noah was blessed and told to "be fruitful, and multiply, and replenish the earth" (9:1). Adam was placed by God in a garden to "dress and keep it" (2:15), and Noah "began to be an husbandman, and he planted a vineyard" (9:20). It was in the garden that Adam transgressed and fell, and the product of the vineyard was the occasion of Noah's sad fall. The sin of Adam resulted in the exposure of his nakedness (3:7), and likewise we read that Noah "was uncovered within his tent" (9:21). Adam's sin brought down a terrible curse upon his posterity (Rom. 5:12), and so did Noah's (Gen. 9:24, 25). Immediately after the Fall of Adam a remarkable prophesy was given, containing in outline the history of redemption (3:15): and immediately after Noah's fall a remarkable prophecy was uttered, containing in outline the history of the great divisions of our race.

Genesis 9 and 11 take up the history of the postdiluvian earth. They show us something of the ways of men in this new world—revolting against God, seeking to glorify and deify themselves. They make known the carnal principles by which the world-system is now regulated. Since 10:8-12,. and 11:1-9 interrupt the course of the genealogies given there, they should be regarded as an important parenthesis: the former one explaining the latter. The first is concerned with Nimrod, and of him we learn that: 1. He was a descendant of Ham, through Cush (10:8), and therefore of that branch of Noah's family on which the curse rested. 2. Nimrod signifies "the rebel." 3. "He began to be a mighty one in the earth," which implies that he struggled for the pre-eminence and by force of will obtained it. 4. "In the earth" intimates conquest and subjugation, becoming a leader of and ruler over men. 5. He was a mighty hunter (10:9): three times over in Genesis 10 and again in 1 Chronicles 4:10, is the term "mighty" used of him—the Hebrew word also being tendered "chief" and "chieftain." 6. He was a mighty hunter *before the Lord*: compare that with "the earth also was corrupt before God" (6:11) and we get the impression that this proud rebel pursued his ambitious and impious designs in brazen defiance of the Almighty. 7. Nimrod was a king and had his headquarters in Babylon (10:10).

From the opening verses of Genesis 10 it is clear that Nimrod had an inordinate desire for fame, that he lusted after supreme dominion or the establishment of a world empire (10:10, 11), and that he headed a great confederacy in open rebellion against Jehovah. The very word "Babble" signifies "the gate of God," but afterwards, because of the Divine judgment inflicted on it, it came to mean "confusion." By putting together the different details supplied by the Spirit, there can be little doubt that Nimrod not only organized an imperial government, over which he presided as king, but that he also instituted a new and *idolatrous worship*. Though not mentioned by name in Genesis 11, it is evident from the foregoing chapter that he was the leader of the movement here described. The topographical reference in 11:2 is just as significant, morally, as is "going *down* into Egypt" and "*up* to Jerusalem": "they journeyed *from the east*" connotes that they turned their backs on the sunrise. God had commanded Noah to "multiply, and replenish the earth," but here we read: "And they said, Go to, let us build us a city and a tower, whose top may reach unto Heaven: and let us make us a name, *lest* we be scattered abroad upon the face of the whole earth" (11:4). That was directly contrary to God, and He at once intervened, brought to naught Nimrod's scheme, and "scattered them abroad upon the face of all the earth" (11:9).

At the Tower of Babel another crisis had arrived in the history of the human race. There mankind was again guilty of apostasy and declared defiance of the Most High. The Divine confounding of man's speech was the origin of the different nations of the earth, and after the overthrow of Nimrod's effort we get the formation of "the world" as it has existed ever since. This is confirmed in Romans 1, where the Apostle supplies proof of the guilt of the Gentiles. In verse 19 we read of "that which *may be* known of God"—through the display of His perfections in the works of creation. Verse 21 goes farther, and states, "when they *knew God* [i.e., in the days of Nimrod], they glorified Him not as God, neither were thankful; but became vain in their imaginations, and their foolish heart was darkened. Professing themselves to be wise, they became fools [in connection with the Tower of Babel], and changed the glory of the incorruptible God into an image made like to corruptible man." It was then that idolatry commenced. In what follows we are told three times over that "God gave them up" (vv. 24, 26, 28). It was then that He abandoned them and "suffered all nations to walk in their own ways" (Acts 14:16).

The next thing after that great crisis in human affairs recorded in Genesis 11 was the Divine call of Abraham, the father of the nation of Israel; but before turning to that, let us consider some of the effects of the former. The first of the Gentile nations about which Scripture has much to say are the Egyptians, and they made their depravity clear by ill-treating the Hebrews and defying the Lord. The seven nations which inhabited Canaan when Israel entered that land in the days of Joshua were devoted to the most horrible abominations and wickedness (Lev. 18:6-25; Deut. 9:5). The characters of the renowned empires of Babylon, Medo-Persia, Greece and Rome are intimated in Daniel 7:4-7, where they are likened to wild beasts. Outside the narrow bounds of Judaism the whole world was heathen, completely dominated by the Devil. Having turned their backs on Him who is light, they were in total spiritual darkness, given up to ignorance, superstition and vice. One and all sought their happiness in the pleasures of earth, according to their various desires and appetites. But whatever "happiness" was enjoyed by them, it was but an animal and fleeting one, utterly unworthy of creatures made for eternity. They were quite insensible of their real misery, poverty and blindness.

It is true that the arts were developed to a high degree by some of the ancients, and that there were famous sages among them, but the masses of the people were grossly materialistic, and their teachers propagated the wildest absurdities. They one and all denied a Divine creation of the world, holding for the most part that matter is eternal. Some believed there was no survival of the soul after death, others in the theory of transmigration—the souls of men passing into the bodies of animals. In short, "the world by wisdom knew not God" (1 Cor. 1:21), and where there be ignorance of Him there is always ignorance of ourselves. They realized not that they were victims of the great deceiver of souls, who blinds the minds of those who believe not. No nation of old was as highly educated as the Greeks, yet the private lives of her most eminent men were stained by the most revolting crimes. Those who had the ear of the public and talked most about setting men free from their passions, and were held in the highest esteem as the teachers of truth and virtue, were themselves the abject slaves of sin and Satan, and, morally speaking, society was rotten to the core.

The whole world festered in its corruption. Sensual indulgence was everywhere carried to its highest pitch, gluttony was an art, fornication was indulged in without restraint. The Prophet shows (Hosea 4) that where there is no knowledge of God in a land there is no mercy and truth among its inhabitants: instead, selfishness, oppression and persecution bear all down. There is scarcely a page in the annals of the world which does not furnish tragic illustrations of the greed and grind, the injustice and chicanery, the avarice and conscienceessness, the intemperance and immorality to which fallen human nature is so horribly prone. Oh, what a sad spectacle does history present of our race! Abundantly does it bear witness to the Divine declaration, "Surely men of low degree are vanity, and men of high degree are a lie: to be laid in the balance, they are altogether lighter than vanity" (Psa. 62:9). Modern infidels may paint a beautiful picture of the virtues of many of the heathen, and out of their hatred of Christianity exalt them to the highest seats of intellectual attainment and moral excellence, but the clear testimony of history definitely refutes them.

The earth has been made an Aceldama by its murders and fightings, deluging it with blood. "The dark places of the earth are full of the habitations of cruelty" (Psa. 74:20). In ancient Greece, parents were at liberty to expose their children to perish from cold and hunger, or to be eaten up by wild beasts; and though such exposures were frequently practiced they passed without punishment or censure. Wars were prosecuted with the utmost ferocity, and if any of the vanquished escaped death, lifelong slavery of the most abject kind was the only prospect before them. At Rome, which was then the metropolis of the world, the court of Caesar was steeped in licentiousness. To provide amusement for his senators six hundred gladiators fought a hand-to-hand conflict in the public theatre. Not to be outdone, Pompeii turned five hundred lions into the arena to engage an equal number of his braves, and "delicate ladies" sat applauding and gloating over the flow of blood. The aged and infirm were banished to an island in the Tiber. Almost two-thirds of the "civilized" world were slaves, their masters having absolute power over them. Human sacrifices were frequently offered on their temple altars. Destruction and misery were in their ways, and the way of peace they knew not (Rom. 3:16, 17).

The "Deists" of the seventeenth and eighteenth centuries dilated much upon the charming innocence of the tribes which dwelt in the sylvan bowers of primeval forests, untainted by the vice of civilization, unpolluted by modern commerce. But when the woods of America were entered by the white man, he found the Indians as ferocious and cruel as wild beasts, so that, as one expressed it, "The red tomahawk might have been emblazoned as the red man's coat of arms, and his eyes of glaring revenge regarded as the index of his character." When travelers penetrated into the interior of Africa, where it was hoped to find human nature in its primitive excellence, they found, instead, primitive devilry. Take the milder races. To look into the gentle face of the Hindu one would suppose him incapable of brutality and bestiality, but let the facts of the Sepoy rebellion of last century be read, and you will find the mercilessness of the tiger. So too of the placid Chinaman: the Boxer outbreak and atrocities at the beginning of this century witnessed similar inhumanities. If a new tribe were discovered, we should know it too must be depraved and vicious: simply to be informed that they were *men* would oblige us to conclude that they were "hateful, and hating one another."

The depravity of the Gentiles may not excite surprise, since their religions, instead of restraining it, furnished a stimulus to the most horrible vices, in the examples of their profligate gods. But were the Jews any better? In considering their case we shall not only turn from the general to the particular, but also have before us that people which was designed by God to be a *specimen* of human nature. The Divine Being singled out and separated them from all other nations: showered upon them His benefits, strengthened them with many encouragements, wrought miracles on their behalf, awed them with the most fearful threatenings, chastised them severely and frequently, and inspired His servants to give us an accurate account of their response. And what a wretched response it was! Excepting the conduct of a few individuals among them, which, being the effect of Divine grace, makes nothing against what we are here demonstrating—in fact only serves to intensify the sad contrast—the entire history of the Jews was nothing but a series of rebellions and continued departures from the living God. No other nation so highly favoured and richly blessed by Heaven, and none made such a wretched return unto the Divine goodness.

Provided with a Law which was drawn up and proclaimed by God Himself, which was enforced by the most winsome and also the most awesome sanctions, within a few days of its reception the whole nation was engaged in obscenely worshipping a golden calf. Unto them were vouchsafed the Divine oracles and ordinances, but they were neither appreciated nor heeded. In the wilderness they greatly provoked the Holy One by their murmurings, their lustings after the flesh-pots of Egypt when supplied with "angels' food" (Psa. 78:25), their prolonged idolatry, (Acts 7:42, 43), and their unbelief (Heb. 3:18). After they received for an inheritance the land of Canaan, they soon evinced their base ingratitude, so that the Lord had to say to His sorrowing servant, "they have not rejected thee, but they have rejected Me, that I should not reign over them" (1 Sam. 8:7). So averse were they to God and His ways that they hated, persecuted and slew the messengers which He sent to reclaim them from their wickedness. "They kept not the covenant of God, and *refused* to walk in His law" (Psa. 78:10). They declared, "I have loved strangers, and after them will I go" (Jer. 2:25).

After furnishing proof in Romans 1 of the total depravity of the Gentile world, the Apostle turned to the case of privileged Israel, and from their own Scriptures demonstrated that they were equally polluted, equally beneath the curse of God. Asking the question, "What then? are we better than they?" he answered, "No, in no wise: for we have before proved both Jews and Gentiles, that they are all under sin" (Rom. 3:9). So too in 1 Corinthians 1, where the utmost scorn is thrown upon that which is highly esteemed among men, the Jew is placed upon the same level as the Gentile. There we are shown how God views the arrogant pretensions of the intellectual of this world. When he asks "Where is the wise?" reference is made to the Grecian philosophers, who dignified themselves with that title. His very question is a pouring of contempt on their proud claims. With all your boasted knowledge, have you discovered the true and living God? They are challenged to come forth with their schemes of religion. After all that you have taught others, what have you accomplished? Have you found out the way to eternal felicity? Have you learned how guilty sinners may have access to a holy God? So far from being wise men, God declares that such sages as Pythagoras and Plato were fools.

Then Paul asks "where is the scribe?" (1 Cor. 1:20), who was the wise man, the esteemed teacher, among the Jews. He too was at just as great a distance from and just as ignorant of the true God. So far from possessing any true knowledge of Him, he was a bitter enemy to the same when it was proclaimed by His incarnate Son. Though the scribes enjoyed the inestimable advantage of possessing the Old Testament Scriptures, they were, in general, as ignorant of God's salvation as were the heathen philosophers. Instead of pointing to the death of the promised Messiah as the grand sacrifice for sin, they taught their disciples to depend upon the laws and ceremonies of Moses, and traditions of human invention. When Christ was manifested before them they were, therefore, so far from being the first to receive Him that they were His most bitter persecutors. Because He appeared before them in the form of a servant, that suited not their proud hearts. Though He was "full of grace and truth," they saw no beauty in Him that they should desire Him. Though He announced glad tidings, they refused to hearken thereto. When Christ performed miracles of mercy before them, they would not believe in Him. Though He sought only their good, they returned Him naught but evil. Their language was, "We will not have this man to reign over us" (Luke 19:14).

The general neglect and even contempt which the Lord Jesus met with among the people affords a very humbling view of what our fallen human nature is: but the awful depths of human depravity were the most plainly evidenced by the scribes and Pharisees, the priests and elders. Though well acquainted with the Prophets, and professing to wait for the Messiah, yet with desperate and merciless malignity they sought His destruction. The whole course of their conduct shows that they acted *against* their convictions that Jesus Christ was the Messiah: certainly they had full knowledge of His innocence of all which they charged against Him. This is evident from the plain intimation of the One who read their hearts, and who knew that they were saying within themselves. "This is the heir, come, let us kill him" (Matt. 21:38). They were as untiring as they were unscrupulous in their malice. They, or their agents, dogged His steps from place to place, hoping that in His more unguarded intercourse with His disciples they might more readily entrap Him, or find something in His words or actions which they could distort into a ground of accusation. They seized every opportunity to poison the minds of the public against Him, and, not content with ordinary aspersions of His character, gave it out that He was ministering under the immediate inspiration of Satan.

Whence did such wicked treatment of the Son of God proceed? Whence but from the vile corruptions of their own hearts? "They hated Me without a cause" (John 15:25), declared the Lord of Glory. There was nothing whatever in either His character or His conduct which merited their vile contempt and enmity. They loved the darkness, and therefore hated the light. They were infatuated by their evil lusts and delighted to gratify the same. So, too, with their deluded followers, who gave a ready ear to false prophets who said, "peace, peace" to them, flattered them, and encouraged them in their carnality. Consequently, they could not tolerate that which was disagreeable to their depraved tastes and condemned their sinful ways; and therefore did "the people" as well as their chief priests and rulers cry out, "Away with this man, and release unto us Barabbas" (Luke 23:18). After they had hounded Him to a criminal's death, their ill will pursued Him to the grave, for they came to Pilate and demanded that he secure His sepulchre. When their effort was proved to be in vain, the high Sanhedrin of Israel bribed the soldiers who had attempted to guard the tomb, and with premeditated deliberation put a fearful lie into their mouths (Matt. 28:11-15).

Nor did the enmity of Christ's enemies abate after He departed from this scene and returned to Heaven. When His ambassadors went forth to preach His Gospel, they were arrested and forbidden to teach in the name of Jesus, and then released under threat of punishment (Acts 4). Upon the Apostles' refusal to comply, they were again beaten (Acts 5:40). Stephen they stoned to death. James was beheaded, and many others were scattered abroad to escape persecution. Except where God was pleased to lay His restraining hand upon them, and those in whom He wrought a miracle of grace, Jews and Gentiles alike despised the Gospel and willfully opposed its progress. In some cases their hatred of the Truth was less openly displayed than in others, yet it was none the less real. It has been the same ever since. However earnestly and winsomely the Gospel be preached, it gains not those who hear it: for the most part they are like those of our Lord's day—they "made light of it, and went their ways, one to his farm, another to his merchandise" (Matt. 22:5). The great majority are too unconcerned to seek after even a doctrinal knowledge of the Truth. There are many who regard this sottishness of the unsaved as mere indifference, but actually it is something much worse than that, namely dislike of the heart for the things Of God, direct antagonism to Him.

Their hostility is made evident by the way in which they treat the people of God. The closer the believer walks with his Lord, the more will he be grate upon and be ill-treated by those who are strangers to Him. But "Blessed are they which are persecuted for righteousness' sake" (Matt. 5:10). As one pointed out, "It is a strong proof of human depravity that men's curses and Christ's blessings should meet on the same persons. Who would have thought a man could be persecuted and reviled, and have all manner of evil said of him for *righteousness*' sake?" But do the ungodly really hate justice and integrity, and love those who defraud and wrong them? No, they do not dislike righteousness as it respects *their own* interests, it is only that species of it which owns the rights of God. If the saints would be content with doing justly and loving mercy, and would cease walking humbly with God, they might go through the world not only in peace, but with the approbation of the unregenerate; but "all that will *live godly* in Christ Jesus shall suffer persecution" (2 Tim. 3:12), because such a life reproves the ungodliness of the wicked. If compassion moves the Christian to warn his sinful neighbours of their danger, he is likely to be insulted for his pains. His best actions will be ascribed to the worst motives. Yet, so far from being cast down by such treatment, the disciple should rejoice that he is counted worthy to suffer a little for his Master's sake.

The depravity of men appears in their disowning of the Divine Law set over them. It is the right of God to be the acknowledged Ruler of His creatures, yet they are never so well pleased as when they invade His prerogative, break His laws, and contradict His revealed will. How little is it realized that it is all the same to repudiate His sceptre and to repudiate His being: when we disown His authority we disown His Godhead. There is in the natural man an averseness to having any acquaintance with the rule under which his Maker has placed him: "Therefore they say unto God, Depart from us; for we desire not the knowledge of Thy ways. What is the Almighty, that we should serve Him? And what profit should we have, if we pray to Him?" (Job 21:14, 15). That is seen in their unwillingness to use the means for obtaining a knowledge of His will: however eager they be in their quest for all other kinds of knowledge, however diligent in studying the formation, constitution and ways of creatures, they refuse to acquaint themselves with their Creator. When made aware of some part of His will, they endeavour to shake it off: they do not "like to retain God in their knowledge" (Rom. 1:28). If they succeed not, they have no pleasure in the consideration of such knowledge, but do their utmost to dismiss it from their minds.

If there be a class of the unregenerate who are exceptions to the general rule, those who attend church, make a profession of religion, and become "Bible students," they are motivated by pride of intellect and reputation. They are ashamed to be regarded as spiritual ignoramuses, and desire to have a good standing in religious circles. Thereby they secure a cloak of respectability, and often the esteem of God's own people. Nevertheless, they are graceless. They "hold the truth in unrighteousness" (Rom. 1:18): *they* hold it, but it does not grip, influence and transform them. If they ponder it, it is not with delight; if they take pleasure therein, it is only because their store of information is increased and they are better equipped to hold their own in a discussion. Their design is to inform their understanding, not to quicken their affection. There is far more hypocrisy than sincerity within the pale of the Church. Judas was a follower of Christ because he "had the bag, and bare what was put therein" (John 12:6), and not out of any love for the Saviour. Some have the faith or truth of God "with respect of persons" (James 2:1): they receive it not from the Fountain, but from the channel, so that very often the same truth delivered by another is rejected, which, when coming from the mouth (and fancy) of their idol, is regarded as an oracle. That is to make man and not God their rule, for though it be the truth which is acknowledged, yet it is not received in the love of the truth, but rather as what is given out by an admired instrument.

The depravity of human nature is seen in the sad and general *reversion to darkness* of a people after being favoured with the light. Even where God has been made known and His truth proclaimed, if He leaves men to the working of their evil hearts, they quickly fall back into a state of ignorance. Noah and his sons lived for centuries after the flood to acquaint the world with the perfections of God, yet all knowledge of Him soon disappeared—Abram and his father were idolaters (Josh. 24:2). Even after a man has experienced the new birth and become the subject of immediate Divine influence, how much ignorance and error, imperfection and impropriety still remains!—just because he is not completely subject unto the Lord. The backslidings and partial apostasies of genuine Christians are an awful demonstration of the corruption of human nature. Our proneness to fall into error after Divine enlightenment is solemnly illustrated by the Galatians. They had been instructed by Paul, and through the power of the Spirit had believed in the Saviour he proclaimed. So rejoiced were they that they received him "as an angel of God" (4:14); yet in the course of a few years many of those converts gave such ear to false teachers, and so far renounced their principles, that the Apostle had to say of them, "I stand in doubt of you" (4:20). Look at Europe, Asia, Africa, after the preaching of the Apostles and those who immediately followed them. Though the light of Christianity illuminated most sections of the Roman empire, it was speedily quenched, and gave place to the darkness. The greater part of the world fell victim to Roman Catholicism and Mohammedanism.

Nothing more forcibly exhibits the sinfulness of man than his *proneness to idolatry*: no other sin so strongly denounced or so severely punished by God. Idols are but the work of men's hands, and therefore inferior to themselves: how irrational then to *worship them*! Can human madness go farther than for men to imagine they can manufacture gods? Those who have sunk so low as to confide in a block of wood or stone have reached the extreme of idiocy. As Psalm 115 points out, "they have mouths, but they speak not: eyes have they, but they see not . . . They that make them are like unto them"— as stupid, as incapable of hearing and seeing those things which belong to their salvation. Romanists and their imitators are no better than the Bible-less heathen, for they pervert the spirituality and simplicity of Divine worship by childish performances. God requires the worship of the soul, and they offer Him that of the body. He asks for the heart, they give Him the lips. He demands the homage of the understanding, and they mock Him with altars and crucifixes, candles and incense, gorgeous vestments and genuflections.

The corruption of human nature discovers itself in *little children.* As our fathers were wont to say, "That which is bred in the bone comes out in the flesh." And at what an early date does it do so! If there were any innate goodness in man, it would surely show itself during the days of his infancy, before virtuous principles were corrupted, and evil habits formed by his contact with the world. But do we find infants inclined to all that is pure and excellent, and disinclined to whatever be wrong? Are they meek, tractable, yielding readily to authority? Are they unselfish, magnanimous when another child seizes their toy? Far from it. The unvarying result of growth in human beings is that as soon as they be old enough to exhibit any moral qualities in human action they display *evil ones.* Long before they are old enough to understand their own wicked tempers, they manifest self-will, greediness, deceitfulness, anger, spite and revenge. They cry and fret for what is not good for them, and are indignant with their elders on being refused, often attempting to strike them. Those born and brought up in the midst of honesty are guilty of petty pilfering before ever they witness an act of theft. These blemishes are not to be ascribed to ignorance, but to their variance with the Divine Law—to which man's nature was originally conformed—to that horrible change which sin has wrought in the human constitution. Human nature is seen to be tainted from the beginning of its existence.

The universal prevalence of *disease and death* witnesses unmistakably to the Fall of man. *All* the pains and disorders of our bodies, whereby our health is impaired and our passage through this world rendered uneasy, are the consequences of our apostasy from God. The Saviour made plain intimation that sickness is the effect of sin when He healed the man with the palsy, saying, "Thy sins be forgiven thee" (Matt. 9:2); as the Psalmist also linked together God's pardoning the iniquities of His people and healing their diseases (103:3). "There is one event that happeneth to all." Yes, but why should it? Why should there be wasting away and then dissolution? Philosophy offers no explanation. Science can furnish no satisfactory answer, for to say that disease results from the decay of nature only pushes the inquiry farther back. Disease and death are *abnormalities*. Man is created by the eternal God, endowed with a never-dying soul; why, then, should he not continue to live here forever? The answer is, Because of the Fall: death is the wages of sin.

Man's ingratitude unto his gracious Benefactor is yet another evidence of his sad condition. The Israelites were a woeful sample of all mankind in this respect. Though the Lord delivered them from the house of bondage, miraculously conducted them through the Red Sea, led them safely across the wilderness, they appreciated it not. Though He screened them with a cloud from the heat of the sun, gave them light by night in a pillar of fire, fed them with bread from Heaven, caused streams to flow in the sandy desert, and brought them into the possession of a land flowing with milk and honey, they were continually murmuring and repining. And *we* are no better. The mercies of God are received as a matter of course. The hand that so bountifully ministers to their needs is not acknowledged or even recognized by men. None is satisfied with the place and portion Providence has assigned him: he is ever coveting what he has not. He is a creature given to changes: stricken with a malady which Solomon termed "the wandering of the desires" (Eccl. 6: 9).

"Every dog that snaps at me, every horse that lifts up its heel against me, proves that I am a fallen creature. The brute creation had no enmity against man before the Fall. Creation rendered a willing homage to Adam (Gen. 2:19). Eve no more dreaded the serpent than we would a fly. But when man shook off allegiance from his God, the beasts by Divine permission shook off allegiance from man" (J. Berridge, *The Christian World Unmasked*). What a proof of his degradation that the sluggard is exhorted to "go to the ant" and learn from a creature so much lower in the scale of being! Consider *the necessity* of human laws, fenced with punishments and terrors to restrain men's lusts: yet despite the vast and costly apparatus of police forces, law courts and prisons, what little success attends their efforts to repress human wickedness! Neither education, legislation nor religion is sufficient.

Finally, take the unvarying *experience of the saints*. It is part of the Spirit's office-work to open blind eyes, to discover unto souls their wretchedness, and make them sensible of their dire need of Christ. And when He thus brings a sinner to realize his ruined condition by imparting an experiential knowledge of sin, his comeliness is at once turned into corruption, and he cries, "Behold, I am vile." Though grace has entered his heart, his native depravity has not been expelled. Though sin no longer has dominion over him, it rages and often prevails against him. There is a ceaseless warfare within between the flesh and the spirit. There is no need for us to enlarge thereon, for every Christian groans within himself, and because of the plague of his heart cries, "O wretched man that I am." Wretched because he lives not as he earnestly longs to do, and because he does so often the very things he hates, groaning daily over evil imaginations, wandering thoughts, unbelief, pride, coldness, pretence.

THE DOCTRINE OF HUMAN DEPRAVITY
Its Corollaries

In the introductory chapter of this book we intimated that we should endeavour to show that our present subject is one of immense doctrinal importance and of great practical value. In view of all that has been advanced in our subsequent discussions, that fact should be clearly apparent. The teaching of Scripture thereon supplies us with a Divinely accurate diagnosis of man's present condition. It shows us, as nothing else can or does, why the entire course of human history has been what it is, and explains why all the remedial methods and measures of man's wit to effect any radical improvement in society are thorough failures. It accounts for the fact that man, in the twentieth century, is essentially the same as in the first, that the like moral features pertain to white and black, yellow and red races, that no change of environment or "living conditions" can transform a sinner into a saint—the removing of thistles and nettles from stony ground and transplanting them into the most fertile soil and lovely surroundings will not cause them to bear fragrant flowers or edible fruit. Human nature is fundamentally the same whether men live in mansions or hovels. Man does what he does because of what he is.

The deep importance of this doctrine of man's total depravity also appears in the close bearing which it has upon other aspects of the truth, and the light which it tends to cast upon them. Reject what is revealed in Genesis 3 and the remainder of the Bible becomes entirely meaningless; but accept what is there recorded and everything else becomes intelligible and is seen to be in its proper place. The whole scheme of redemption manifestly proceeds in view of the ruination of their race by our first parents: our defection in Adam and our recovery by Christ plainly stand or fall together. It is just because he is a sinner that man needs a Saviour, and being so great a sinner none but a Divine Saviour is sufficient for him. Since sin has corrupted the whole of his constitution, vitiating and debasing all his faculties, man is utterly incapable of doing anything to raise himself out of the horrible pit into which the Fall has plunged him: sooner will the Ethiopian change his skin or the leopard his spots than those who are at enmity with God evolve any love to Him or do that which is pleasing in his sight. If then such a one is to be made fit to dwell forever with the thrice Holy One, then obviously a miracle of grace must be wrought in him.

Equally real and great is the practical value of this doctrine. Nothing else is so well calculated to humble the proud heart of the creature and bring him into the dust before his Maker, crying "Behold, I am vile." Nothing else is so well calculated to demonstrate the utter futility of the sinner's attempting to appease God and obtain His approbation by any efforts of his own, or to gain an acceptance with Him by his own performances: as well might a murderer standing in the dock seek to win the judge's favour by means of his smiles and flatteries. Nothing is so well calculated to convince us that, since our hearts be rotten to the core, our very righteousnesses are as filthy rags. And nothing else will so deeply impress upon the heart of a believer his entire dependence upon the Lord as a feeling sense of what he is by nature: that God must work in him both to will and to do of His good pleasure if ever he is to perform His bidding, that nothing but daily supplies of grace can preserve him in the narrow and upward way. But let us now proceed to particularize what has just been summarized.

Since the entire being of the natural man be under the dominion of sin, it follows that *his will is in bondage thereto*. Anyone who denies that fact evinces that he does not understand or believe in the total depravity of man, for in effect he is asserting that one of the most important of his faculties has not been debased by the Fall. But as the whole of man's body is corrupt, so his entire soul is inclined unto evil only, and so long as he remains in the state of nature his will is in captivity thereto. The power of the will can only extend itself to things within its own province and cannot act above it—all actions and powers of action are limited by the nature and capacity of their agent. As creatures below man cannot put forth a rational act, neither can those who lack a holy principle (which all do till born again) put forth any spiritual action. Before Divine grace works upon and within the heart, man's will is enslaved by sin, he is "in the bond of iniquity" (Acts 8:23), the servant of those lusts and pleasures which he chooses and delights in. Christ must make us free (John 8:36) before there is or can be any deliverance from our moral captivity.

The Lord Jesus declared, "Whosoever committeth sin is the servant ["bondman of sin"] (John 8:34)—sin is his master, ordering all his actions. Nevertheless, he voluntarily assents thereto: that is why it is termed "the will of *the flesh*" (John 1:13), for it is defiled. It is "without strength" (Rom. 5:6) unto that which is good. Since the tree itself be corrupt, no good fruit will be borne by it. Romans 8:7 not only declares that the carnal mind is enmity against God and that it is not subject to the Law of God, but adds, "neither indeed can be," which would not be the case were the will of fallen man free, or had power unto good. Even when the understanding is convinced and sees the Truth, the will obstinately opposes and rejects it. Rightly did G. H. Bishop (of the Dutch Reformed Church) say, "Man can no more turn to God than the dead can sit up in their coffins. He can no more originate a right desire than he can create a universe. God the Holy Spirit alone, by sovereign, special interference, calls dead sinners to life and creates within them 'the desires of their hearts'—the first faint fluttering of a breath toward holiness."

Some may reply, But my own experience refutes what you have said. I am clearly conscious of the fact that my will accepted the offer of the Gospel, that I freely came to Christ as a lost sinner and accepted Him as my own Saviour. Fully admitting that, if you go a little *further back*, you will find that your very experience confirms what we have written above. Previous to conversion, your will was opposed to God, and you refused to come to Christ. Though the time arrived when that was reversed, *who* produced or caused that change—you or God? In every conscious act he performs, man necessarily wills. In repenting he wills, in believing he wills: in turning from his evil ways and in turning unto God in Christ he wills. But does the sinner make himself willing, or does God? The question at issue is, Does salvation begin by self-movement or Divine? Scripture is plain on the matter. God alters the bent or bias of the will, by communicating a principle of grace and holiness. A supreme will overcomes man's. He who said "Let there be light: and there was light" (Gen. 1:3) says, Let rebellion and opposition cease, and it does so. "So then it is not of him that willeth [originally], nor of him that runneth, but of God that showeth mercy" (Rom. 9:16). As He loved us before we loved Him, so His will goes before ours in conversion.

Because the natural man is dead in trespasses and sins, *he is quite insensible of his wretched plight*. This is indeed one of the most terrible elements in the fatal malady which has smitten him: that he is so morally paralyzed as to be quite unaware of his desperate state. At this juncture it is necessary to point out that there is a difference between being totally ignorant of our condition and being quite insensible thereof. The unregenerate may acquire a theoretical knowledge of man's total depravity, yet they are still without any feeling sense of the same. They may hold the theological belief that sin is the transgression of the Divine Law, but they have no inward horror and anguish over their vileness. That deadly insensibility is in all sinners, and at all times. Their natural emotions may be stirred as they listen to a portrayal of the sufferings of Christ on the Cross—like they shed tears over some particularly touching incident recorded in the newspapers, or a pathetic episode acted on the stage—but they weep not over their awful enmity against God, nor mourn because of their contrariety to His holiness. They are quite incapable of so doing, for they have a *stony heart* (Ezek. 36:26) Godward, and realize not that His wrath abides upon them.

This it is which explains why sinners generally are so secure and happy. It has always appeared strange, as well as grievous, to the saints to see the ungodly so unconcerned and light-hearted, though under sentence of death. Job understood not how the wicked could "take the timbrel and harp, and rejoice at the sound of the organ," spending "their days in mirth, and in a moment go down to the grave" (21:12, 13, margin). The Psalmist was perplexed when he "saw the prosperity of the wicked" and observed that they were "not in [soul] trouble as other men" (73:3, 5). Amos was astonished at the sinners in Zion, who "put far away the evil day," and who lay "upon beds of ivory . . . eat the lambs out of the flock . . . invent to themselves instruments of music . . . drink wine in bowls, and anoint themselves with the chief ointments" (6:3-6), but were thoroughly unconcerned about their souls. Though natural men differ from one another in so many respects, in *this* they are very much alike: they generally live as though there be no God to whom they must yet render an account, and who will pass sentence of eternal damnation upon them. Such stupidity in rational and immortal creatures can be explained only on the ground of their insensibility. They have eyes, but see not; ears, but hear not; hearts, but perceive not. Thus it is not at all strange that those who neither discern nor *feel* their danger should *fear* none.

Those who deny the moral insensibility of sinners are but proclaiming their own insensibility, for they repudiate not only what Scripture maintains, but that which universal observation confirms. Nothing but their crass stupidity can account for the conduct of the great majority of mankind, who are saying peace and safety while exposed to instant and eternal destruction. They are completely unconcerned that their hearts are desperately wicked, their understandings darkened, and their wills in bondage to evil. They are unaware of Satan's malignant dominion over them, and know not that he is perpetually causing them to sin. The Devil employs a multitude of devices to ensnare them. He knows how to take full advantage of their sottishness, yet though they be led captive by him from day to day they perceive not his wiles and influence. Even though they recognize the objects which he employs to seduce them, they realize not his seducing power. They are ignorant that they are continually walking in the paths of the destroyer, who is leading them blindfold to Hell. They know not, or if they do they care not, that the friendship of the world is enmity with God, and that to follow a multitude to do evil is the direct road to endless woe. Hence it is that they are not sensible of stumbling at one another. They are united in their disaffection to God, and in their love of sin. They join hand in hand: all lead, and are led.

Their very numbers inspire them with courage and resolution, and encourage them to walk together in the path of ruin.

In view of all that has been advanced, it is crystal clear that *fallen man is in a lost and perishing condition.* He is obnoxious to God: alienated from His life (Eph. 4:18), cast out of His favour (Gen. 3:24), cut off from communion with Him (Eph. 2:12). He is given up to the Devil, to be led captive by him as he pleases. He is dead in trespasses and sins, and that means (among other things) that he is utterly powerless where spiritual things be concerned, quite unable to do anything in regard of them: yet he is powerful with respect to that which is carnal and devilish. Entirely averse to all that is good and holy, his will desperately set against the Truth; but prone to and in love with whatever be sinful and evil. Lying in a horrible pit of corruption, unable to break the cords of sin which hold him fast, so infatuated with his iniquities as to regard them as his benefactors (Hosea 2:5, 12). His heart is so calloused that the mercies of God melt him not, nor do His threatenings and judgments awe him. Instead of the Divine goodness leading him to repentance, it leads him to deeper impenitence, unbelief and presumption, for since he sees the sun shining and the rain falling on the evil and on the good and God suffering all things to come alike to the one as to the other, he concludes that He will treat them all alike in the next world.

Man's plight is very much worse than is generally recognized, even in those sections of Christendom which are still regarded as being orthodox. Quite recently we read a piece entitled "Individual Salvation" wherein things were thus presented. "Imagine a situation in which an island is affected by some calamity, say a raging fire, and that the only escape is by means of a bridge to the mainland. The bridge is swiftly erected. Once erected it offers the possibility of escape, of salvation, for the entire island—but only a possibility. The concrete realization of the possibility is a matter for each individual man, woman, and child. The bridge does not offer automatic salvation, but simply the opportunity. If some individual citizen deems that the fire will die down, and that he proposes to remain in the conflagration, the possibility of escape by the bridge is nullified. It is true that he can be carried by force over the bridge to safety. But God does not effect the soul's salvation by compulsion. Unless the individual wills acceptance he perishes." Then, after quoting John 3:16, the writer added, "The individual must himself decide to cross the bridge."

How far below the desperateness of the sinner's case and situation does such an illustration fall! It ignores the fact that sin has such a stupefying effect upon the whole soul of the natural man that he is oblivious to his peril and insensible of his dire need. It loses sight of the fact that the sinner is not only in gross darkness, but has no *desire* to be enlightened: that he is stricken with a deadly malady, and is quite *unwilling* to be healed. He is highly displeased if someone tells him of his awful danger, resenting anything which disturbs his false peace and comfort. Sinners could not bear to hear the plain preaching of either God's Prophets or His incarnate Son: they stoned the former and crucified the latter. So it is now: they refuse to give a hearing unto one who declares them to be *totally depraved*. Even though mentally convinced of the urgency of his situation, the sinner has no eyes to see "the bridge," and if another offered to lead him it would be of no avail, for he is "without strength." True, God does not effect the soul's "salvation by compulsion," but He *does by* a miracle of grace: making His people willing in the day of His power (Psa. 110:3), imparting life, light and strength to them.

Since man be totally depraved, how *great is his need of salvation!* The guilt of Adam's transgression is charged to his account, the polluted nature of our first parents transmitted to him, he is shapen in iniquity, conceived in sin, and enters this world a child of wrath, estranged from God from his mother's womb (Psa. 58:3). Born with a heart that is deceitful above all things and desperately wicked, from earliest childhood he pursues a course of self-will and self-pleasing, treasuring up to himself wrath against the day of wrath. His iniquities are more in number than the hairs of his head (Psa. 40:12) and his "trespass" [or "guiltiness"] is grown up unto the heavens" (Ezra 9:6). He lies beneath the death sentence of the Law, and that curse cannot be removed until full satisfaction has been rendered to it, and such satisfaction the guilty culprit is utterly powerless to render. Nor can any of his fellows, no, not his nearest and dearest relatives, discharge his incalculable debt. "None of them can by any means redeem his brother, nor give to God a ransom for him: for the redemption of their soul is precious" (Psa. 49:7, 8), or "costly" as the same word is rendered in 1 Kings 8: 9, 10. And the sinner is a moral bankrupt, with no good thing to his credit, without a penny to discharge his liabilities.

Manifest it is that such a one is utterly unfit for Heaven, and even if he were permitted to enter it he would at once desire to depart therefrom, for he would be entirely out of his element, having nothing whatever in common with the ineffable holiness of its atmosphere and society. Not only so, he is already ripe for Hell, fit only for the company of the damned. Thus the natural man is in a perishing condition. Not only does he need delivering from the curse of the Law, the wrath of God, and the captivity of the Devil, but he requires *saving from himself*: from the guilt, the dominion and the pollution of his sins. He needs to be saved from his hard, impenitent and unbelieving heart, from his love of the world, from his self-righteousness. Divine justice requires not only that he be clear of any accusation the Law can bring against him, but that he possess a perfect obedience which constitutes him righteous before the Law, and thus has a title to the reward of endless felicity. But his righteousnesses are as filthy rags, and the wearer of them a moral leper. His plight is desperate beyond the power of words to express: there is but a step betwixt him and death, and beyond that lies "the blackness of darkness forever" (Jude 13).

It is equally evident that the lost sinner is *incapable of contributing anything toward his salvation*. Can a foul and filthy fountain send forth clean and pure waters? Neither can a polluted creature offer anything which is acceptable unto the Holy One. "The sacrifice of the wicked is an abomination to the LORD" (Prov. 15:8), as He made clear at the beginning, when He had not respect unto Cain and his offering. Instead of a pleasing service to God, it is an insulting provocation, for it lacks that principle without which it is impossible to please Him. The supplications of the unregenerate are rejected by Him. "And when ye spread forth your hands, I will hide Mine eyes from you: yea, when ye make many prayers, I will not hear" (Isa. 1:15). And why? Because such "praying" is the howling of those in pain (Hosea 7:14) rather than the breathings of loving devotion. Or it can be likened to the wishing and cravings of those who would have their lusts gratified (James 4:3) rather than their souls ministered unto; or bold presumptions for things unwarranted by the Divine promises—they would have mercy without holiness, sins forgiven without forsaking them: or but the perfunctory exercises of those who have a form of godliness but are strangers to its power. Likewise are their fastings rejected (Isa. 58:3-7).

"We can no more be voluntarily serviceable to God while our serpentine nature and devilish habits remain in us, than we can suppose that the Devil can be willing to glorify God while the nature he contracted by his fall works powerfully in him. Our nature and will must be changed, that our actions may regard God as our end, that we may delightfully meditate on Him, and draw the motives of our obedience from love" (Charnock). The imperative necessity of that radical change in the soul, a change so great and complete as to be like unto a second birth, was expressed by Christ when He declared, "Ye must be born again," having prefaced the same by stating "Except a man be born again, he cannot see the kingdom of God . . . Except a man be born of water and of the Spirit, he cannot enter into the kingdom of God" (John 3:3, 5, 7). There must be a spiritual and supernatural principle in us before we can live a spiritual and supernatural life. The new birth is indispensable, yet what can one who is dead in sin do to effect it? As Nicodemus asked, "How can a man be born when he is old?" "Ye must be born again" at once reveals the utter futility of all self-effort. Such a demand withers all fleshly pretensions and bars the gates of Heaven against all the unregenerate. It is designed to crush pride and make man realize his helplessness.

As the sinner cannot regenerate himself, neither can he produce any evangelical repentance, for "godly sorrow worketh repentance" (2 Cor. 7:10), and of godliness he has not a spark. Until he be born again he can neither hate sin nor abhor himself. Nor is he capable of exercising faith: how can he confide in One to whom he is a total stranger, trust in One whom he regards as his enemy, love One with whom he is at enmity? The obstacles in the way to salvation are absolutely insurmountable by any efforts of the sinner. He might as easily turn back the tide as deliver his soul. That solemn fact was shown by Christ when in answer to His disciples' question, "who then can be saved?" He averred, "with men this is *impossible*" (Matt. 19:26). What a shattering word was that to all creature sufficiency! How it should bring the sinner to despair of saving himself!

Since man be totally depraved it necessarily follows that if ever he is to be saved it can be only *by Divine grace and power*. Grace is a truth which is peculiar to Divine revelation. It is a concept to which the unaided powers of the human mind can never reach. Proof of that is found in the fact that where the Bible has not gone it is quite unknown. But not only is grace taught in God's Word, it is given great prominence there. Holy Writ declares that salvation is by grace from first to last: it issued from grace, it is received by grace, it is maintained by grace, it is perfected by grace. Divine grace is bestowed upon those who have no merits, and from whom no recompense is demanded; nay, more, it is given to those who are full of demerit and ill-desert. How thoroughly grace sets aside every thought of worthiness in its object is evident from a single quotation: "being justified *freely* by His grace" (Rom. 3:24). The Greek word is yet more impressive and emphatic, and might be rendered "gratuitously," "for nothing," the same term being translated "for naught" in 2 Thessalonians 3:8 and "without a cause" in John 15:25, there being nothing whatever in the beneficiary to attract it, but rather everything to repel it. "None eye pitied thee . . . to have compassion upon thee . . . when I passed by thee and saw thee polluted in thy blood, I said unto thee . . . Live" (Ezek. 16:5, 6).

Divine grace is the sinner's only hope, for it is not searching for good men whom it may approve, but the guilty and lost whom it may save. It comes not to those who have done their best and are quite presentable, but rather to those who have done their worst, and are in rags and tatters. Grace ever draws near to the sinner with his condition fully exposed. Grace recognizes no distinctions either social or moral: the chaste virgin is on the same level as the confirmed harlot, the religious professor with the wildest profligate. Grace is God's provision for those who are so corrupt that they cannot better their conduct, so averse to God that they cannot turn to Him, so dead that He must open their graves and bring them on to resurrection ground. Unless men be saved by grace, they cannot be saved at all. Equally true is it that the salvation of sinners must be by Divine power. Their crass stupidity and insensibility is irremovable by any human means. Nothing but God's might can dispel the darkness from their minds, take away their hearts of stone, or free their sin-enslaved wills. All the faculties of the natural man are opposed to the offers and operations of Divine grace until Divine power saves him from himself. None ever yet turned unto God but who was turned by Him.

From all that has been before us it should be quite apparent that the *sinner lies entirely at God's disposal*. If He sees fit to leave him in his sins, he is undone forever: yet God has a perfect right so to do. Had He precipitated the whole race to Hell, as He did the fallen angels the day they sinned, it would have been no excess of severity but simply an act of justice, for they deserved eternal damnation. In its ultimate analysis salvation is a matter of God's choice and not of ours, for we are merely clay in His hands to be molded into a vessel of honour or dishonour entirely as He pleases (Rom. 9:21). Sinners are in the sovereign hand of God to save or to destroy them according to His own will. That is His Divine prerogative: "Therefore hath He mercy on whom He will have mercy, and whom He will He hardeneth" (Rom. 9:18); and so far from offering any apology, He bids us observe and ponder that solemn fact, saying, "See now that I, even I, am He, and there is no god with Me: I kill, and I make alive: I wound, and I heal: neither is there any that can deliver out of My hand" (Deut. 32:39). Such a One is not to be spoken lightly about, but held in the utmost awe.

In the very nature of the case, mercy is not something which can be claimed as a right—least of all from Him whom we have wronged far above all others: but lies entirely at the discretion of the one who is pleased to exercise it. "Because He is a sovereign God, infinitely happy in Himself without us, it is at His option to manifest mercy or not, to save or not, as much as it was His option to make man or not" (R. Erskine). "He doeth according to *His will* in the army of Heaven, and among the inhabitants of the earth: and none can stay His hand,

The Doctrine of Human Depravity

or say unto Him, What doest Thou?" (Dan. 4:35). Therefore He exercises sovereignty in the cause *why* He shows mercy, even because He "will show mercy": sovereign not only in the ones He saves, but in the time when, the instrument by whom, and the means by which He saves them. Such teaching alone accords to God His proper place, as it likewise cuts away all ground of creature merits and boasting of his free will; and at the same time deepens the wonderment and gratitude of the redeemed. God can never act unjustly, but, He can and does bestow His favours on whom He pleases, and in so doing exercises His high prerogative: "Is it not lawful for Me to do what I will with Mine own?" (Matt. 20:15).

The exemption of any sinner from the everlasting burning is an act of sovereign mercy and free grace, and therefore God consults none but exercises His own mere good pleasure as to those on whom He bestows the same. "Many widows were in Israel in the days of Elias . . . when great famine was throughout all the land, but unto none of them was Elias sent, save unto Sarepta a city of Sidon, unto a woman that was a widow. And many lepers were in Israel in the time of Eliseus the prophet: and none of them was cleansed, saving Naaman the Syrian" (Luke 4:25-27). If some are brought to believe in Christ, while others are left in their unbelief, it is sovereign grace alone which makes the one to differ from the other. And if it be right for God to make such a difference in time, it could not be wrong for Him to purpose doing so from eternity. They who balk at sovereign and unconditional election believe in neither the total depravity of man nor the God of the Bible. One the one hand, He hides these things from those who are wise and prudent in their own conceits; on the other, He reveals them to babes (Matt. 11:25). There cannot be an election without a rejection: "the one shall be taken, and the other left" (Matt. 24:40, 41): "the election hath obtained it, and the rest were blinded" (Rom. 11:7); "Jacob have I loved, but Esau have I hated" (9:13).

Inasmuch as the sinner's will is enslaved by sin, then God *must overcome his opposition* before he will submit to Him. But both Scripture and observation make it evident that He does not bring all rebels into subjection, but only a favoured few. As Psalm 110:3 declares, "Thy people shall be willing in the day of Thy power." Though "by nature the children of wrath, even as others" (Eph. 2:3), equally depraved and guilty; yet even in their unregenerate state "God's people." They are His by sovereign election, His by eternal decree, His by covenant relationship. He loved them with an everlasting love (Jer. 31:3), chose them in Christ before the foundation of the world (Eph. 1:4), predestinated them to be conformed to the image of His Son (Rom. 8:29). Accordingly, in the day of His power, He quickens them into newness of life, puts the soul into a condition to receive the Truth and cordially embrace it. That putting forth of Divine power upon and within the vessels of mercy takes place at a definite season, for there is a "set time" for God to show favour unto the members of Zion (Psa. 102:13). As the length of Israel's captivity in Babylon was so Divinely fixed that none could any longer detain them when that time had expired, likewise must His elect be delivered from their bondage to sin and Satan when the appointed moment arrives. He who ordered the day of our birth and death (Eccl. 3:2) does not leave us to decide the day of our conversion—still less whether we shall be converted or not.

"Thy people shall be willing" unto whom? To do what? Willing unto that to which previously they were completely averse. Willing to submit their intellect wholly to God's Word, so that they receive with childlike simplicity all that is revealed therein. Willing to lean no more unto their own understanding, but to accept without question the mysteries of the Faith. High imaginations and lofty reasonings against the knowledge of God are now cast down, and every thought brought into captivity to the obedience of Christ. Miracles which infidels scoff at, aspects of Truth which Arminians term contradictory, precepts which run counter to the lusts of the flesh, are meekly accepted. Willing to bow to God's way of salvation, so that they freely abandon their idols, renounce the world, repudiate all merits of their own, and come as empty-handed beggars, acknowledging themselves to be deserving only of Hell. Willing to receive Christ as Prophet to instruct, as Priest to atone for their sins, as King to rule over them. Willing to receive Him as their Lord, to take His yoke upon them, to follow the example He has left them. Willing to bear reproach for His sake, to be given the cold shoulder, to be hated and persecuted. Willing to be on the side of the minority, to be cast out of the synagogue if need be, to lay down their very lives rather than deny Him.

Obviously, a miracle of grace must be wrought within them before they will choose what is so contrary to fallen human nature. That wonderful change from unwillingness to willingness is not the result of creature effort, but of Divine operation; it is not of self-improvement, but the effect of God's work in the soul. Thus we read of "the exceeding greatness of His power to us-ward who believe, according to the working of His mighty power" (Eph. 1:19). That putting forth of His power does not violate man's constitution or responsibility. Instead of destroying the freedom of his will, it liberates it from its native bondage. God's people are not dragged to Christ, but "drawn" (John 6:44), and by "the bands of love" (Hosea

The Doctrine of Human Depravity

11:4). That acting of His power has reference to that blessed time when the effectual inworking of the Spirit delivers the soul from the dominion of sin and Satan, when the influences of grace prevail over the corruptions of the flesh, when the Lord opens the heart to receive His Word (Acts 15:14), when the affections are turned from the world to Christ, and the soul gladly gives up itself to Him. It is life-giving and liberating power which delivers from death in sin. It is the communicating of a new disposition which causes its recipient cordially to yield himself to God. It is convincing power which convicts the individual of his wickedness, wretchedness, and need. It is God working in him "both to will and to do of His good pleasure" (Phil. 2:13).

The Lord made the Egyptian jailer show kindness unto His servant. How? By giving "him favour in the sight of the keeper of the prison" (Gen. 39:21). When Saul had been anointed king as he returned to his home "there went with him a band of men." And who were they? Men "whose hearts God had touched" (1 Sam. 10:26). When the appointed time of Israel's captivity expired, "the Lord stirred up the spirit of Cyrus" to make a gracious decree inviting the Jews to return unto Jerusalem. But a small minority accepted. Who were they? And why did they act differently from their fellows? They were those "whose spirit God had raised, to go" (Ezra 1:1-5). In like manner, in the day of His power God gives the antitypical Joseph favour in the eyes of His people who formerly had seen no beauty in Him that they should desire Him. He touched their hearts, so that they willingly submit to follow the One whom He has anointed to be King over them. He raises up their spirit, which previously had been sunk in bondage, so that now they desire a better country (Heb. 11:16). Unless He did so none would be saved: "except the Lord of Saboath had left us a seed, we had been as Sodoma" (Rom. 9:29). It is by their willingness to deny self, take up their cross and follow Christ that God's people are distinguished from the children of the Devil. As the Christian looks back to the time of God's power, he sings:

> "O happy day that fixed my choice
> On Thee, my Saviour and my God!
> Well may this glowing heart rejoice,
> And tell its raptures all abroad.
> 'Tis done, the great transaction's done,
> I am my Lord's, and He is mine;
> He drew me, and I followed on.
> Charmed to confess His voice Divine."

The vile condition of mankind *heightens the marvel of Christ's mediation.* It was by no means incumbent upon God to recover those who had turned their backs upon Him. As He was not obliged to prevent their defection, neither was He obliged to restore any of those who had revolted. When He permitted the whole human race to offend in Adam, it had been no undue severity on His part had He left them to be buried in the ruins of their Fall, and to sink utterly beneath the weight of their iniquities. He might well have reserved all in those chains which they fully deserved, and left them to feed upon the fruits of their evil doings, without lifting a finger for their deliverance. Nay, to go farther back: as God might forever have left men in their nothingness without bringing them into being, so He could have left them all in their contracted misery. There was no more reason why the Lord should save any of Adam's posterity than there was for Him to bring back the fallen angels to their original obedience and bliss. The blessedness of God Himself had no more been infringed by the eternal destruction of our entire race than it was by the everlasting ruin of devils. It was wholly at His own option whether He provided a Saviour or withheld Him.

There was no reason why God should not have abandoned all mankind. He certainly was not bound in justice to intervene on their behalf, for as the righteous Governor of the world He might well have proceeded to uphold the majesty of His law by executing its penalty on the disobedient, thereby making them an example of vengeance to all other intelligences in the universe. Nor did His *goodness* oblige Him to rescue His refractory subjects from their misery, for He had previously given full proof of that in their creation, as it is still made manifest in the happiness enjoyed by all His loyal subjects. Nor did any consideration of *His glory* require that He should show them mercy, "The glory of God does not depend upon the manifestation of any particular attribute, but upon the manifestation of them all on proper occasions and in full harmony. He is glorified when He bestows blessings upon the righteous, and is equally glorified when He inflicts punishment upon the wicked" (J. Dick). What would the loss of this world be unto Him in whose sight it is nothing, yea, less than nothing and vanity? The provision of a Saviour was a matter of His free grace, and grace is something which none can claim as a right.

God was pleased to act in a manner which will cause both the holy angels and redeemed sinners forever to marvel and adore. His way of salvation is the wonder of all wonders, whether we consider the dignity of the Mediator's Person, the nature of His work, the things it accomplished, or the beneficiaries thereof. The Saviour was none other than the Lord of Glory, the co-equal and beloved of the Father. His work necessitated a journey from Heaven to earth, the assumption of human nature, the being made under the Law, and the enduring of unspeakable humiliation. It required Him to become the Man of Sorrows, so that the whole of His life in this scene was one of suffering and grief. It involved His becoming the Substitute of His people, so that the iniquity of them all was placed upon Him, and He paid the wages due them. It entailed His laying down His life to ransom them, dying a cruel, shameful and accursed death, during which He was separated from God Himself. So infinitely meritorious and efficacious was Christ's death that it appeased the wrath of God against His people, satisfied every demand of His justice, removed the guilt of their transgressions from them as far as the east is from the west, conquered Satan and spoiled him of his dominion over them, procured the Spirit to quicken and indwell them, opened Heaven for them, so that they have access to and fellowship with God, ensured their preservation in time and fullness of joy for eternity.

And on whose behalf did the Son of God suffer such awful indignities? Not for the fallen angels, whose original habitat was Heaven, but for creatures of the earth who are but breathing dust and animated clay. The best of men compared with Christ are less in His sight than a worm is in ours, yea, in Job 25:6, He actually terms them worms. It is for the unworthy, the unholy, the unlovely that such was ordained. Oh, what an amazing thing that the Lord should set His heart upon them! Upon those who in their fallen estate were quite incapable of doing anything to please or honour Him. The objects of His mediation were despicable not only in their beings, but in their actions also. As man is nothing comparatively, so he can do nothing to glorify Christ, though much to provoke and dishonour Him. How can one who is lame and blind walk or work, or one who is dead act? Such were His people when He entertained thoughts of mercy toward them: destitute of any good qualities or fruit, and lacking any spiritual principle or nature to yield the same. And when Christ has bestowed such upon His people, they cannot act but as they are acted. They cannot stand, except He uphold them. They cannot move unless He draws them. Christ must work all their works in them (Isa. 26:12).

Not only impotent, but poverty-stricken: man is nothing, can do nothing, and has nothing. He not only has "no money" (Isa. 55:1) but is heavily in debt. He is in a famishing condition, feeding on nothing but wind and husks, for such are the vanities and pleasures of this world. He has not so much as to cover his shame, for though he may, like the Laodiceans, imagine himself to be rich and in need of nothing, yet in God's sight he is poor and naked. He cannot rightly say that his soul is his own, for he has given it over to Satan, sold himself to work wickedness. What a marvel that Christ should love such forlorn creatures! But more: man is not only a bankrupt, but a hideous object. Poverty alone will not hinder love, especially if there be beauty; but who can admire deformity? Yet such is the sinner in the eyes of holiness: full of revolting loathsomeness,—no human pen can depict the obnoxiousness of defiled man. Created fair and very good, adorned with the beauty of God's image; but not only is all of that erased, but the horrible image of Satan has displaced it. His light has been turned into darkness, his comeliness into corruption—instead of sweet savour there is a stench, and burning instead of beauty (Isa. 3:24).

That which makes the soul most unlovely is its being *dead*. When life expires all beauty expires with it. Abraham loved Sarah dearly while she lived, but when she was dead he could not endure the sight of her. A dead soul is as repulsive to God as a dead body is to us. But men are not only hateful to Christ but *haters of Him*. They hate His Person, His offices, His precepts. They hate His very image, and the more resemblance to Him any of His followers have the more are they detested. Yet there is not in Christ the least occasion of hatred: He is altogether lovely—Divinely glorious, humanly perfect. Nor does He give any cause to be hated: all His administrations are righteous, so that His justice ought to be admired as much as His mercy. It is an unmixed hatred, without any degree of love, yea, without the slightest inclination or tendency to it. It is a deadly hatred, so that when He was delivered into their hands they murdered Him. It is an unvarying and inveterate hatred, firmly rooted in their hearts, expressed by continual acts of rebellion against Him. Oh, what a truly amazing thing it is that Christ should voluntarily lay down His life for such creatures! Yet the Spirit tells God's people, "when we were *enemies*, we were reconciled to God by the death of His Son" (Rom. 5:10). Behold what manner of love. Behold, and wonder!

The total depravity of all mankind *explains the opposition which the Gospel generally meets with*. When one considers what the Gospel is in itself—namely a message of good news unto lost sinners—one would naturally suppose that it will be universally and cordially received. Will not those condemned to eternal damnation welcome a reprieve? Will not those perishing from a deadly malady be glad to avail themselves of an effectual remedy? Will the naked scorn the garments of salvation, the poverty-stricken refuse the unsearchable riches of Christ, the famishing decline an invitation to a feast? One had not thought so. The Evangel contains the most illustrious display of the Divine character which has ever been given to this world, and therefore is it designated "the glorious Gospel of the blessed God" (1 Tim. 1:11). It makes known to us how Divine wisdom has so perfectly adjusted His attributes that God can at the same time be both just and merciful in saving a Hell-deserving sinner, that He can lavish upon him the riches of grace without in any wise compromising His holiness. Such a marvel is so far beyond human conception that it evidences itself to be truly Divine. It is indeed "worthy of all acceptation." It announces the inestimable blessings of pardon, holiness and joy, and therefore should be cordially welcomed by all who hear it.

The love of God which the Gospel publishes, and the sufferings of Christ for sinners, ought to melt the hardest heart and cause every hearer fervently to cry, "Thanks be unto God for His unspeakable gift." It is a message of glad tidings proclaiming peace. It tells of deliverance from condemnation and promises eternal life to all who receive it. Yet the fact remains that the great majority of those who sit under it are but little affected and obtain no lasting advantage to their souls; and *that* perplexes many Christians. How often we hear them saying, after the most winsome notes of the Gospel have been struck, I cannot see how it is possible for any hearer to reject such an appeal. But the total depravity of man fully explains that lamentable event. There is nothing whatever in a heart that is desperately wicked upon which the Gospel can seize that will evoke any echo to it: nay, its contents are directly opposed to the opinions and inclinations of the fallen creature. If it informed men of how great worldly honours could be secured gratis, or how large sums of money could be obtained for nothing, it would be heartily welcomed. If it assured men how they could indulge their lusts with impunity and live in sin without fear of death and Hell, it would indeed be good news to them. But a *holy Gospel* suits not their tastes, being quite foreign to their longings.

If God were to leave men entirely to themselves in their response to the Gospel, it would be universally rejected. There is a deeply rooted contrariety to God in their very natures which makes them turn a deaf ear to His voice, though they are ready enough to listen to the least whispers of Satan. As there be plants which are attractive to the eye but poisonous to the stomach, so even though the Gospel be a pleasant sound to the ear it is repulsive to a corrupt heart. The Gospel requires men to renounce their own wisdom and become as little children, to repudiate their own righteousness and accept that of Another, to cease from self-pleasing and submit to the will of God. The Gospel is designed to transform the inner man and regulate the outer man, and that is quite unacceptable to the unregenerate. No exhortations will reconcile a wolf and a lamb. No logical arguments will tame a fierce lion. Though man be a rational creature, he follows the promptings of his lusts rather than the dictates of his judgment. One who is wholly in love with sin and Satan desires not to enter into the service of Christ. To turn unto God in Christ is altogether contrary to the stream of corrupt nature, and therefore it requires to be overcome by a flood of almighty grace, as the stream of the river is by the tide of the sea.

There is a certain class of writers who represent the heart of fallen man as painfully conscious of its burden and sighing for deliverance. But to say that the natural man is eager to escape from the ruin and degradation to which sin has reduced him is but the figment of fancy, unsupported by a single fact of experience. The natural man does indeed encounter conflicts, yet his struggles are not for deliverance from indwelling corruption, but to escape from the accusations of conscience. Man's misery is that he cannot sin without unpleasant consequences. There is nothing whatever in him that predisposes him to welcome the Gospel, or to give it joyful acceptance when it is made known to him. The heart of man is more unwilling to embrace the Evangel than it is to acknowledge the equity of the Law. "The Law puts man upon his own strength, the Gospel takes him off from his own footing. The Law acknowledges him to have a power in himself, and to act for his own reward: the Gospel strips him of all his proud and towering thoughts (2 Cor. 10:5), brings him to his due place, the foot of God, and orders him to deny himself as his own rule, righteousness, and end, and henceforth not to live unto himself (2 Cor. 5:14). This is the reason why men are more against the Gospel than against the Law: because it doth more deify God and debase man" (Charnock).

As there needed to be a forerunner for Christ to "prepare His way" before Him, so the Holy Spirit must first work upon the heart ere it is ready to receive the Gospel: not until He renews the soul is any real sense of need awakened: and until its sickness be felt the Great Physician is undesired. Before the heart has been Divinely prepared for its reception, the Word of God can find no permanent place in it. That is very evident from our Lord's parable of the sower, wherein He likened those who heard the Word unto several kinds of ground. The seed sown was the same in each case: it was the soils that differed. The seed which fell on the wayside, the stony ground and the thorny ground was abortive. The heart has to be made "honest and good" (Luke 8:15) before there will be any increase or fruit. None but the Holy Spirit can produce in the soul a hatred of sin and the desire to be saved from it because of its intrinsic vileness. It is owing to the distinguishing and astonishing grace of God that *any* are brought to repent and believe the Gospel. One whose affections are chained to the things of earth cannot seek those things which are above. Nothing more clearly demonstrates the fact of human depravity than that without a special and Divine operation no heart ever did or ever will savingly receive the Gospel.

In view of the total depravity of man *we need not be the least surprised at what we behold in Christendom itself.* A change of clothes effects no alteration in the character of the wearer, neither does a person's taking upon him a profession of religion better his heart. In many, indeed, it fosters a spirit of hypocrisy, and causes them to take more pains to hide from the eyes of their fellows what they are by nature; but it will not cleanse their souls from indwelling sin. Thus, while there be more open wickedness in the profane world, there is far more secret and cloaked wickedness in the professing world. Error is bound to be much more popular than Truth unto the unregenerate, and therefore to render the Truth in any wise acceptable to them, it has to be watered down, wrested, and perverted; and there are always those who, for the sake of filthy lucre, are ready to perjure their souls. Hence it is that heretical sects and systems abound on every side. What delusions are cherished about the character of God! What erroneous ideas are entertained about His way of salvation! What false notions are held of man's dignity, greatness, free will, even by many who call themselves Christians! Because of the unbelief, selfishness and impiety of men's hearts, the false prophets, who speak smooth and flattering things, are assured of a ready hearing.

Here, then, is the explanation of the babble of tongues which is now to be heard in Christendom. When the natural man takes it upon himself to handle the things of God, they are sure to be corrupted. How can those who are devoid of Divine grace, in love with sin, deal faithfully with that which unsparingly condemns sin? For the same reason, those who are without true piety will prefer to hear and follow those whose preaching gives them the most license to gratify their carnality. Moreover, Satan will see to it that his emissaries cater to the worldly minded. What is Roman Catholicism, with its "indulgences," its gorgeous pageantry, its dogma of purgatory, but an appeal unto the flesh? What are Universalism and Annihilationism but opiates to remove the dread of eternal punishment? What is Antinomianism, with its bald fatalism and repudiation of the moral law as the believer's rule of life, but an attempt to set aside the unpalatable truth of man's responsibility? What are the great majority of present-day "missions" and "revivals," with their musical attractions and sensational methods, but a pandering to those who love emotionalism and sensationalism? Higher Criticism and Modernism are but devices to banish the authority of Holy Writ, and get rid of the supernatural.

Arminianism panders blatantly to human pride, for it is virtually the *deification of man*, making *him* the architect of his life and the determiner of his destiny.

How the depravity of mankind *makes evident the infinite patience of God*! "The LORD is slow to anger, and great in power" (Nahum 1:3). How significant is the conjunction of those Divine perfections! It is not because God is indifferent unto men's wickedness that He does not speedily take vengeance upon them; still less because He lacks the ability to do so. No, it is because God is not at the command of His passions as men are. He can restrain His anger when under great and just provocation to exercise it. His power over Himself is the cause of His slowness to execute wrath (Num. 14:17): nevertheless, His might to punish is as great as His patience to spare. And oh, what fearful provocations, insults and injuries God meets with daily from mankind. "How many millions of practical atheists breathe every day in God's air and live upon His bounty, who deserve to be inhabitants of Hell rather than possessors of earth! An infinite holiness is opposed, and infinite justice provoked, yet an infinite patience forbears the punishment, and infinite goodness relieves our wants" (Charnock). What a wonder it is that God has protracted human history until now, and that He still "maketh His sun to rise on the evil and on the good, and sendeth rain on the just and unjust." Patience is as truly a Divine attribute as are holiness, wisdom, faithfulness.

What a mercy that God does not strike dead those who brazenly defy Him and take His holy name in vain! Why does He not suddenly cut off every blatant infidel, as He did Ananias and Sapphira? Why does He not cause the earth to open her mouth and swallow the persecutors of His people, as He did when Dathan and Abiram rebelled against Moses and Aaron? Why does He tolerate the ten thousand abominations in Christendom which are now being perpetrated under the holy name of Christ? Only one answer is possible: because He endures "with much longsuffering the vessels of wrath fitted to destruction" (Rom. 9:22). There are many ways in which the patience of God is manifested in this world. First, by publishing His vengeance before He strikes. "Because there is wrath, beware lest He take thee away with His stroke: then a great ransom cannot deliver thee" (Job 36:18), thereby affording them "space to repent." Second, by delaying the judgments which He has threatened. How long was the ark being prepared before He sent the great deluge (Gen. 6:3)! Third, in executing His judgments by degrees, as He sent plague after plague upon Egypt before He commissioned the angel of death to slay all her firstborn; and as the Shekinah glory departed slowly from an apostate

Israel, retiring stage by stage (Ezek. 9:3; 10:4, 19; 11:23), as though reluctant to leave.

Consider how great are our provocations against the Most High—His authority and majesty. Consider how many are our transgressions against the Law. Consider how long-continued they have been: no improvement in their manners during the course of time, but each succeeding generation as bad as the former, nay, "evil men and seducers; waxing worse and worse." Consider how fearfully God is insulted and offended by the world's treatment of His Gospel. He proclaims mercy unto the chief of sinners, but they scoff thereat. He entreats them to turn unto Him that they may live, but they are determined to destroy themselves. What an indescribably dreadful state men must be in who prefer their idols to Christ, and have no desire to be saved from their sins! What proof of His longsuffering that God has already prolonged this day of salvation for almost five hundred years more than the Mosaic economy lasted! Yet so far from appreciating such clemency the unregenerate misinterpret and abuse it: "Because sentence against an evil work is not executed speedily, therefore the heart of the sons of men is fully set in them to do evil" (Eccl. 8:11). When His rod was laid heavily upon them they "blasphemed the God of Heaven because of their pains and their sores, and repented not of their deeds" (Rev. 16:11). How it should astonish us that God not only preserves in this life such a multitude of monsters, but continues to spread their tables!

How clearly the depravity of mankind *demonstrates the necessity for Hell*! What can be the future of stout-hearted rebels who throughout life defied their Maker and Ruler and died in impenitence? Shall such a Being be despised with impunity? If, by the common consent of all right-minded people, one who *is* guilty of treason against an earthly monarch be worthy of death, what punishment can be too great for those who prefer themselves to the King of kings, and daily invade His prerogatives? Sin is a challenge to the government of God, and insurrectionists must be dealt with. Sin has to be paid the wages which it has so hardly earned: equity requires that each one should reap as he has sown. The time of God's patience has an end. He has wrath to punish as well as patience to bear. Because God is holy He hates all sin, and as the moral Governor it becomes Him to deal with revolters. How could He be the Sum of all excellence were He to make no distinction between good and evil and to treat virtue and vice alike? Christ bade His hearers, "Fear Him, which after He hath killed hath power to cast into Hell: yea, I say unto you, Fear Him" (Luke 12:5). He knew as none other did that God is the enemy of sin and the avenger of those who set at naught all His counsels.

God will yet fully vindicate His throne and make evident what a fearful thing it is to despise Him. It is meet that He should display His governmental supremacy and make a footstool of all those who rise up against Him. Though He "endures [not "loves"!] with much longsuffering the vessels of wrath fitted to destruction," yet in the day to come He will "show His wrath, and make known His power," and that wrath will be no greater than the mercy which they abused. The highest contempt merits the greatest anger, and it is fitting that those who refuse to make God their happiness should be made to feel everlastingly the misery of their separation from Him. Eternal life and eternal death were plainly set before them, and since they chose the latter they cannot justly blame any but themselves when they are cast into the same. God's veracity requires Him to fulfill His threatenings: and His very goodness to separate eternally the wicked from the righteous, for the latter could not enjoy perfect peace and happiness if they lived forever with the reprobate. It is just that those who freely serve the Devil should be cast into the same prison and tormented with him. How could those who hate God, whose very natures are averse to Him, be admitted into Heaven? What *must be* the portion of those who would destroy the Deity were it in their power to do so?

The total depravity of our race *sheds much light on Providence.* Many of God's dealings with men present insoluble riddles unto carnal reason. There is a Divine handwriting on the wall of human affairs which, like that in Belshazzar's palace, is indecipherable by human wisdom. Unto those who are unacquainted with what is recorded in Genesis 3, God's ways with our race cannot but be most mysterious: but the whole subject is at once illumined when the doctrine of human depravity is understood. The whole brood of ills which now afflicts mankind has sprung from the pregnant womb of sin. The wrecked and wretched condition in which man now finds himself is the inevitable consequence of his Fall. The frowning aspect of Providence which so often darkens this scene and appalls our minds receives its only adequate solution in the fact that Adam's offence fearfully changed the relation of God and the creature. Our nature being what it is, we cannot expect history to be written in any other inks than those of tears and blood. Hospitals and mental homes, the discords and strifes among men, the warring between nations, unprincipled politicians, conscienceless preachers—all are the effects of the corruption of human nature.

Here is the key to the problem of suffering: all the misery in the world proceeds from sin. But not only are the governmental ways of God with men what they are because of what the race is, they are also designed to make more evident the real character of fallen man.

The Doctrine of Human Depravity

While Providence sets bounds to the exercise of human depravity, at the same time it permits sufficient manifestations thereof to leave no candid observer in doubt of the same. God causes men to reveal what they are by suffering their insubordination to His Law, their rejection of His Gospel, their perverting of His Truth, their persecutions of His people. How many others, who were regarded as upright, are by some sudden temptation shown to have been all along corrupt at heart. Many a merchant, lawyer, bank official, yea, even minister of the Gospel, who was highly respected is permitted to fall into open sin, that the long-cherished depravity of his soul might be exposed. How remarkably does Providence often bring to light the hidden things of darkness: as in the case of Abraham's deception, of Joseph's brethren, the discovering of Judah's secret sin (Gen. 38:15-17), of Achan's, of David's.

Belief of this doctrine *ought to have a beneficial effect upon the children of God*. A sense of our native depravity should engender deep humility. What a state we were in when God plucked us as brands from the burning! The realization of that ought to make us take and maintain a very lowly place before Him. "That thou mayest remember, and be confounded, and never open thy mouth any more [in self praise] because of thy shame, when I am pacified toward thee, for all that thou hast done, saith the LORD God" (Ezek. 16:63). Pride should be forever hidden from us, and that acknowledgment of Jacob's be our constant confession, "I am not worthy of the least of all the mercies, and of all the truth, which Thou hast showed unto Thy servant" (Gen. 32:10). Again, as we look back to the hole of the pit from which we were dug, what fervent praise and thanksgiving should be awakened in our hearts! How we should adore the One who opened our prison doors, for none but His hand could loose the bolts and shoot back the many locks which held us captive. How our hearts should be melted and filled with wonderment at the amazing grace which has saved us from the dominion of Satan and made us kings and priests unto God, which has elevated beggars to be "heirs of God, and joint-heirs with Christ."

Once more, how this solemnizing doctrine ought to convince the saint that he cannot keep himself alive! If, being a mutable creature, sinless Adam, when left to himself, brought about his destruction, how much more so would the mutable believer, with a fallen and corrupt nature still within him, unless an Almighty hand preserved him! So perverse are we by nature, and so weak as Christians, that without Christ we can do no good thing (John 15:5). Sustaining and preserving grace must be sought by us hourly. We are treading a slippery path and need to pray, "Hold Thou me up, and I shall be safe" (Psa.

119:117). Finally, the knowledge of this truth ought to beget in us a spirit of complete dependence on God. How beautifully is that state depicted in the description given of the Church of old: "Who is this that cometh up from the wilderness, leaning upon her beloved?" (Song. 8:5). So ignorant and wayward are we that "we know not what we should pray for as we ought" (Rom. 8:26). It is only by the gracious operations of the Spirit that our affections are raised above this world, faith is strengthened, and we are enabled to lay hold of a Divine promise. So shut up are we to God, that, in all things, He must work in us both to will and to do of His good pleasure.

THE DOCTRINE OF HUMAN DEPRAVITY
Its Remedy

Perhaps some of our younger and more impatient readers are inclined to demur: "Why devote a separate chapter to this? We already know all about it: the remedy for ruined man is to be found in God's salvation." But that is a very superficial view to take, and a wrongful one too; for the greatest and grandest of all the wonderful works of God ought never to be spoken of so lightly or dismissed so cursorily. Moreover, the matter is very far from being as simple as that, and since there be such widespread ignorance concerning the disease itself it is needful to examine closely and enter into some detail upon a description of the cure for the same. The fact needs to be deeply realized at the outset that to all natural wit the condition of fallen man is beyond repair, that so far as self-help or human skill is concerned his case is hopeless. Yea, none other than the Son of God Himself declared, "With men this is impossible" (Matt. 19:26), and it is only as we perceive, to some extent at least, the various respects in which that impossibility lays that we can begin to appreciate the miracle of grace which secures the recovery of lost sinners.

The deadly disease which has seized man is not a simple but a compound one, consisting of not a single element but a combination, each of which is fatal in itself. Look at some of them. Man's very nature is thoroughly corrupt, yet he is in no wise horrified because of it. Not only is sin part and parcel of his being, but he is deeply in love with it. He is filled with enmity against God, and his heart is as hard as a stone. He is wholly paralyzed Godward, and completely under the dominion and sway of Satan. He is not only devoid of righteousness, but a guilty sinner—without a spark of holiness—a moral leper. He is quite incapable of helping himself, for he is "without strength" (Rom. 5:6). The wrath of God abides upon him, and he is dead in trespasses and sins. Fallen man is not merely in danger of ruin and destruction, but is already sunk in the same. He is like a brand on the very edge of a raging fire, which will swiftly be consumed unless the Divine hand plucks him thence (Zech. 3:2). His condition is not only wretched but desperate, inasmuch as he is altogether incapable of devising any expedient for his cure.

The sinner is guilty, and no creature can make an atonement for him. He is an outcast from God, terrified by His very perfections, and therefore does his best to banish Him from his thoughts. No tongue can express or heart be suitably affected with the woeful plight and abject misery of the natural man. And such will be his case forever unless God intervenes. Yet all of this presents but one side of the problem—and the easier one—which stands in the way of man's recovery. To finite intelligence it would seem that a creature so vile and polluted, so wayward and rebellious, so obnoxious to the righteous curse of the Law, is beyond all hope—that it would not comport with the Divine honour to save such a wretch. How a transgressor could be pardoned consistently with the requirements of that Law which he had despised and flouted, and be delivered from the penalty which it justly demands, and how he could be recovered unto God's favour in concord with the maintaining of the Divine government, presented a difficulty which no angelic wisdom could solve. It was a secret hid in God till He was pleased to make it known.

There are those—with no regard to the Word of Truth—who suppose that God must pardon and receive to favour those who throw down the weapons of their rebellion against Him and sue for mercy. But the solution to the problem is far from being as simple a matter as that. Meeting such people on their own ground, it is to be pointed out that human reason can advance no valid and sufficient argument why God should forgive the sinner merely because he repents, or that this could be done consistently with His moral government. Rather is the contrary evident. The contrition of a criminal will not exonerate him in a human court of law, for it offers no satisfaction and reparation for his crimes. Any sinner who cherishes the idea that his repentance gives him a claim to Divine clemency and favour demonstrates that he is a total stranger to true repentance: and never will he repent until he abandons such presumption. Universal experience and observation, as well as Scripture, fully attest the fact that none of mankind ever repent while they be left to themselves, and are not made the subjects of those Divine operations to which they have no claim, and which mere reason is incapable of concluding that God will grant them.

That an adequate remedy for the complicated and fatal malady by which man is stricken must be *of God* is very obvious: it must needs be of His devising, His providing, His applying, His making of the same effectual. That is but another way of saying it must be *wholly of Him* from start to finish, for if any part thereof be left to the sinner, at any stage, it is certain to fail. Yet it requires to be pointed out once more that God was under no obligation whatever to make such provision, for when man deliberately apostatized from Him he forfeited all favourable reward from his Maker. Not only might God now righteously inflict the full penalty of His broken law upon the entire human race, but suitably unto His holy nature, He could have left all mankind to perish eternally in that condemnation whereinto they had cast themselves. Had He utterly forsaken the whole of Adam's apostate posterity and left them as remediless as the fallen angels, it had been no reflection whatever upon His goodness, but rather a display of His inexorable justice. Wherefore, whenever redemption is mentioned, it is constantly described as proceeding from sovereign grace and mere mercy (Eph. 1:3-11).

Yet something more than a gracious design was required on God's part in order for any sinner to be saved. Grace is indeed the source thereof, yet it was not sufficient of itself. One may be filled with the most amiable intentions, yet be unable to carry them out. How often is the fond love of a mother impotent in the presence of their suffering child! There has to be the putting forth of Divine power also if the purpose of grace is to be accomplished. And no ordinary power either, but, as Scripture affirms, "the exceeding greatness of His power to usward who believe, according to the working of His mighty power" (Eph. 1:19). It calls for the exercise of far more might to re-create a fallen creature than it did to create the universe out of nothing. Why so? Because in that there was no opposition, nothing to resist His working: whereas in the case of fallen man there is the hostility of his will, the alienation of his heart, the inveterate enmity of his carnal mind to be overcome. Furthermore, there is the malice and opposition of Satan to be neutralized, for he endeavours with all his might to retain his hold upon his victims. The Devil must be despoiled of the advantage which he had gained, for it consists not with the glory of God that he should be left to triumph in his success.

But something more than the exercise of God's power was still required: omniscience must be exercised as well as omnipotence. Strength itself will not build a house: there must also be art to contrive and proportion the materials. Skill is the chief requirement of an architect. Let that faintly illustrate what we are here endeavouring to express. Those who are saved are not only the products of God's amazing grace and almighty power, but they are also "His workmanship" (Eph. 2:10). Wondrously does God's wisdom appear in the beautiful fabric of His grace, in the spiritual temple which He erects for His own residence. He has "wrought us for the selfsame thing" (2 Cor. 5:5): as stones are carved and polished, so believers are made "living stones" in that edifice in which God will dwell forever. Now that which is exquisite in execution serves to make manifest excellent skill in the planning of the same. The counterpart of God's Law in the hearts of His quickened children is no less the fruit of His wisdom than the writing of it on the tables of stone: wisdom in the first framing of it, wisdom also in the imprinting of it upon the understanding and the affections.

It is neither in the marvels of creation nor in the mysteries of Providence that the depths and riches of God's wisdom are to be found: rather is it in the plan and fruits of redemption that they are most fully and illustriously revealed. This is clear from several Scriptures. It is in the God-man Mediator that "are hid all the treasures of wisdom and knowledge" (Col. 2:3): yea, He is expressly denominated "the wisdom of God" (1 Cor. 1:24). "Unto the principalities and powers in heavenly places" is now being made known by means of "the church the manifold wisdom of God" (Eph. 3:10). The devising of a method whereby a part of mankind should be recovered out of their miserable estate is indeed the masterpiece of Divine wisdom: naught but omniscience itself could have found a way to effect such a triumph in a manner suited to all the Divine perfections. The wise men of this world are termed "princes" (1 Cor. 2:6, 8), but angels are designated "principalities and powers in the heavenlies," because of their superior dignity, wisdom and strength. Yet though they be so great in intelligence, always beholding the face of the Father, yet a new and grander discovery of God's wisdom is made to them through the Church, for His work in the redemption of it far transcends their native understanding.

The celestial hierarchies had witnessed the dishonour which had been done to the authority of God and the discord brought into the sphere of His government by the sin and rebellion of Adam. It was therefore necessary, morally speaking, that that defiance of God's rule should be dealt with, and that that affront to His throne should be rectified. This could not be done except by the infliction of that punishment which in the unalterable rule and standard of Divine justice was due thereunto. The dismissal of sin on any other terms would leave the rule of God under unspeakable dishonour and confusion. "For where is the righteousness of government if the highest sin and provocation that our nature was capable of, and which brought confusion on the whole creation below, should forever go unpunished? The first express intimation that God gave of His righteousness in the government of mankind was His threatening punishment equal unto the demerit of disobedience if man should fall into it: 'In the day that thou eatest thereof thou shalt surely die.' If He revoke and disannul this sentence, how shall the glory of His righteousness in the rule of all be made known? But how this punishment should be undergone, which consisted in man's eternal ruin. and yet man be eternally saved, was a work for Divine wisdom to contrive" (John Owen).

Not only was it necessary unto the honour of God's righteousness, as He is the moral Governor and supreme Judge of all the earth, that sin should be summarily punished, but it was required that there should be an obedience unto God, and such an obedience as would bring more glory unto Him than the dishonour and reproach which resulted from the disobedience of man. "This was due unto the glory of His holiness in giving the Law. Until this was done, the excellency of that Law as becoming the holiness of God, and as an effect thereof, could not be made manifest. For if it were never kept in any instance, never fulfilled by any one person in the world, how should the glory of it be declared? How should the holiness of God be represented by it? How should it be evident that the transgression of it was not rather from some defect in the Law itself, than from any evil in them that should have yielded obedience unto it? If the Law given unto man should never be complied withal in perfect obedience by any one whatever, it might be thought that the Law itself was unsuited unto our nature, and impossible to be complied withal" (John Owen). It did not become the Rector of the universe to give unto man a law whose spirituality and equity should never be exemplified in obedience. That law was not imposed, primarily, that man might suffer justly for its transgression, but rather that God should be glorified in its performance. But since Adam's offence brought ruin upon all his posterity, so that they are incapable of meeting its requirements, how could a perfect obedience be rendered to it? Omniscience alone could supply the answer.

O, what a truly amazing thing it is, Christian reader, that the wisdom of God has, by our redemption, made that which is the greatest possible dishonour to Him the occasion of His greatest glory! Yet such is indeed the case. Nothing is so displeasing to the Most High as sin, nothing so dishonouring to Him, for it is in its very nature enmity against Him, contempt of Him. Sin is a reproach to His majesty, an insult to His holiness, an insurrection against His government. And yet this "abominable thing" which He hates (Jer. 44:4), upon which He cannot look but with infinite disfavour (Hab. 1:13), is made the occasion of the greatest possible good. What a miracle of miracles that the Lord makes the wrath of man to praise Him (Psa. 76:10), that the very evil which aims at dethroning Him is transmuted into the means of magnifying Him: yea, that thereby He has made the grandest manifestation of His perfections that ever was. Sin casts contempt upon the Law of God, yet through redemption that law is made supremely honourable. Never was the King of Heaven so grievously slighted as when those made in His image and likeness broke out into revolt against Him: never was such honour paid unto His throne as by the way He chose to effect the salvation of His people. Never was the holiness of God so slighted as when man preferred to render allegiance to that old serpent the Devil: never did God's holiness shine forth so illustriously as in the victory He has gained over Satan.

Equally wonderful is it, Christian reader, that God contrived a way whereby a flagrant transgressor should become not guilty, and that he who is completely destitute of righteousness should be justified or pronounced righteous by the Judge of all the earth. Had such things as these been submitted for solution, they had forever appeared to be irreconcilable contradictions to all finite understandings. It seems to be utterly impossible for a condemned culprit to be cleared of any charge against him. Sin necessarily entails punishment: how then can any transgressor escape the "due reward" of his deeds (Luke 23:41), except by a manifest violation of justice? God has declared plainly that He "will by no means clear the guilty" (Exo. 34:7). He has determined by an unalterable decree that sin shall be paid its wages: then how can the guilty be exempted from the sentence of death? Nor is the problem any less formidable of how God can, with perfect equity, declare righteous those who have not themselves met the requirements of the Law. To adjudge entitled to the reward of obedience those whose record is a lifelong disobedience appears to be something worse than an anomaly. Nevertheless, Omniscience contrived a solution to both of these problems, a solution which is, in every respect, a perfect and a glorious one.

Without that solution, the restoration of any of mankind into the favour of and unto fellowship with and the enjoyment of God Himself was utterly impossible. It was so not only because of the total depravity of man himself, but because of the concernment of the glory of the Divine perfections in our sin and apostasy. Not only were they stricken with a fatal disease, from which there was not the slightest hope of deliverance unless a supernatural remedy be provided, but the government of God had been so grievously outraged by our revolt therefrom that full compensation must be made to His insulted sceptre, and complete satisfaction offered to His broken Law, before the throne of Heaven could be satisfied. Great beyond conception to finite intelligence as was the difficulty of repairing the damage wrought in the whole of our constitution and being by sin, yet greater far were the obstacles which stood in the way of the exercise of God's grace and mercy in the restoring of the outcast. That way of restoration must be one wherein God was magnified: His justice vindicated, His threatenings realized, His holiness glorified. The manner in which all of those ends were achieved and those results secured is the adoring marvel alike of the redeemed and of the angels.

As others before us have pointed out, if the Divine government were to be vindicated the whole work of our recovery must be performed *in our nature*, and the very nature of those who had sinned, and which was to be recovered from the ruins of the Fall and bought to everlasting felicity: in human nature that was not only free of any pollution. but intrinsically holy. In order to the salvation of sinners, no satisfaction could be made unto the glory of God for the vitiation of apostate man's nature, with all the evil fruits thereof, but in the nature of those who had sinned and were to be saved. Since God's giving of the Law unto our first parents was itself an effect of His wisdom and holiness, wherein could the glory of them be exalted if that rule of righteousness be complied with by a nature of a totally different kind? Should an angel fulfill it, his obedience would be no proof that the Law was suited unto man's nature, whereunto it was originally prescribed: rather would an angel's compliance with the Law have been a reflection upon the Divine goodness in giving it to men. Nor could there have been the necessary relation between the nature of the substitute and those on whose behalf he acted and suffered, and therefore such an arrangement had not magnified the Divine wisdom, but had been at best an unsatisfactory expedient.

The Scriptures are very explicit in their teaching about the necessity of the same nature in the surety and those whom he represented, as being condecent unto God's wisdom. Speaking of the way of our relief, the Apostle declared, "Forasmuch then as the children are partakers of flesh and blood, He [the Deliverer] also Himself likewise partook of the same" (Heb. 2:14). It was human nature—here expressed by "flesh and blood"—that was to be delivered, and therefore it was human nature in which this deliverance was to be wrought. The Apostle enters into considerable detail upon this point in Romans 5:12-21, the sum of which is, "as by one man's disobedience many were made sinners, so by the obedience of one ["by one man," v. 15] shall many be made righteous": the same nature that transgressed must work out the remedy for the same. Again, in 1 Corinthians 15:21, "For since by man came death, by man came also the resurrection of the dead." Our ruin could not be retrieved, nor deliverance from our guilt be effected, except by one in our own nature.

It is further to be observed that the deliverance to be secured must be wrought by one whose substance was derived from the common stock of our *first parents*. It had not met the exigencies of the case for God to create a second man out of the dust of the ground, or out of anything which was different in nature from ourselves, for in such a case there had been no nexus and relation between him and us, and therefore we could be in no wise concerned in anything he did or suffered. That alliance depended solely hereon, that God "hath made of one blood all nations of men" (Acts 17:26). But at this point a further difficulty was presented, one which again had proved insurmountable unto all created intelligences had not "the only wise God" revealed

His provision for the resolving of the same. Any deliverer of sinful men must derive his nature from their original stock, yet he must not bring along with it the least taint of corruption or the same liability as we unto guilt upon his own account: for if his nature were defiled, if it lacked the image of God, it could do nothing that should be acceptable unto Him: and were he subject to the penalty of the Law on his own account, then he could make no satisfaction for the sins of others. But since every descendant of Eve is shapen in sin and conceived in iniquity how could any of *her seed* be sinless? Only Omniscience could bring an immaculately clean thing out of thorough uncleanness.

Nor must we lose sight of *the grounds* on which defilement and guilt adhere unto our nature, as they do in all individuals alike. First our entire nature, as to the participation of it, was in Adam as our covenant head and federal representative. Therefore his offense was ours also, and justly imputed unto us. Because we sinned in him, we became "by nature the children of wrath"—the subjects of God's judicial displeasure. Second, we derived our nature from Adam by way of natural generation, so that his defilement is communicated to all his offspring. We are the degenerate plants of a degenerate stock. Thus, still another difficulty was presented: the nature of a deliverer for fallen man must, as unto its substance, be derived from our first parents, yet so as *not* to have been in Adam as a legal representative, *nor* be derived from him by natural generation. But how could this be: that his nature should relate as truly unto Adam as does ours, yet so as neither to partake of the guilt of his transgression nor to participate in his pollution? Such a prodigy was utterly beyond the concept of every finite mind.

We have dwelt upon some of the difficulties, yea, seemingly impossibilities which stood in the way of the recovery of any of the fallen sons of Adam, showing that there required to be something more than a benign purpose of grace on God's part to effect the same, something more than the putting forth of His mighty power—that the obstacles which needed to be removed were so many and so great that "the manifold wisdom of God" (Eph. 3:10) must also needs be called into play. The difficulty from the human side was the desperate state of the sinner: how his darkness could be changed into light, his enmity into love, his unwillingness into willingness, without any violence being done to his moral agency. The obstacles from the Divine side were how the Most High could restore such wretches to His favour, and yet not compromise His perfections: how He could have dealings with moral lepers without sullying His holiness, clear the guilty without repudiating His Law, exercise mercy consistently with His justice. To provide a remedy for such a malady, and to do so in a way that honoured the throne of God, was far beyond the reach of created intelligence.

We saw that in order to save a law-cured and Hell-deserving sinner it was necessary that some method and means be devised whereby he should be delivered from all the consequences of the Fall, and at the same time meet all the requirements of the Divine government. Sin had to be dealt with unsparingly, yet transgressors be exempted from their merited doom. Full conformity unto the Law must be rendered, yet by one in *the same nature* as those who had violated it. That was clearly adumbrated under the Old Testament types: the redeemer had to be a *kinsman* of those he befriended (Lev. 25:25; Ruth 4:4-6). Moreover, the requirements of the Law could be met only by one whose nature was derived from *the same stock* as those on whose behalf he transacted, yet his humanity must not be tainted in the least degree by their common defilement. It was required that he be a man of the seed of Adam (Luke 3:38) and of Eve (Gen. 3:15), yet an absolutely pure and holy man, for none other could personally and perpetually obey in thought, word and deed. But none such existed: "there is not a just man upon earth, that doeth good, and sinneth not" (Eccl. 7:20), nor would there ever have been one had the human race been left to itself. Naught but the manifold wisdom and miracle-working Power of God could produce him.

Yet one who was *more than man,* even though a perfect one, yea, far superior to those heavenly beings who veil their faces in the presence of Deity, was needed in order to discharge the liabilities of depraved sinners, and renew them in holiness. This is evident from several considerations. The most exalted creature, simply because he is a creature, is *obligated* to render perfect obedience unto his Maker, and therefore could merit nothing on the behalf of others. If he fully performed his duty, he would indeed work out a righteousness and be entitled to the reward of the Law; but he would need that righteousness *on his own account,* and therefore it would not be available for imputation unto another—and still less unto many others. Again, the work he had to do—pay in full that incalculable debt incurred by those who were to be saved, make expiation for all their sins, reconcile them to God, restore them to His favour, make them meet for the inheritance of the saints in light—was far beyond the compass of any mere creature, no matter how high his rank in the scale of being. Moreover, any deliverer of the apostate sons of Adam must be essentially and infinitely holy, for none less could be qualified to put away the infinite guilt of their countless iniquities.

In order for any portion of mankind to be eternally saved *unto the glory of* God, it was necessary that not only a flawless obedience be rendered unto God's Law, but such an obedience as brought more honour unto His holiness than was dishonour cast upon it by the disobedience of all—to affirm that it matters little what becomes of the glory of God so long as poor sinners be saved in some way or other is naught but the blasphemous belching of the carnal mind. Where God be revered and loved above all, very different will be the sentiments of such a one; namely, better far that the whole of Adam's race perish than that the character of Deity be sullied and the foundations of His throne undermined. But such an obedience could not be rendered by any mere creature, no matter how pure his nature or eminent his rank, for there must needs be somewhat of *the Divine* in it, in order for his performance to possess an infinite value. Nor must that obedience be constrained, but rather a voluntary one, for that which is forced proceeds not from love and is valueless. Nor must his conformity unto the Law be one which he was personally *responsible* to render unto it, for in such case it could not be accepted as a due compensation for the disobedience of all.

It was not a single individual who was to be recovered from the Fall and be brought unto Glory, but "ten thousands" (Jude 14), and each of them had more sins to his account than the hairs upon his head: and every sin had in it an immeasurable guilt, since it was committed against the infinite Majesty of Heaven. The woe unto which all of them were obnoxious was also infinite, the duration thereof being eternal—everything unspeakably dreadful and painful which our nature is capable of suffering. Nor could they be delivered from the awful consequence of their sin without an adequate satisfaction being made to the offended justice of God. To assert the contrary is as if one has to say it matters not to God whether He be obeyed or disobeyed, whether He be honoured or dishonoured in and by His creatures, and that would be to deny His very being, seeing it is directly contrary to the glory of all His perfections. But where was the person qualified to make and capable of making the requisite propitiation for sin? Where was the one fitted to act as mediator between God and men, between the Holy One and the unholy? Where was the one who could bestow life on the dead and merit everlasting blessedness for them?

If a remedy be provided for sinners, it must be one that restores them unto the same state and dignity wherein they were placed before the Fall. To recover them unto any lesser honour and blessedness than that which was theirs originally would not consist with either the Divine wisdom or bounty. "Yea, seeing it was the infinite grace, goodness and mercy of God to restore him, it seems agreeable unto the glory of the Divine excellencies in their operations that he should be brought into a better and more honourable condition than that which he had lost" (John Owen). In his primitive state man was subject unto none but his Maker. Though he was less in dignity than the angels, yet he owed them no obedience: they were his fellow servants of the Lord God. Obviously [as Owen also pointed out], if the sinner were saved by any mere creature, he could not be restored to his first state and dignity, for in such a case he would owe allegiance and subservience unto that creature who had redeemed him—he would become the property of the one who bought him. That would not only introduce the utmost confusion, but the sinner would be in a still worse case than he was before the Fall, for he would not be in the position wherein he owed subjection and honour unto God *alone*.

From the foregoing it will be seen that the only sufficient deliverer of fallen men must be one possessed of infinite dignity and worthiness, in order that he might be capable of meriting infinite blessings. He must be a person of infinite power and wisdom, for the work he must perform could be successfully accomplished by none less. But more, it was requisite that he should be a person who was infinitely dear to God the Father, in order to give an infinite value to his transactions in the Father's esteem, and that the Father's love to him might balance the offense and provocation of our sins. He must also be a person who could act in this matter in his own right, that in himself he be not a servant and subject of the Most High; otherwise he could not merit anything for those he would save. Moreover, he must be a person possessed of infinite mercy and love, for none other would voluntarily undertake a task so arduous, so humiliating, and involving such unspeakable suffering, for creatures so unworthy and foul as fallen men. But where in all the universe was such a one to be found? No created person possessed the necessary qualifications. When the Apostle John beheld (in vision) the seven-sealed book, we are told that he wept much, because no man in Heaven or earth was found worthy to open the book (Rev. 5:1-4), and had not the manifold wisdom of God found the solution to all these problems, men and angels alike had forever been nonplussed by them.

The various elements in the complicated problem of salvation for any of Adam's children are far from being exhausted in those already pointed out. Man was made to serve and glorify God. In spirit and soul and body, in all his faculties and powers, in all that was given to and entrusted with him, he was not his own, but in the place of a servant. The same was equally the case with the angels. A creature and one who is in all respects in subjection to his Maker are convertible terms. But from that condition and status the human race in Adam revolted, determining to be "as gods"—lords over themselves. There is something of *that* in every sin: a preferring of self-will to the will of the Almighty. By his insurrection, man fell into complete bondage to sin and Satan. In order to free the sinner from his captivity, it was necessary for any deliverer to take the position man originally occupied: he must enter the place of *absolute subjection to* God, entirely subordinating his own will to His, for in no other way could adequate compensation be made to the outraged government of God, and the damage wrought by our first parents be repaired. But how could any uncreated being occupy the position of a creature? With what propriety could one possessed of infinite dignity and excellence suffer such humiliation? How could one who was above all law come under the Law and render obedience to it?

Again, in his original state man had naught but what his Creator has bestowed upon him. Made out of the dust of the ground, he was endowed with intelligence and moral agency—but to be employed in the Divine service. He was also dependent upon his Maker for every breath he drew. That state of need and dependence he deliberately forsook, determining to enrich himself and assume absolute dominion. But his awful crime brought upon him and all whom he represented the loss of his original endowments: he lost the image of God, his right unto creatures here below, his own soul. Consequently, any saviour for him must needs experience *the degradation and poverty* which the sinner had brought upon himself, so that he would not have where to lay his head. But how was such an experience possible for anyone who was infinitely rich in himself, and in his own right? Since Adam stood for and transacted on the behalf of all whom he legally represented, it follows that any saviour must serve not in a private capacity but as the covenant head of those whom he was to recover. Finally, since God made the first man lord of the earth, giving him dominion over all creatures therein, which dominion he forfeited upon his Fall, then a deliverer must be capable of recovering the lost estate. But where was one that was able to purchase so vast an inheritance?

"The things which are impossible with men are possible with God" (Luke 18:27). Omniscience found a solution to all those problems which had forever baffled the minds of men. Scripture throws not a little emphasis upon this. It is referred to as "the wisdom of God in a mystery, even the hidden wisdom, which God ordained before the world unto our glory"—i.e., our salvation (1 Cor. 2:7). "In a mystery" connotes that which is undiscoverable by human reason, incomprehensible to the finite capacity, completely concealed until Divinely revealed, and even then beyond our powers to comprehend fully. In Ephesians 1:8, we are told of it: "Wherein He hath abounded

Its Remedy

toward us in all wisdom and prudence." The word "abounded" has the force of gushing out, overflowing. It is called "all wisdom" for its excellency. It was not a single concept or act, but a conjunction of many excellent ends and means to the glory of God. Unto wisdom is added "prudence": the former refers to the eternal contriving of a way, the latter to the ordering of all things unto the accomplishment of God's counsel or purpose—wisdom in devising, prudence in executing. In Ephesians 3:10, it is designated "the manifold wisdom of God" because of its complexity and variety: the salvation of sinners, the defeat of Satan, the full discovery of the blessed Trinity in Their different Persons, separate operations, combined actions and expressions of goodness; and because of the vastness of its extent.

That manifold wisdom of God, now exhibited before the angels in the redemption of the Church, is said to be "according to the eternal purpose which He purposed in Christ Jesus our Lord" (Eph. 3:11). The eternal Son of God, predestined to be the God-man mediator, is the grand medium, means and manifestation of the Divine omniscience, and therefore is He called "The Word of God" (Rev. 19:13), and "the wisdom of God" (1 Cor. 1:24). "Having made known unto us the mystery of His will, according to His good pleasure which He hath purposed in Himself: that in the dispensation of the fullness of times He night gather together in one all things in Christ, both which are in Heaven, and which are on earth; even in Him" (Eph. 1:9, 10). "The mystery of the will of God is His counsels concerning His own eternal glory in the sanctification and salvation of the Church here below, to be united unto that above. The absolute original hereof was in His own good pleasure, or the sovereign acting of His wisdom and will. But it was all to be effected in Christ, which the Apostle twice repeats: He would gather 'all things into a head in Christ, even in Him,' that is, in Him alone.

"Thus it is said of Him with respect unto His future incarnation and work if mediation that 'the LORD possessed Me in the beginning of His way, before His works of old. I was set up from everlasting, from the beginning, or ever the earth was' (Prov. 8:22, 23). The eternal personal existence of the Son of God was supposed in these expressions . . . without it none of these things could be affirmed of Him. But there is a regard in them both unto His future incarnation and the accomplishment of the counsels of God thereby. With respect thereto, God 'possessed Him in the beginning of His way, and set Him up from everlasting. God possessed Him eternally as His essential wisdom, as He was always and is always in the bosom of the Father, in the mutual, ineffable love of the Father and Son, in the eternal bond of the Spirit. But He signally possessed Him in the beginning of

His way as His wisdom acting in the production of all the ways and works that are outwardly in Him. The beginning of God's way before His works are His counsels concerning them, even as our counsels are the beginning of our ways with respect unto future works. And He set Him up from everlasting as *the foundation* of all the counsels of His will, in and by whom they were to be executed and accomplished" (J. Owen).

The eighth chapter of Proverbs is an exceedingly profound chapter, but a most blessed one. In it, as the first verse shows, the voice of "wisdom" is heard speaking. That it is a *person* who is there in view is evident, again, from verse 12: "I wisdom dwell with prudence," and verse 17: "I love them that love me." That it is a *Divine* person may be seen from verse 15: "by me kings reign." But it is equally clear from the language of verses 24 and 25, "I was brought forth," and "I was by Him [the Father], as one brought up with Him" (v. 30), that such expressions could not be predicated of the Son of God absolutely, that is as co-eternal and co-equal with the Father. No, "wisdom" is here to be understood of the Son as the God-man Mediator in His *two natures*, as the One ordained to be the incarnate "wisdom of God" (1 Cor. 1:24). When He declares: "The Lord possessed Me: the beginning [the Hebrew is without the "in"] of His way, before His works of old," it is the Mediator speaking in the covenant subsistence which He had before God ere the universe was called into union with the eternal Son, was "the beginning" (cf. Rev. 1:8) of the Triune God's "way," for in all things He must "have the pre-eminence" (Col. 1:18).

The *first counsel* of God had respect unto the Man Christ Jesus, for He was appointed to be not only the Head of His Church, but "the firstborn of every creature" (Col. 1:15), the One whom the Lord of hosts addresses as "the man, My fellow" (Zech. 13:7) was predestinated unto the grace of Divine union and glory. "In the head [Greek] of the book it is written of Me" (Heb. 10:7). He being the Object and Subject of God's original decree. "Our Redeemer came forth of the womb of a decree from eternity, before He came out of the womb of the Virgin in time. He was hid in the will of God before He was made manifest in the flesh of a Redeemer. He was a Lamb slain in purpose before He was slain upon the Cross. He was possessed by God in the beginning or the beginning of His way (the Head of His works), and set up from everlasting to have His delights among the sons of men" (Charnock). The person of the God-man Mediator was the origin of the Divine counsels. As such, the triune Jehovah "possessed" or embraced Him, as a Treasury in which all the Divine counsels were laid up, as an efficient Agent for the execution of all His works. Christ was God's first Elect (Isa. 42:1) and then the Church was chosen in Him (Eph. 1:4).

"I was set up, from everlasting." That declaration concerns Him not essentially as God the Son, but economically as the Mediator: "set up" or literally "anointed" by a covenant constitution and by Divine subsistence before the mind of God. Before all worlds, in the "counsel of peace" (Zech. 6:13), Christ was appointed and anointed to His official character. Before God planned to produce any creature, He first "set up" Christ as the great Archetype and Original. "Then I was by Him as one brought up, and I was daily His delight, rejoicing always before Him" (Prov. 8:30). It was not the Father's complacence in the second Person in the Trinity (as such) which is there in view, but His satisfaction and joy in the Mediator, as God contemplated Him in the glass of His decrees as the Repository of all His designs. The Hebrew word for "brought forth" also signifies "master-builder," and is so rendered in the Revised Version—how blessedly it described Him who could be relied upon to carry out the Father's purpose! In His eternal thoughts and primitive views, the Man Christ Jesus was the object of God's love. By Him all things were to be created. By Him vessels were to be formed for His glory. By Him the grand remedy was to be provided for sin's victims.

It is indeed lamentable that so few of the Lord's people have been instructed in these "deep things of God" (1 Cor. 2:10), for they have been revealed for their edification and consolation. What we have sought to explain in Proverbs 8 throws light on other passages. For example, how many a thoughtful reader has been puzzled by John 6:62, "What and if ye shall see the Son of *man* ascend up where *He* was before?"—in what sense had He been in Heaven as Man before He became incarnate? But though *we* be ignorant of this wondrous truth, the Old Testament saints were not, as is clear from Psalm 80:17—"Let Thy hand be upon the man of Thy right hand, upon the Son of man whom Thou madest strong for Thyself." Though the Man Christ Jesus had no historical existence then, He *had* a covenant subsistence before the Father, as taken into union with the second Person of the Trinity. As faith gives a present "substance" (the Greek word means "a real subsistence") in the believer's heart and mind of the things hoped for, so that he has a present enjoyment of things yet future, so in the mind of Him before whom all things are ever present Christ as incarnate was ever a living reality. Thus, when God said. "Let Us make man in Our image (Gen. 1:26) the ultimate reference was to the God-man, who is *par excellence* the image of the invisible God" (Col. 1:15).

Let us pause here and admire and adore the glorious wisdom of God, which found a way to save His people in a manner that was infinitely becoming and honouring to Himself, and let us bow in wonderment and worship before the Lord Jesus, who, notwithstanding the unspeakable shame and suffering involved therein, delighted to do the Father's will. The manifold wisdom of God is seen in *His choice* of the One to be the Head and Saviour of the Church, in that He was in every respect fit to perform that office and work, possessed of all the necessary qualifications: and in that He was the *only* Person suited thereunto. God's abounding wisdom appeared in His knowing that Christ *was* a fit Person. Naught but omniscience itself could have thought of God's dear Son becoming the Redeemer of Hell-deserving sinners.

God's choice of the Person who was to be the Restorer of His honour, the Vanquisher of Satan, the Victor of death, and the Deliverer of His fallen people, was one that naught but omniscience itself had made. Who but One endowed with infinite wisdom had ever thought of selecting His only begotten Son for such a fearful undertaking? For Christ, as God, is one of the eternal Three who was offended by sin, and from whom men had revolted. They were His avowed enemies, and of Him they deserved infinite woe. Who, then, had conceived *of Him* as One who should set His heart upon depraved wretches, who should exercise infinite love and pity toward them, should be willing to provide an all-sufficient remedy for all their ills? But when that choice was made, insurmountable difficulties seemed to stand in the way of its realization. How was it possible for a Divine Person to enter the place of ruined sinners, to come under the Law and render perfect obedience to it, and so work out a perfect righteousness for those who had none? And how could it be possible for the Holy One to be made a curse, for the Lord of Glory to suffer the penalty of the broken Law, for the Beloved of the Father to experience the fires of Divine wrath, for the Lord of life to die? Such problems as those had forever baffled all created intelligences. But Divine wisdom found a solution.

First, the manifold wisdom of God ordained that His dear Son should be constituted the last Adam, that as He made a Covenant of Works with the first man who was of the earth, so He would make a Covenant of Grace with "the second Man," who is the Lord from Heaven. That as the first Adam stood as the covenant head and federal representative of all his posterity, so the last Adam should stand as the covenant Head and Representative of all His seed. But as the first Adam broke the Covenant of Works and brought ruin upon all those he acted for, so the last Adam should fulfill the terms of the

Covenant of Grace, and thereby secure the everlasting felicity of all on whose behalf He transacted. Accordingly, a covenant was entered into between the Father and the Son, the Former promising a glorious reward upon the Latter's meeting all the conditions thereof. That wondrous transaction is referred to in Psalm 89:3-5, "I have made a covenant with My chosen, I have sworn unto [the antitypical] David [which means "the Beloved"] My servant. Thy seed will I establish forever, and build up thy throne to all generations. Selah. And the heavens shall praise Thy wonders, O LORD: Thy faithfulness also in the congregation of the saints." That passage, like Proverbs 8, takes us back to the eternal counsels of God, for Psalm 89:19 declares, "Then Thou spakest in vision to Thy holy one and saidst, I have laid help upon one that is mighty"—fully able to accomplish My vast and gracious designs.

That Covenant of Grace was a mutual compact which was voluntarily entered into between the Father and the Son, the One promising a rich reward in return for the fulfillment of the terms agreed upon: the Other solemnly pledging Himself to carry out its stipulations. Many are the Scriptures which speak of Christ in connection with the covenant. In Isaiah 42:6, we hear the Father saying to Him, "I the LORD have called Thee in righteousness, and will . . . give Thee for a covenant of the people." In Malachi 3:1, Christ is designated "the messenger of the testament" because He came here to make known its contents and proclaim its glad tidings. In Hebrews 7:22, He is designated "a surety of a better covenant," in 9:15, "the mediator of the new testament," while in 13:20, we read of "the blood of the everlasting covenant." In that covenant the Son agreed to be the Head of God's elect, and do all that was required unto the Divine glory and the securing of their eternal blessedness. To that, reference is made in "His own purpose and grace, which was given us in Christ Jesus before the world began" (2 Tim. 1:9)—a federal relation then subsisted between Christ and the Church, though the same was not made fully manifest until He became incarnate. It was then that the Son was appointed unto the mediatorial office, when He was "set up" or "anointed," when He was "brought forth" from the everlasting decree (Prov. 8:23, 24) and given a covenant subsistence before the triune God.

It was proposed and freely agreed upon that the Beloved of the Father should take upon Him the form of a servant and be made in the likeness of sin's flesh. Accordingly, when the fullness of time was come, He was "made of a woman," taking a human spirit and soul and body into perpetual union with Himself. As the body of Adam was supernaturally made out of the virgin earth by God's immediate hand, so the body of Christ was supernaturally made out of the Virgin's substance by the immediate operation of the Holy Spirit. So too the union of soul and body in Adam shadowed forth the Hypostatic union of our nature with the Son of God, so that He is not two persons in one, but one Person with two natures, those natures not being confounded, but each preserving its distinctive properties. Well did Owen remark, "His conception in the womb of the Virgin, as unto the integrity of human nature, was a miraculous operation of the Divine power. But the prevention of that nature from any subsistence of its own, by its assumption unto personal union with the Son of God, in the first instance of its conception, is that which is above all miracles, nor can be designated by that name. A *mystery* it is, so far above the order of all creating or providential operations, that it wholly transcends the sphere of them that are most miraculous. Herein did God glorify all the properties of the Divine nature, acting in a way of infinite wisdom, grace and condescension."

He who was the Lord of all, and owed no service or obedience to any, being in the form of God and equal unto Him, descended into a condition of absolute subjection. As Adam deliberately forsook the place of complete submission unto God, which was proper to his nature and suited unto God, aspiring after lordship, so the Son of God left that state of absolute dominion which was His by right, and took upon Him the yoke of servitude. The Son's descent involved far greater humiliation unto Himself than did the glory of that ascent unto which the first man aspired in his pride. As others have shown, this self-abasement of the Lord of Glory unto an estate of entire subjection is referred to by the Apostle in Hebrews 10:5, where Christ is heard saying "a body hast Thou prepared Me." Those words are an explanatory paraphrase of "Mine ears hast Thou opened"—margin "digged"—in Psalm 40:6: which, in turn, looks back to Exodus 21:6, where a statute was appointed to the effect that one who voluntarily gave himself up to absolute and perpetual service signified the same by having his ear bored with an awl. Thus, Hebrews 10:5, in the light of Psalm 40:6, and Exodus 21:6, imports that Christ's body was prepared for Him with the express design of His absolute service unto God therein.

By His assumption of human nature, not only was Christ fitted to render subjection unto God, but He became qualified to serve as *Mediator* between God and men. For it is required that a mediator be related unto *both* of the parties he would reconcile, and be the equal of each of them—thus an angel would not be qualified for this office, since he possesses neither the Divine nor the human nature. It was necessary for Christ to be real man as well as God in order to perform the work of redemption: the former so that He should be susceptible of suffering, qualified to offer Himself as a sacrifice, be capable of dying. So too the assumption of human nature fitted Christ to be *the Substitute* of His people, to act not only on their behalf, but in their room and stead: actually to take their law-place and render full satisfaction thereto by obeying its precepts and enduring its penalty. But that, in turn, required that He be their Surety and Sponsor: that is, be so related to them legally and federally that He could fittingly serve as their Substitute. As there was a federal and representative oneness between the first Adam and those he stood for, so there must be a like oneness between the last Adam and those for whom He transacted: that as the guilt of the former was charged to the account of his posterity, so the righteousness of the Latter might be imputed unto all His seed.

Yet the truth concerning the position which the Son of God took is not fully expressed by the above statements. It is not sufficient to say that He became their Surety and Substitute, but we must go farther back and ask, What was it that rendered it meet that He *should serve* as the Sponsor of His people before their offended Lawgiver and Judge? And the answer is, *Their covenant union.* Christ served as their Surety and Substitute because He was one with them, and therefore could He and did He assume and discharge all their liabilities. In the Covenant of Grace Christ had said to the Father, "I will declare Thy name unto My brethren, in the midst of the church will I sing praise unto Thee. And again, I will put My trust in Him. And again, Behold I and the children which God hath given Me" (Heb. 2:12, 13). Most blessedly is that explained in what immediately follows: "Forasmuch then as the children are partakers of flesh and blood, He also Himself likewise took part of the same," and therefore is He not ashamed to call them brethren. *Federation is* the root of this amazing mercy, *identification* the key which unlocks it. Christ came not to strangers, but to His "brethren": He assumed human nature, not in order to procure a people for Himself, but to secure a people already His (Eph. 1:4; Matt. 1:21).

Since a union has existed between Christ and His people from all eternity, it inevitably followed that when He came to this earth He took upon Himself their debts, and now He has gone to Heaven they must be clothed (Isa. 61:10) with all the rewards of His perfect obedience. This is very much more than a technicality of theology, being the strongest buttress of all in the walls of Truth which protect the Atonement, though it is one of the most frequently and fiercely assailed by its enemies. Men have argued that the punishment of the Innocent as *though* He were guilty was an outrage upon justice. In the human realm, to punish a person for something when he is neither responsible nor guilty is beyond question, unjust. But that objection is invalid and entirely pointless in connection with the Lord Jesus, for He voluntarily entered the place and lot of His people in such an intimate way that it could be said, "For both He that sanctifieth and they who are sanctified are *all of one*" (Heb. 2:11). They are not only one in nature, but are also so united in the sight of God and before His Law as to involve an identification of legal relations and reciprocal obligations and rights. "By the obedience of One shall many be made [legally constituted] righteous" (Rom. 5:19).

It was required from the Surety of God's people that He should not only render a full and perfect obedience to the precepts of the Law, and thereby provide the meritorious means of their justification, but that He should also make full satisfaction for their sins by having visited upon Him the curse of the Law. But before that penalty could be inflicted, the guilt of the transgressors must be transferred unto Him: that is to say, their sins must be judicially imputed to Him. To that arrangement the Holy One willingly consented, so that He who "knew no sin" was legally "made sin" for them (2 Cor. 5:21). God laid upon Him the iniquities of them all, and then the sword of Divine justice smote Him (Zech. 13:7), exacting full satisfaction. Without the shedding of blood there is no remission. The blotting out of transgressions, procuring for us the favour of God, the purchase of the heavenly inheritance, required the death of Christ. That which demanded the death sentence was the guilt of our sins: let *that* be removed, and condemnation for us is gone for-ever. But how could guilt be "removed"? Only by its being transferred to another. The punishment due to the Church was borne by her Surety and Substitute. God charged upon Him all the sins of His elect and proceeded against Him accordingly, visiting upon Him His judicial wrath.

How marvellous are the ways of God! As death was destroyed by death—the death of God's Son—so sin by sin, the greatest that was ever committed—the crucifixion of Christ—putting it away as far as the east is from the west. Because God imputed the trespasses of His people unto their Surety, Christ was condemned that they might be acquitted. Christ took upon Him their accumulated and incalculable debt, and by His discharging the same they are forever free and solvent. By His precious blood all their iniquities were expiated, so that the triumphant challenge rings out, "Who shall lay anything to the charge of God's elect?" (Rom. 8:33). Throughout His life and by His death Christ was repaying and repairing all that injury which the sins of the Church had done unto the manifestative glory of God. God now remits the sins of all who truly believe in Christ, because Deity

Its Remedy

has received a vicarious but full satisfaction for them in the Person of their Substitute. Through Christ they are delivered from the wrath to come. Necessarily so, for God's acceptance of the Lamb's sacrifice obtained the eternal redemption of all for whom it was offered. Just as a dark cloud empties itself upon earth and then melts away under the rays of the sun, so when the storm of Divine judgment had exhausted itself upon the Cross, our sins disappeared from before God's face, and we are received into His everlasting favour.

Wondrous as was the work that the incarnate Son performed for His people, yet something more was still needed in order to provide a *complete* remedy for their complicated ruin, for *that* covered only the legal aspects of their woe. A miracle of grace required to be wrought *in them* in order to make them experientially meet for everlasting glory: yea, such is absolutely indispensable to fit them to commune with God in this life. His elect need to be quickened into newness of life, their enmity against God destroyed, their darkness dispelled, their wills freed, their love of sin and hatred of holiness rectified. In a word, they must experience a thorough change of heart, a principle of grace be communicated to them, and them made new creatures in Christ. That miracle of grace is performed by the Holy Spirit in those who are "by nature the children of wrath, even as others" (Eph. 2:3). But how little is this realized today—insistence thereon has well-nigh disappeared from the modern pulpit, even in those who pride themselves upon being orthodox. The work of the Spirit *in the saving of sinners* has no place in the creed of the average churchgoer, and where it be nominally acknowledged, it possesses no real weight and exerts no practical influence.

In the majority of places where the Lord Jesus is still formally owned as the only Saviour, the current teaching is that He has made it *possible* for men to be saved, but that they themselves must decide whether or not they shall be saved; and thus the greatest of all God's works is left contingent on the fickle will of men as to whether it be a success or a failure. Narrowing the circle to those places where it is still held that the Spirit has a mission and ministry in connection with the Gospel, the general idea prevailing is that, when the Word is faithfully preached, the Spirit convicts men of sin and reveals to them their need of a Saviour; but beyond that, very few are prepared to go. The popular view is that the sinner has to *co-operate* with the Spirit: that he must yield himself to His "striving," or he will not and cannot be saved. But such a pernicious and God-insulting concept repudiates two cardinal facts: to affirm that the natural man is capable of co-operating with the Spirit is to deny that he is "dead in trespasses and sins," for a dead man is powerless to do any good; while to say that the specific operations of the Spirit in a man's heart and conscience are capable of being so resisted as to thwart His endeavours is to deny His omnipotence.

The solemn and unpalatable fact is, my reader, that were the Spirit of God to suspend His operations, not a single person on earth would savingly benefit from the redemptive work of Christ. The natural man is such an enemy to God and so obstinate in his rebellion that he dislikes a holy Christ, and remains opposed to His way of salvation until his heart be Divinely renewed. That criminal darkness and delusion which fills every soul wherein sin reigns cannot be removed by any agent but God the Spirit—by His giving a new heart and enlightening the understanding to perceive the exceeding sinfulness of sin. There are indeed thousands of people ready to respond to the fatal error that sinners may be saved without throwing down the weapons of their warfare against God: who receive Christ as their Saviour, but who are unwilling to surrender to Him as their Lord. They would like His rest, but they refuse His "yoke," without which His rest cannot be had. His promises appeal to them, but for His precepts they have no heart. They will believe in an imaginary Christ who is suited to their corrupt nature, but they despise and reject the Christ of God. Like the multitudes of old, they are pleased with His loaves and fishes, but for His heart-searching, flesh-withering, sin-condemning teaching they have no appetite. Naught but the miracle-working power of the Spirit can change them.

"Man is utterly and entirely averse to everything that is good and right. 'The carnal mind is enmity against God, for it is not subject to the law of God. Neither indeed can be' (Rom. 8:7). Turn through all Scripture, and you will find continually the will of man described as being contrary to the things of God. What said Christ in that text so often quoted by the Arminian to disprove the very doctrine which it clearly states? What did Christ say to those who imagined that men would come *without* Divine influence? He said, first, 'No man can come unto Me, except the Father which hath sent Me draw him': but He said something more strong—'Ye *will not* come unto Me that ye might have life.' Herein lies the deadly mischief: not only that he is powerless to do good, but that he is powerful enough to do that which is wrong, and that his will is desperately set against everything that is right. Men *will not come*; you cannot force them to by all your thunders, nor entice them by all your invitations. Until the Spirit draw them, come they neither will, nor can" (Spurgeon).

The manifold wisdom of God is just as evident in the official task assigned to the Holy Spirit as in the work that the Son was commissioned to perform. The miracles of regeneration and sanctification are as wonderful as the obedience and sufferings, the death and resurrection of Christ were; and the saint is as truly and as deeply indebted to the one as he is to the other. If it were an act of amazing condescension for God the Son to leave Heaven's glory and assume unto Himself human nature, equally so was it for God the Spirit to descend to this earth and take up His abode in fallen men and women; and if God signalized the marvel and importance of the one by mighty wonders and signs, so did He in connection with the latter—the song of the angelic choir (Luke 2:13) having its counterpart in the "sound from Heaven" (Acts 2:2), the Shekinah "glory" (Luke 2:9) in the "tongues like as of fire." If we admire the gracious and mighty works of Christ in cleansing the leper, strengthening the palsied, giving sight to the blind and imparting life to the dead, no less is the Spirit to be adored for His supernatural operations in quickening lifeless souls, in illuminating their minds, delivering them from the dominion of sin, removing their enmity against God, uniting them to Christ, and creating in them a love of holiness.

From all that has been before us it will be seen how complete and perfect is the remedy which the grace and wisdom of God has provided for His people. As they were federally in Adam, and therefore held responsible for what he did, they are federally in Christ, and therefore enjoy all the benefits of His meritorious work. As they were ruined by the breaking of one covenant, so they are restored by the keeping of another. As they were rendered guilty by Adam's disobedience being charged to their account, so they are justified before the Throne of God because the righteousness of their Surety is imputed to them. As they fell under the curse of the Law, were alienated from God and became children of wrath, through Christ's redemption they are entitled to the reward of the Law, reconciled to God and restored to His favour. As they inherit a corrupt nature from their first head, so they receive a holy nature from their second Head. In every respect the remedy answers to the malady.

THE DOCTRINE OF HUMAN DEPRAVITY
Conclusion

The entrance of evil into the domain of God is admittedly a deep mystery, nevertheless sufficient is revealed in the Scriptures to prevent our forming erroneous views thereon. For instance, it is flatly contrary to the Word of Truth to entertain the notion that either the fall of Satan and his angels or that of our first parents took God by surprise, or wrecked His plans. From all eternity God designed that this earth should be the stage on which He would display His perfections: in creation, in providence, and in redemption (1 Cor. 4:9). Accordingly, He foreordained everything which comes to pass in this scene (Acts 15:18; Rom. 11:36; Eph. 1:11). God is no idle spectator, looking on from a fardistant world at the happenings of this earth, but is Himself ordering and shaping everything to the ultimate promotion of His glory—not only in spite of the opposition of men and Satan, but by means of them, everything being made to serve His purpose. Nor did the introduction of evil into the universe take place simply by the bare permission of the Most High, for nothing can come to pass that is contrary to His decretive will. Rather must we believe that, for wise and holy reasons, God foreordained to suffer His mutable creatures to fall, and thereby afford an occasion for Him to make a further and fuller exhibition of His attributes.

From *God's* standpoint the result of Adam's probation was left in no uncertainty. Before He formed him out of the dust of the ground and breathed into his nostrils the breath of life, He knew exactly how the appointed testing of Adam would eventuate. But more: He had *decreed* that he should eat of the forbidden fruit. That is certain from 1 Peter 1:19, 20, which tells us that the shedding of Christ's blood was verily "foreordained before the foundation of the world" (cf. Rev. 13:8). As Witsius rightly affirmed of Adam's sin, "if foreknown it was also predestinated: thus Peter joins together 'the determinate counsel and foreknowledge of God' (Acts 2:23)." In full harmony with that fact, it is to be remembered that it was God Himself who placed in Eden the tree of the knowledge of good and evil! Moreover, as the celebrated Moderator of the Westminster Assembly asked, "Did not the Devil provoke Eve and Adam to sin against God in Paradise? Could not God have kept the Devil off? Why did He not? Doth it not manifestly appear that it was God's will to have them tempted, to have them provoked unto sin? And why not?" (W. Twisse, 1653). God overruled it unto a higher manifestation of His glory. Just as without night we could not admire the beauty of day, sin was necessary as a dark background on which the Divine grace and mercy should shine forth the more resplendently (Rom. 5:20).

It has been asserted, most dogmatically, by Romanists and Arminians, that God could not have prevented the Fall of our first parents without reducing them to mere machines. It is argued that since the Creator endowed man with a free will he must be left entirely to his own volitions: that he cannot be coerced, still less compelled, without destroying his moral agency. That may sound to be good reasoning, yet it is refuted by Holy Writ! God declared unto Abimelech concerning Abraham's wife, "I also *withheld thee* from sinning against Me, therefore suffered I thee not to touch her" (Gen. 20:6). Thus it is very plain that it is not *impossible* for God to exert His power upon man without destroying his responsibility, for *there is* a case in point where He restricted man's freedom to do evil and prevented him from committing sin. In like manner, He *prevented Balaam* from carrying out the wicked desires of his heart (Num. 22:38; 23:2, 20); yea, He prevented kingdoms from making war upon Jehoshaphat (2 Chron. 17:10). Why, then, did not God exert His power and prevent Adam and Eve from sinning? Because their Fall the better served His own wise and blessed designs.

But does that make God the Author of sin? The culpable Author, no, for as Piscator long ago pointed out, "Culpability is a failing to do what ought to be done." Clearly it was the Divine will that sin should enter this world, or it had not done so, for not only had God the power to prevent the same, but nothing ever comes to pass save what He has decreed. "Though God's decree made Adam's Fall infallibly necessary *as to the event,* yet not by way of efficiency, or by force and compulsion on the will" (J. Gill). Nor did God's decree in any wise excuse the wickedness of our first parents, or exempt them from punishment. They were left entirely free to the exercise of their nature, and therefore fully accountable and blameworthy for their actions. While the tree of the knowledge of good and evil and the solicitations of the serpent to eat thereof were *the occasions* of their sinning, yet they were *not the cause* thereof—that lay in their voluntarily ceasing to be in subjection to the will of their Maker and rightful Lord. God is not the efficient Author of the sins of men as He is of whatever works of holiness they perform.

That God decreed sin should enter this world was a secret hid in Himself. Of it our first parents knew nothing, and that made all the difference so far as their responsibility was concerned, for had they been informed of the Divine purpose and the certainty of its fulfillment by their actions, the case had been radically altered. They were quite unacquainted with the Creator's secret counsels. What concerned them was God's *revealed* will, and *that* was quite plain. He had forbidden them to eat of a certain tree, and that was enough. But

He went farther. The Lord even warned Adam of the dire consequences which should follow his disobedience—death would be the penalty. Thus, transgression on his part was entirely excuseless. God created him morally "upright," without any bias toward evil. Nor did He inject any evil thought or desire into Eve. No, "God cannot be tempted with evil, neither tempteth He any man" (James 1:13). Instead, when the serpent came and tempted Eve, God caused her to remember His prohibition! Admire, then, the wonderful wisdom of God, for though He had predestinated the Fall of our first parents, yet in no sense was He the Instigator or Approver of their sins, and their accountability was left entirely unimpaired.

These two things we must believe if the Truth is not to be repudiated: that God has foreordained everything that comes to pass; that He is in no way to be blamed for any of man's wickedness—the criminality thereof being wholly his. The decree of God in no wise infringes upon man's moral agency, for it neither forces nor hinders man's will, though it orders and bounds its actions. Both the existence and operations of sin are subservient to the counsels of God's will, yet that lessens not the evil of its nature or the guilt of the transgressor. "Though He esteems not evil to be good, yet He accounts it good that evil should be" (W. Perkins, 1587); nevertheless sin is "that abominable thing" (Jer. 44:4) which the Holy One ever hates. In connection with the crucifixion of Christ there was the agency of God (John 19:11; Acts 4:27, 28), the agency of Satan (Gen. 3:13; Luke 22:53), and the agency of men; yet God neither concurred nor co-operated with the internal actions of their wills, and God charged the latter with the wickedness of their deed (Acts 2:23). God overrules evil unto good (Gen. 44:8; Psalm 76:10), and therefore He is as truly sovereign over sin and Hell as He is over holiness and Heaven.

God cannot will or do anything that is wrong: "The LORD is righteous in *all* His ways, and holy in all His works" (Psa. 145:17). He therefore stands in no need whatsoever of vindication by any of His puny creatures. Yet even the finite mind, when illumined by the Spirit of Truth, can perceive how that God's admittance of evil into this world provided an occasion for Him to display His ineffable perfections in a manner and to a degree which otherwise He had not, to magnify Himself by bringing a clean thing out of an unclean, and by securing to Himself a revenue of praise from redeemed sinners such as He receives not from the unfallen angels. Horrible and terrible beyond words was the revolt of man against his Maker, and fearful and total the ruin which it brought upon him and all his posterity. Nevertheless, the wisdom of God contrived a way to save a part of the human race in such a manner that He is more glorified therein than in and by all His works of creation and providence, and so that the misery of sinners is made the occasion of their greater happiness; such is a never-ending wonder.

That way of salvation was determined and defined in the terms of the everlasting Covenant of Grace. It was one by which each of the Divine persons is exceedingly honoured. As the renowned Jonathan Edwards long ago pointed out, "Herein the work of redemption is distinguished from all the other works of God. The attributes of God are glorious in His other works; but the three Persons of the Trinity are *distinctly glorified* in no other work as in this of redemption. In this work every distinct Person has His distinct parts and offices assigned Him. Each one has His particular concernment in it agreeably to Their distinct personal properties, relations, and economical offices. The redeemed have an equal concern with and dependence upon each Person in this affair, and owe equal honour and praise to each of Them. The Father appoints and provides the Redeemer, and accepts the price of redemption. The Son is the Redeemer and the price—He redeems by offering up Himself. The Holy Spirit immediately communicates to us the thing purchased; yea, and He is the good purchased. The sum of what Christ purchased for us is holiness and happiness. Christ was 'made a curse for us . . . that we might receive the promise of the Spirit through faith' (Gal. 3:13, 14). The blessedness of the redeemed consists in partaking of Christ's fullness, which consists in partaking of that Spirit which is not given by measure unto Him. This is the oil that was poured upon the Head of the Church, which ran down to the members of His body (Psa. 133:2)."

It is a serious mistake to regard the Lord Jesus as our Saviour to *the excluding of* the saving operations of both the Father and the Spirit. Had not the Father eternally purposed the salvation of His people, chosen them in Christ and bestowed them upon Him, had He not entered into an everlasting compact with Him, commissioned Him to become incarnate, and redeemed them, His Beloved had never left Heaven in order that He might die, the Just for the unjust. Accordingly, we find that He who so loved the world that He gave His only begotten Son has ascribed unto Him the salvation of the Church: "Who hath *saved us*, and called us . . . according to His own purpose and grace, which was given us in Christ Jesus before the world began" (2 Tim. 1:9). Equally necessary are the operations of the Holy Spirit to actually apply to the hearts of God's elect the good of what Christ did for them: He it is who convicts of sin and imparts faith to them. Therefore is their salvation also ascribed to Him: "God hath from the beginning chosen you to salvation *through* sanctification of the Spirit and belief of the truth" (2 Thess. 2:13). A careful reading of

Titus 3:4-6 shows the three Persons acting together in this connection: "God our Saviour" in verse 4 is plainly the Father, and "He saved us by the washing of regeneration, and renewing of the Holy Spirit" (v. 5), "which He shed on us abundantly through Jesus Christ our Saviour" (v. 6)—compare the doxology of 2 Corinthians 13:14!

It is very blessed to ponder the many *promises* which the Father made unto and respecting Christ. Upon the Son's acceptance of the exacting terms of the Covenant of Grace, the Father agreed to invest Him with a threefold office, thereby authenticating His mission with the broad seal of Heaven: to the prophetic (Deut. 18:15, 18, and see Acts 3:22), to the priestly (Heb. 5:5; 6:20), and to the kingly (Jer. 22:5; Psa. 89:27). Thus Christ did not run without being sent. He promised to furnish and equip the Mediator with a plentiful effusion of the graces and gifts of the Holy Spirit (Isa. 42:1, 2, and see Acts 10:38; Matt. 12:27, 28). He promised to strengthen Christ, supporting and protecting Him in His execution of the tremendous work of redemption (Isa. 42:1, 6; Psalm 89:21). His undertaking would be attended with such difficulties that creature power, though unimpaired by sin, would have been quite inadequate for it: therefore did the Father assure Him of all needed help and succour, to carry Him through the opposition and trials He would encounter. Precious it is to mark how the incarnate Son rested upon those promises: Psalm 22:10; Isaiah 69:4-7; Psalm 16:1; Isaiah 1:6-9.

The Father promised to raise the Messiah from the dead (Psa. 21:8; 102:23, 24; Isa. 53:10), and most blessed is it to observe how Christ laid hold of the same (Psa. 16:8-11). Promise of His *ascension* was also made to Him (Psa. 24:3, 7; 67:18; 89:27; Isa. 52:13): that too was appropriated by the Saviour while still on earth (Luke 24:26). Having faithfully fulfilled the terms of the covenant, Christ was highly exalted by God, and made to be Lord and Christ (Acts 2:36), God seating Him at His own right hand. That is an economical lordship, a dispensation committed to Him as the God-man. The One whom men crowned with thorns, God has crowned with glory and honour. The "government" is upon His shoulder.

Christ was assured of a *"seed"* (Isa. 53:10)—His crucifixion must not be regarded as an infamy unto Him, since it was the very means ordained by God whereby He should propagate a numerous spiritual progeny: unto this He referred in John 12:24. The "seed" promised Christ occupies a prominent place in Psalm 89, see verses 3, 4, 31-36 and cf. 22:30. Thus, from the outset, Christ was assured of the success of His undertaking. As there were two parts to the covenant, so the elect were given to Christ in a twofold manner. As He was to fulfill its terms, they were entrusted to Him as a *charge*; but in fulfillment thereof the Father promised to bestow them upon Him as a *reward*. In the former sense, they are regarded as fallen, and Christ was held responsible for their salvation: they were committed to Him as stray and lost sheep (Isa. 53:6), whom He must seek out and bring into the fold (John 10:16). In the latter sense, they are viewed as the fruit of His travail, the trophies of His victory over sin, Satan, and death; as His crown of rejoicing in the day to come (when He shall be "glorified in His saints, and to be admired in all them that believe"— 2 Thess. 1:10); as the beloved wife of the Lamb.

Finally, God made promise of *the Holy Spirit to Christ*. He rested upon Him during the days of His flesh, anointing Him to preach the Gospel (Isa. 61:1) and work miracles (Matt. 12:28). But He received the Spirit after another manner (Psa. 45:7; Acts 2:33) and for a different purpose after His ascension, namely that the God-man Mediator has been given *the administration* of the Spirit's activities and operations both world-ward in providence and Church-ward in grace, John 16:7 makes it clear that the Spirit's advent was dependent upon Christ's exaltation. That assurance was also appropriated by Christ ere He left this scene: on the point of His departure, He said unto His disciples, "Behold, I send the promise of My Father upon you" (Luke 24:49), which was duly accomplished ten days later. In full accord with what has just been pointed out, we hear the Saviour saying from Heaven, "These things saith He that hath the seven Spirits of God" (Rev. 3:1)—"hath" to communicate unto His redeemed individually, and to His churches corporately.

The grand design in the Spirit's descent to this earth is to glorify Christ (John 16:14). He is here to witness unto the Saviour's exaltation, Pentecost being God's seal upon the Messiahship of Jesus. The Spirit is here to take Christ's place. That is clear from His own words to the Apostles: "I will pray the Father, and He shall give you *another* Comforter, that He may abide with you forever" (John 14:16). Until then the Lord Jesus had been their Comforter, but He was on the eve of returning to Heaven; nevertheless, He graciously assured them, "I will not leave you orphans: I will come to you" (John 14:18, marginal rendering)—fulfilled spiritually in the advent of His Deputy. The Spirit is here to further Christ's cause. The word *Paraclete* (translated "Comforter" in John's Gospel) is rendered "advocate" at the beginning of the second chapter of his Epistle, and an advocate is one who appears as the *representative* of another. The Spirit is here to interpret and vindicate Christ, to administer for Christ in His kingdom and Church. He is here to make good His redeeming purpose, by applying the benefits of His sacrifice unto those in whose behalf it was offered. He is here to endue Christ's servants (Luke 24:49).

Conclusion

It is of first importance to recognize and realize that the Lord Jesus not only obtained for God's people redemption from the *penal consequences* of sin, but has also secured their *personal sanctification*. Alas, how little is this emphasized today. In far too many instances those who think and speak of the "salvation" which Christ has purchased attach no further idea thereto than that of deliverance from condemnation, *omitting* deliverance from the love, dominion, and power of sin. But the latter is no less essential, and is as definite a blessing as the former. It is just as necessary for fallen creatures to be delivered from the pollution and moral impotency which they have contracted as it is to be exempted from the penalties which they have incurred; so that when reinstated in the favour of God they may at the same time be capacitated to love, serve, and enjoy Him forever. And in this respect also the Divine remedy meets all the requirements of our sinful malady (see 2 Cor. 5:15; Eph. 5:25-27; Titus 2:14; Heb. 9:14). This is accomplished by the gracious operations of Christ's Spirit: begun in regeneration, continued throughout their earthly lives, consummated in Heaven.

Not only is the triune God more honoured by redemption than He was dishonoured by the defection of His creatures, but His people also are *greatly the gainers*. How that too magnifies the Divine wisdom! It had been wonderful indeed had they been merely restored to their original estate, but it is far more wonderful that they should be brought to a much higher state of blessedness—that the Fall should be the occasion of their exaltation! Their sin deserved eternal woe, yet everlasting bliss is their portion. They are now favoured with a greater manifestation of the glory of God and a fuller discovery of His love than otherwise they would have had, and in those two things their happiness principally consists. They are brought into a much closer and endearing relation to God. They are now not merely holy creatures, but heirs of God and joint-heirs with Christ. The Son having taken their nature upon Him, they have become His "brethren," members of His body, yea, His spouse. They are thereby provided with more powerful motives and inducements to love and serve Him than they had in their unfallen condition. The more we apprehend of God's love, the more we love Him in return: throughout eternity the knowledge of God's love in giving His dear Son to and for us, and Christ's dying in our stead, will fix our hearts upon Him in a manner which His favours to Adam had never done.

Now it is in *the Gospel* that the wondrous remedy for all our ills is made known. That glorious Gospel proclaims that Christ is able to save unto the uttermost them that come unto God by Him. It tells us that the Son of man came to seek and to save that which was lost. It announces that *sinners*, even the chief of sinners, are the ones that are freely invited to come. It publishes liberty to Satan's captives and the opening of doors to sin's prisoners. It reveals that God has chosen the greatest of sinners to be the everlasting monuments of His mercy. It declares that the blood of Jesus Christ, God's Son, cleanses believers from all sin. It furnishes hope to the most hopeless cases. The prodigies which Christ performed on the bodies of men were types of His miracles of grace on sinners' souls. No case was beyond His healing. He not only gave sight to the blind and cleansed the leper, but delivered the demon-possessed and bestowed life on the dead. He never refused a single appeal made to His compassion. Whatever be the reader's record, if he will trust in the atoning sacrifice of Christ he will be saved, now and forever.